Into the
World of Light

Into the World of Light

AN ANTHOLOGY OF MAORI WRITING

Edited by
Witi Ihimaera and D. S. Long

Heinemann

Heinemann Publishers
Cnr College Road and Kilham Avenue, Auckland 9, New Zealand
The Windmill Press, Kingswood, Tadworth, Surrey KT20 6TG, England
4 Front Street, Exeter, New Hampshire 03833, U.S.A.

Also at Edinburgh, Melbourne, Johannesburg, Ibadan,
Nairobi, Lusaka, New Delhi, Hong Kong, Singapore,
Kuala Lumpur, Kingston, Port of Spain

ISBN 0 86863 580 4

© 1982 Witi Ihimaera, D. S. Long
First Published 1982
Reprinted 1983

Printed in Hong Kong

The cover illustration is entitled Cape Colville and is taken from *Rei Hamon — Artist of the New Zealand Bush — His Life and His Drawings* (Auckland, Collins Bros & Co Ltd, 1971).

Ki o tatou iwi
To our people

The publisher and the editors wish to express their gratitude to Margaret Orbell, who acted as Maori language consultant for the first draft of this anthology and whose *Contemporary Maori Writing*, published eleven years ago, remains a landmark in the field; and to Bill Parker, who was Maori language consultant when the book was in its final form: also to the Alexander Turnbull Library, the Drama Department of Radio NZ, the University of Queensland Press, the Maori Artists' and Writers' Society; Michele Taylor, Jane Smiler, and Cass Tangaere; all of whom offered invaluable help and advice over the eight years during which the anthology was in preparation.

The publication of the anthology was made possible by assistance from the NZ University Students' Arts Council and the NZ Literary Fund.

Contents

* First published in this anthology

A Glossary of Maori words is not provided in this anthology. The reader unfamiliar with Maori may turn to either H. W. Orsman's *Heinemann New Zealand Dictionary* (1979) or Herbert W. Williams' *A Dictionary of the Maori Language* which first appeared in 1844 and which has been revised many times since.

    Maori, like English, has more than one dialect. In this anthology we have followed the tribal affiliations of the writer — and their own original manuscripts. Thus 'Ngaati' may be found as 'Kati', the Southern dialect.

Vowel length is not marked unless at the author's request (macron or double vowel e.g. ā or aa to indicate the long vowel). Where the English 's' has been used to make a Maori word plural this also follows the author's form. All translations are the author's unless otherwise noted.

The word 'Pakeha', generally spelt with a small 'p', is most often found in this anthology capitalised.

Because we are dealing with a body of writing which inhabits two cultural traditions our definition of 'writing' or 'literature' may strike some readers as rather wide. In particular, some of our selections incorporate music, but it would be a mistake to label them in the European way as 'songs'. Many contemporary Maori writers might also be called composers. Barry Mitcalfe called his 1974 collection of waiata *Maori Poetry — The Singing Word*. There is no more apt description of the Maori language.

The names of the writers are those by which they wish to be known.

Contemporary Maori Writing: A Context

E nga waka. E nga hau e wha. E nga mana
E nga iwi. E nga manu korero o runga i nga marae
Whakarongo! Whakarongo! Whakarongo!
Ki te tangi a te manu e karanga nei 'Tui, tui, tuituia!'
Tuia i runga, tuia i raro, tuia i roto
Ka rongo te po, ka rongo te po
Tuia i te kawai tangata i heke mai i Hawaiki nui
I Hawaiki roa, i Hawaiki pa-mamao
I te hono ki wairua, ki te whai ao, ki te Ao Marama.

Writers in New Zealand have had to fight against prejudice and distrust to attain literary standing in these small islands. For Maori writers, contrary to popular belief, the fight has been harder — their work has had to win the confidence and critical acceptance not only of a European audience with preconceived notions of what literature is supposed to be like but also from a Maori audience who, until the 1950s, had no consistent tradition of written literature in English.

Most of the writers in this collection have had to create an audience, both Maori and Pakeha, for their work. There is the classic tale of the writer who, when asked by a publisher 'Who will read your books?', responded that Maoris would. The publisher's reply was 'But Maoris don't read books'.

The fact that publishers and a bicultural audience now exist is more a matter of tenacity than luck. Indeed, the development of Maori writing over the last ten years, charted in this anthology, has produced one of the most exciting experiences in modern New Zealand literature. In the process New Zealand literary forms, concerns and directions have been transformed in ways which could hardly have been foretold as little as thirty years ago.

Maori writing has also assisted in halting New Zealand's monocultural perception of itself and it has helped force a reconsideration of the national identity as being bilingual, bicultural and beneficiary of both Maori and Pakeha cultural heritages. It is about time: there has always been a need for New Zealand to take its Maori personality more into account.

This anthology had its own beginnings in 1973, just when Maori written literature burst in its first fullness upon the fish of Maui.

1

Maori literature, of course, began much earlier. In its oral form it had been in existence ever since the first man, the Maori, was created; the chants and waiata have since carried his stories of Creation, Gods and demi-Gods, voyages from Hawaiki to New Zealand, tribal genesis, clan-stories, folktales and, particularly, his great passion for living, to his descendants in the present, so that we are able to understand what we have been and what we are. The coming of the Pakeha two centuries ago introduced a new phase in the history of the Maori, one which was subsequently synthesised and defined within the Maori world view.

The Maori viewpoint has always been accessible, to Maoris that is, and to those who understand the Maori language; in this sense it has been a 'hidden' literature for many years. But it was not until the early 1960s, and via written English, that Maori literature began to unfurl the views of the people, until then participants in virtually the largest underground movement known in New Zealand, into the world of light.

At that time, Maori people formed ten percent of the total New Zealand population, mainly located in the northern half of the North Island. Despite appearances to the contrary, monocultural European methodology had tended to exclude them from the national mainstream, even in New Zealand literature. Under this circumstance it is little wonder that a tradition of Maori literature written in English took so long to eventuate. While some Pakeha writers like Roderick Finlayson, Bill Pearson and Noel Hilliard early identified with Maori concerns, it was not until the 1970s that Maori writing really began to emerge. Before then the body of imaginative work in English had been small: collections of verse by Hone Tuwhare and Alistair Te Ariki Campbell (which must be read beside their work included here), a handful of poems by others, Reweti Kohere's *The Autobiography of a Maori* and fifty short prose pieces, all of them except for some by Rowley Habib published since 1955 in *Te Ao Hou*, a Maori Affairs Departmental publication now renamed Te Kaea. Even by 1970, Margaret Orbell's collection, *Contemporary Maori Writing*, could only give a glimpse of the fullness still to come.

Part of the problem was the malaise which affected a people who, although they were undergoing the psychic trauma of Europeanisation after the last century's Land Wars, still held a misplaced confidence that the culture would survive anyway. Rowley Habib has characterised the period as being one in which tranquillisers were dispensed to the Maori people. On one hand they were encouraged to embrace Pakeha ways — at the same time they were given small concessions to Maori ways to keep them happy. Everything looked good and there was no doubt that Maori people were making it. The trouble was that the culture, the small concession, wasn't. What was needed was for Maori people to wake up to the fact that integration of people did not automatically make for integration of culture, and that the Maori cultural base needed to be regained if the Maori was not to become simply a brown Pakeha.

That need came in the early 1960s. Its subsequent impact on the national landscape has been characterised as a *renaissance* of Maori art and culture. It has been more than this — it has been a cultural *revolution*.

By the 1960s a young Maori generation, trained in European techniques and aware of the personal price paid in Maori cultural terms for such training, had evolved. At the same time, Maori culture was reaching a crisis point. Continued alienation of Maori land and of Maori people from their culture meant that the Maori was becoming landless and cultureless in his own country. As well, he was moving in greater numbers from rural areas, the earth-base of his culture, into urban areas where traditional tribal values and transmission of culture by Maori methods could not be sustained; nor were urban areas equipped then for providing for the transmission of the culture.

The result was a dislocation and a disruption to cultural continuity. As the faultline began to widen, the sense of loss — magnified by memories of past injustices and the resolve to assure cultural regeneration for Maori children being born within a Pakeha framework — coalesced into a period of political and cultural protest.

This was the time which saw Nga Tamatoa petitioning Parliment for the establishment of courses in Maori language and culture in all schools *as a gift to the Pakeha from the Maori*. It was the time of sit-ins in Parliament Grounds and annual protests at Waitangi Day celebrations, normally commemorating New Zealand's bicultural nationhood, to draw attention to Maori grievances regarding land, culture, sporting contacts with South Africa, educational and economic under-achievement, the necessity for a bicultural bureaucracy and, particularly, the innate rights of Maoris to be able to have control over their destiny in Aotearoa. It was the time of Land Marches and protests at Bastion Point in urban Auckland and Raglan near Hamilton. It was the time of media communication of issues in a way never available before and of consequent debate between Maori and Pakeha, Pakeha and Pakeha, Maori and Maori, which tested all. A time, ultimately, of the turning of the tide.

In Maori language, for instance, Maori Language Day was initiated in 1972 and helped to alter official attitudes to such an extent that by 1977 the Education Department reported that there were about 45 000 primary schoolchildren learning the Maori language with over 140 secondary schools offering Maori as part of their curriculum. In broadcasting, Radio Aotearoa was established in 1977, a Maori television production unit was set up in 1980, and the medium itself has become more sensitised to Maori

3

programming. In the arts, a Maori and South Pacific Arts Council was inaugurated in 1978. These are some of the achievements — there are more. While there is still a long way to go, particularly with land issues and the establishment of Maoris within the nation's power structure, one thing is certain: there is no turning back by New Zealand from a bicultural course for Maori and Pakeha.

This anthology identifies, from the Maori point of view, some of the preoccupations and concerns of individual men, women, elders and youth who themselves were caught in the cross-currents of the years of the furnace and of the tide's turning. In this sense the emergence of Maori literature written in English became as much a launching point for, as well as a development from, the period of protest during the past twenty years — indeed, the 1970s have been critical years for writing throughout the Pacific.

In New Zealand there is no doubt that the achievement, particularly in the last decade, has been stunning: 1972 *Pounamu, Pounamu* by Witi Ihimaera (the first collection of short stories by a Maori writer); 1973 *Tangi* by Witi Ihimaera (the first novel by a Maori writer); 1973 the Maori Artists' and Writers' Society is formed; 1974 *Te Raukura* by Harry Dansey (the first published play by a Maori writer); 1975 *Waiariki* by Patricia Grace (the first collection of short stories by a Maori woman writer); 1978 *Mahanga* by Vernice Wineera Pere (the first collection of poems by a Maori woman writer); 1978 *Mutuwhenua* by Patricia Grace (the first novel by a Maori woman writer). These were but taller trees in a forest of work not only by other Maori writers but also Pakeha interpreters of Maori life in journals, newspapers, radio and television — and, again, during a time notable for the absence of Maori publications.

For Maori people particularly this is the 'new' literature for the new world and this anthology, in effect, is the first-ever comprehensive survey of the complexity that has claimed them. It is a complexity which while conveying the continuity between the oral and literary forms also reveals the range of subject matter and style from the pastoral tradition established by *Te Ao Hou* in the 1950s to the urban literature of Maori/Pakeha relations and race relations conflict. To take subject matter, the anthology ranges from Pei Te Hurinui Jones' account of Maori ritual, through J.C. Sturm's stories of the shadow-boxing years of the 1950s, to Keri Hulme's perceptions of the present; from Dovey Katene-Horvath's traditional lament for the late Norman Kirk through the anguished poems of Rowley Habib to the lyrical strength of Michael Stevens' 'Let The Moon and The Sea'; from the male-force writing of Pat Heretaunga Baker to the incisive perceptions of Patricia Grace on Maori women and Maori culture. To take style, the anthology includes writing in English, writing in Maori and writing in both of these with translations — to expect all Maori writing in

4

Maori to appear with English translation would be to fail to understand what is happening to New Zealand's no longer monolingual literature.

If one thing is certain from this survey it is that this range in subject matter and style — from waiata composed along traditional lines to the stories, say, of Bub Bridger, which are not on the surface identifiably Maori — reveals a richness of experience and identity which has taken too long to come to the world of light. Nevertheless, this anthology could well have charted a course towards death. Instead, it charts a course towards life.

The contributors to this anthology are arranged, in the main, in order of birth from elders to youth. In so doing the editors have wished to let the generational differences in literary approach and tone speak for themselves without editorial interference. Apart from one or two pieces, the majority of the work has been published or written since 1970.

The authors themselves claim Maori ancestry and, in turn, are claimed by Maoridom as their own. Most of them emerged during a period of thirty years when Maori written literature burst upon the landscape but it would be unfair not to emphasise that their concerns are as artistic as they are Maori. Indeed, one of the major dilemmas faced by the editors of this anthology has been the irony inherent in assembling a collection which to all appearances contributes to keeping Maoris out of the national mainstream, even in New Zealand literature. Let there be no doubt that as far as we are concerned the contributors as artists belong as much to the mainstream as they do to the written tradition of Maori literature.

A few writers for a number of reasons are not featured in this anthology — Apirana Taylor, whose *Eyes Of The Ruru* was published in 1979, and Netana Te Ringa Mangu Mihaka, whose autobiography is still in preparation, are among those who do not appear. Many of us know the work of Rangi T. Harrison, Miritana Hughes, Ngapo and Pimia Wehi, Peter Sharples, Mason Durie, Muru Walters, George Brennan, Rora Pakititi, and Amiria Stirling. To these, and others, this anthology and the times it interprets also belong.

If anything, our own purpose as editors of this anthology is best described in Patricia Grace's memorable story 'Parade'. In it Patricia follows a Maori girl into a parade where she has to perform Maori action songs on the back of a float. But Patricia's character, perhaps like many Maori writers themselves, is watching the crowd:

'They think that's all we're good for ... A laugh and that's all. Amusement. In any other week of the year we don't exist. Once a year we're taken out and put on show, like relics'.

But then old Hohepa speaks, and says, perhaps not just to the girl but perhaps to all of us involved with Maori art and culture of whatever form:

'It is your job, this. To show others who we are'.

5

In 1977, Sydney Moko Mead wrote in *The NZ Listener* that 'it is Maori culture and the special relationship between Maori and Pakeha, for so long the envy of the world, which provides the source for a distinctive New Zealand image.'

It is our hope as editors that with this anthology we have made it possible for others to share something of this new reality as it is for Maoris and as it can be for all New Zealanders — contemporary Maori writing which is also contemporary New Zealand writing — which is surely something of what Sydney Moko Mead and old Hohepa foresaw.

No reira, tena koutou, tena koutou, tena tatou katoa.

O canoes. Four winds, Great ones.
Tribes. Orators of the marae.
Listen! Listen! Listen!
To the cry of the bird calling 'Unite, unite, be one!'
Unite above, unite below, unite within
Unite without, everyone unite in the brotherhood of men
The night hears, the night hears
Unite the descent lines from Great Hawaiki
From long Hawaiki, from Hawaiki far away
Joined to the spirit, to the daylight,
to the world of light.

Witi Ihimaera and D.S. Long

Canberra and Wellington
1981

Wiremu Kingi Kerekere

Taku Waiata

Horahia mai ki au nga taonga tupuna,
Nga kowhaiwhai, nga whakairo, nga pakiwaitara, nga waiata
    Maori tuturu o te ao tawhito,
Tuituia mai ki nga tikanga o toku ao o tenei ra,
Te ao tawhito, te ao hou, Maori, Pakeha,
Homai nga tohu tika, i runga i te aroha.
Tohatohaina tenei kupu ki te ao katoa
Puta ake i te po, ka ao, ka ao, ka marama.

Give to us the treasured arts of our ancestors,
The carvings, the designs and patterns, the stories and the traditional
    chants.
Let us of this generation, try to combine them with what talents we
    have in this changing world of today,
Give to us your greatest gift, 'aroha', love in its many connotations,
It will bring peace, goodwill, friendship among peoples,
And will take us from the world of darkness and ignorance, into the
    light of knowledge and understanding.

WIREMU KINGI KEREKERE (1923; Ngaitai, Mahaki) whose waiata opens this
anthology, was born at Waihirere. He was educated at Waerenga-a-Hika College
and Gisborne High School. He is Radio New Zealand's consultant on Maori
Affairs and lives in Wellington.

He began leading a Maori group performing for radio when he was thirteen and
in 1963 he led the Waihirere Maori Club in a performance of his own compositions
before the Queen. (His compositions were to be presented to the Queen again in
1970 and 1977.) In 1964 Wiremu's work appeared on 'Songs of the Forefathers',
this was the first time modern Maori action songs had been seen on television.
Apart from Waihirere Maori Club, Ngati Poneke Maori Club and Te Kahui
Rangatahi Maori Club have featured his compositions, as have the Maori Opera
Theatre Group, the New Zealand Maori Company, and the Aoteroa Maori Group.

He is best known, perhaps, for his compositions 'Tangihia', 'Karangatia e te Iwi
te Manu Kotuku', and 'Tumaramaranoa'. Wiremu has been awarded an OBE for
his work in this field.

Wiremu has steadfastly refused to allow a collection of his compositions to appear
in book form, believing that his is, above all, an oral art. The waiata which opens
Into the World of Light was specially composed for the occasion.

7

Pei Te Hurinui Jones

Te Hurinui

My second name, Te Hurinui, was the name of my great-great-grandfather who flourished some 150 years ago. Te Hurinui the First, as I shall call him, was a High Priest of Ahurei, the Tainui House of Sacred Learning, at Maketu on the shores of Kawhia Harbour.

At the time of his death, Te Hurinui had been to Kawhia where there had been some animated discussion about the sacred emblems of the Ahurei Temple, which had been deposited there on the arrival of the Tainui Canoe some five hundred years before. Te Hurinui was on his way back to his home at Mangaorongo, near Otorohanga, when he was waylaid by a party of Waikato warriors under a chief named Te Uira. Te Uira had tried to persuade Te Hurinui to disclose the hiding place of the sacred emblems and, failing in his purpose, he had killed Te Hurinui.

This killing led to much bloodshed, and the civil war which ensued engulfed all the Tainui tribes, and it finally led up to the Kawhia tribes of Ngati Toa, Ngati Koata and Ngati Rarua migrating to the south under their leader, the famous Te Rauparaha.

The second of the name, Te Hurinui, was my maternal grandfather's first cousin whose name in full was Te Hurinui Te Wano. He adopted me from infancy.

During my life with this granduncle, Te Hurinui, until his death in 1911, my English schooling was often irregular. My recollection of those schooldays were of visits from the Truant Officer, some tribal meetings in many parts of the country, conferences of tribal elders and attending at sittings of the Maori Land Court at Otorohanga. Our home was at Te Kawakawa, now called Ongarue, a small township among high hills on the bank of the Ongarue River.

I had more than my share of childhood ills. At night I often had vivid dreams ending in nightmares. This would indicate, one would suppose, that my illnesses were in the nature of digestive disorders. Be it as it may, some of these vivid dreams of mine were often followed by the death of some relative — usually a leading tribal figure — whose name I had uttered during my midnight ravings. In time I gained some notoriety, and I was often referred to as te tamaiti moe tohutohu nei, this child with significant dreams. As a last resort, in order to cure me, so I was told by my mother at the time, I had to submit myself to two ancient sacred rites. Later on I learnt that the whole matter had been discussed and arranged by the tribal elders.

The first of these ceremonies took place at Ongarue. I was awakened from sleep to find myself with my granduncle on the western bank of the Ongarue River. I was wrapped up in a blanket, and for a moment I thought I was again having one of my disturbing dreams. The time was the early morning, and the place chosen for the ceremony was on a big bend of the river. Where we were there was a sandy spit, and on the opposite bank was a deep dark pool. On the riverbank above the pool was a sacred or tapu rock, which children were warned not to approach when bathing.

For the ceremony, my granduncle had as his assistant, Te Pou. Te Pou, in later years, achieved quite a reputation as a faith-healing tohunga. My granduncle recited the ritual to the accompaniment of responses from Te Pou who had waded out knee-deep into the river with a branch of koromiko in his hand. Te Pou stood naked as he dipped the branch at intervals into the water. Now and again he would wave it sharply about him: toward the tapu rock, then upstream and lastly downstream. The dawn light was lighting up the valley of the Mangakahu, tributary of the Ongarue, when Te Pou returned to the bank and handed over the wet branch to my granduncle. It was again waved in the same manner as Te Pou had done, but this time above my head, and then it was finally thrown into the river. As I watched the drifting branch float down the river, my granduncle rubbed my wetted head gently and brought the ceremony to an end. This was my Tohinga or Initiation Rite. And, strangely enough, I was never to be troubled with those disturbing dreams again.

The second ceremony took place a year or so later at Taumarunui, sixteen miles south of our home at Ongarue. A tribal gathering was in progress, and our sleeping quarters were in the wharepuni. Our sleeping place was next to the kopa-iti, the lefthand side of the doorway. Again I was awakened from sleep. This time it was my mother who awakened me.

Next to me, in the corner, was the sleeping place of Hakiaha, the chief of the local tribe of Ngati Haua and the host for the occasion, a relative of ours. Across the kauhanga nui, the centre-way, in the iho nui, on the right hand side of the doorway, was the sleeping place of Te Naunau Taonui, a first cousin of my mother's grandfather. After waking me from sleep, my mother hurriedly whispered in my ear not to be afraid of my koroua, at the same time indicating Taonui, who was by this time sitting up on his couch. As I rubbed the sleep from my eyes my mother told me that I had to cross over to the foot of Taonui's sleeping place and, without further ado, she left the building.

Sitting round about were several tribal elders. As was the case with the Tohinga ceremony, the time was again early morning, and it was some time before I was properly awake. It seemed that all eyes were on me, and I was self-conscious and nervous. I knew Taonui was a very important person, and this knowledge did not help matters. He was, I learnt later, paramount chief of the Maniapoto tribe, and he lived at Te Kuiti. Te Hurinui, my foster father, was sitting next to Taonui (they were first cousins once removed), and this reassured me somewhat. I stood for a moment or two outside the paepae, the beams fronting Taonui's couch. He motioned me to step over and to sit down at the foot of his couch. After I sat down, Taonui remained silent for quite a time. Then in a low solemn voice he began to recite a ritual.

With my eyes on his moving lips I listened, only comprehending a word here and there and wondering how long it was all going to be. It seemed his karakia would last for a very long time, but suddenly he stopped and, pulling his blanket aside, he motioned for me to lean forward towards his left food which he thrust toward me. Then, pointing to his big toe, he said 'Ngaua!' Bite!

I placed my mouth over his toe, and in the rather awkward position I was in I tried hard not to bite the toe too hard. The ceremony was becoming quite an ordeal and I could not help thinking that I must look rather ridiculous with the big toe in my mouth. It seemed that the ritual would never end, but quite gently Taonui withdrew his toe and the ceremony came to an end. At the same time as he pulled his foot away he said quietly, 'Kau mutu'. It is finished.

That ceremony was the Tohi-whakaara, The Raising Up. The toe-biting part was the Whakangungu, The Strengthening Rite. My impression of the ceremony, in retrospect, is that it was somewhat impromptu. However, one may suppose that allowing for changing circumstances as the result of European influences, it was inevitable there should have been some modification in these ancient ceremonies. Then again, perhaps, much had preceded my awakening in the early morning. It was noticeable that there were no women left in the building after the departure of my mother.

From the time of that Tohi-whakaara ceremony, my granduncle often would recall me from my youthful games and set me to work on his manuscript books. These books contained genealogical tables, tribal traditions, ancient songs, and ritual. The task I was first set to do was to copy pages of manuscript into new books. He flattered and encouraged me in this work by words of admiration for my handwriting.

At times I found the task most irksome, and it was hard to put up with the shouting and laughter of my companions in their play. The temptation was strong to rush off and leave my granduncle's books behind. In time, however, I became very interested in the subject matter of my writing.

When I started to question my granduncle about some of the rather obscure passages in the stories or the songs, a look of deep contentment came over his smiling face before he went on to answer me. From those early years I became so absorbed in the study of ancient ritual, tribal traditions, waiata, and the esoteric lore of our people that it became a passion with me.

It was in this way, at a comparatively early age, that my grandfather implanted in me and I acquired an abiding love for the ancient lore of our Maori people.

I shall now bring this account to an end with a ritualistic epilogue which is part of one of the earliest karakia I was taught. It was chanted on important occasions when one was about to undertake some arduous or dangerous enterprise to Waere i te Ara, Clear the Way. It may also be addressed to Tawhirimatea, God of Wind and Storms, to cause the tempest to Whakataha, to pass by, to cease.

I have only ritually pronounced this karakia twice, and on both occasions it was efficacious. The first occasion was on the Turangawaewae marae at Ngaruawahia, in drenching rain at dawn on Monday, 23rd May, 1966. This was the day of the funeral of King Koroki and the traditional crowning ceremony of the Maori Queen, Arikinui Dame Te Ata-i-rangikaahu. The rain stopped for the funeral service and the crowning, and this enabled both ceremonies to be carried out in the presence of several hundred tribespeople, with all due dignity and solemnity.

The second occasion was during the Royal Tour, when the Maori welcome was held at Gisborne on Sunday, 23rd March, 1970. The early morning radio weather forecast was for high winds with rain. As I was to give the address of welcome on an open-air platform, to be followed by the Queen in reply, I was rather worried the day might be spoilt.

During my speech and as I recited the karakia in Maori, some heavy rain drops fell accompanied by strong gusty winds, and I noticed that the Duke of Edinburgh was making quick glances at the sky, and he had a worried look I thought. On the spur of the moment, and before I gave my English rendering of the ritual, I interpolated a few words of explanation and said: 'Your Royal Highness the ancient ritual I have spoken in Maori will placate Tawhirimatea, God of Wind and Storms.'

The Gisborne Herald of Monday, 23rd March, 1970, carried a front page coverage of a 'Memorable Day', and about the rain, the ritual, and my speech the paper reported (I quote parts only):
'In spite of one small shower of rain during the Maori welcome, the weather favoured the occasion... The show commenced during the address of welcome being given by Dr Pei Te Hurinui Jones, the Vice-president of the New Zealand Maori Council. It also stopped during Dr Jones' speech at a point at which he had just quoted an ancient Maori ritual of welcome in which the words: "Cease O wind from the South" were spoken. From then on sunshine bathed the park for the remainder of the function.'

The ritualistic epilogue:

Whakataka to hau ki te Uru,
Whakataka to hau ki te Tonga!
Kai makinakina i Uta,
Kai mataratara I Tai;
Kai hii ake ana te Ata-kura
He Tio . . .
He Huka . . .
He Hauhunga!

Cease O wind in the West,
Cease O wind in the South!
Let gentle breezes blow o'er the Land,
Let calm seas flow o'er the Ocean;
And let the Red-tipped dawn come
With a Sharpened air . . .
A touch of Frost . . .
And the promise of a Glorious Day!

Katahi ka mutu

PEI TE HURINUI JONES (1898-1976; Waikato, Tuwharetoa, Maniopoto) was a
central figure in the renaissance of Maori culture in the 20th century. Educated at
Ongarue School, he was awarded an OBE in 1961 and an honorary Doctorate in
Literature from the University of Waikato in 1968. Among his works are
Mahinarangi, King Potatau, and *Puhiwahine* in addition to which he translated *The
Merchant of Venice* and *The Rubaiyat of Omar Khayyam* into Maori. With the late
Sir Apirana Ngata he co-edited and translated a three-volume collection of songs of
the Maori, *Nga Moteatea*. He was also chairman of the revision committee for
H.W. Williams' *A Dictionary of the Maori Language*. The autobiographical
fragment in this anthology was written in 1975 especially for this work.

Arapeta Awatere

Kepa Anaha Ehau

i te maruawatea
he wera koroirangi
koopehupehu ana

Kepa Anaha Ehau

in broad daylight
the shimmering heat
strikes down

12

'taku rau kootuku	my kootuku leaf
i te maruahiahi	in the evening
he matangi hehengi	the breeze is gentle
kua parohea ia	but withered is
taku taonga whakaepa	my symbol
tirohia te rangi	see the sky
'parewaikohu ana	mistily weeps
moou raa, e te hoa,	for you, friend,
'takuatetia nei—	lamented by us—
te kaakaa kura	the tried leader
te manu tohikura	the fount of lore
te manu koorero	the orator supreme
kua taaoki naa!	now gone to rest!
kua wehe nei koe	now you are gone
e te puukoorero	wise man of words,
maa wai e taku	who will recite
te hono taatai	the family tree
heke tanga-aa-rangi	rooted in heaven
o Te Arawa iwi?	of Te Arawa people?
maa Muruika pea?	will Muruika speak?
maa Te Papa-i-ouru?	will Te Papa-i-ouru?
takahia e te hoa	follow, friend,
i te ara a Taane	the path of Taane
kia tae naa koe	until you reach
ki Tatau-o-te-poo	Tatou-o-te-poo
ki te whaaioio	and the myriad
kua ruupeke atu	now assembled
hei karanga i a koe	to greet you
ki Te Oii tangotango!	to the Underworld!

ARAPETA AWATERE (1910-1976; Ngati Porou) was a celebrated leader of the New Zealand Maori Battalion; during World War II he was Lieutenant-Colonel. His long career was marked by an active concern for the welfare of the Maori people and for Maori affairs. The poem in this anthology forms part of an extensive collection of writings on aspects of Maoritanga written in his later years while in Mount Eden Prison where he died in 1976. In 1960 the Caxton Press published *Why Birds Don't Cry* by Colin Bell (Patricia Bell's husband) with a translation into Maori by Arapeta. The year 1976 was a sad one for New Zealand literature with the deaths of Arapeta and Pei, two of the last great classical Maori language scholars.

Dovey Katene-Horvath

Te Ra Pouri

Waiata Tangi

E tangi e te tai
I waho i te takutai
Tangi hotuhotu ana
Te hau e puhi mai
E ua e te ua i runga ra
Aue
Rite rawa i nga roimata e

Piri ai ki nga kapua nga manu e rere ra
Ki te rangi piki atu tangi haere e
I kawe mai te rau o te kawakawa e
Hei tipare mo nga iwi o te motu e
Ka hinga te Totaranui e
Ru ana te whenua i hinga i te Tetekura
Haere ki te tini ki te mano e
Haere ki te iwi nui i te po

The Day The Capital Mourned

Lament for the late Prime Minister, Norman Kirk

The sea wept
Out beyond the seashore
Sobbing in sadness
The wind sighed and eddied past
The rain that continually fell,
Alas,
Appeared to be as tears of sorrow.

The birds flying close to the low-lying clouds
Called mournfully as they soared on high
They bore in their beaks the leaves of the kawakawa tree
To fashion the garland of mourning for all people of New Zealand to wear

14

Fallen indeed is the great Totara tree of our time
The earth shook and trembled at the impact of loss
Of a noble and honoured chief
So go forth beloved friend and leader
Go forth to join the hundreds and thousands who have gone before
Go forth to the great tribe, who await us all.

DOVEY KATENE-HORVATH (1912; Ngati Toa, Ngati Tama, Te Atiawa, Te Rarawa) was born and grew up in the Wellington area where she still lives. A tutor of Maori culture, she is the kuia of the Mawai Hakona Cultural Group and a life member of Ngati Poneke. She is one of an increasingly well known group of composers whose compositions for cultural groups have won awards at Polynesian and Maori cultural festivals. 'Te Ra Pouri' was the winning composition in the traditional section of the NZBC Maori Songs Contest (1974). She is a recipient of the Queen's Service Order.

Heretaunga Pananehu Pat Baker

Punahamoa

A Story of the High Priest

Everyone stared at the Sacred Flame.

In hushed whispers, the elders discussed its awful significance — and the frightening portents to come.

In their minds was the thought: 'What has our dear relation Te Paki done that he should die?'

Others asked, 'How many more are to be taken?' While their friends answered, 'Surely one man is enough for a sacrifice!'

'Silence!'

A stentorian bellow rocked the marae — so only the distant murmur of the sea permeated the scene, while the wind cried forlornly between the palisade posts.

All eyes focused as a tall athletic figure emerged from the shadows of the Chief's House and danced before them — his clawlike toes crushing the earth beneath him, and kicking it away in puffs of dust.

15

Punahamoa the High Priest proceeded slowly and deliberately to the centre of the marae, chanting a song to the Sacred Flame — especially dedicated to the tribal War God — the dreaded Tama I Waho.

Masses of tattoo cut into the High Priest's arms, legs, face and body appeared to undulate in rhythm to his every movement as tantalising glimpses from beneath his flowing dogskin cloak. This gave the High Priest a sinister appearance almost as though there were two men walking together in the one body.

Suddenly he stopped chanting and turned to face his people.

'You heard the God scream when I lit the Sacred Flame?' he shouted eyeing the crowd.

'Yes! Yes! We certainly did!' Everyone voiced together — the uncanny scream still echoing in their minds: who could ever forget it!

'I shall explain to you the commands of our War God, Tama I Waho!'

His words came like a thunder clap preceding an icy hailstorm and people shivered as he spoke.

'Every member of the Ngaitai tribe in Hurumua must die! There shall be no exceptions! Tama I Waho in return will place the mantle of power over the weapons of our brave warriors — the Hoko Whitu A Tu — to defeat the gathering hordes of the enemy, under that tattooed lizard, Tu Te Rangikurei!

By midday the Sacred Flame will be extinguished. Then the command of Tama I Waho must be completed — and every Ngaitai dead!'

The voice was cold, unforgiving, commanding.

'But my wife is Ngaitai!'

'My children are from Ngaitai!'

'My father is half Ngaitai!'

'Our mother, our dear mother!'

And so the clamour against the shock pronouncement rose like the roar of an angry sea.

Punahamoa had expected this outburst. He remained immobile on the marae, one hand holding a greenstone mere raised above his head, a sign demanding complete silence.

Slowly the angry shouting and screams against the High Priest died down and some people began fingering their weapons in preparation for rushing onto the marae and cutting their High Priest down where he stood — several had decided no man or woman of any courage would tolerate such a demand, god or no god.

But then these very people who were preparing to attack their priest saw sudden movement around them.

The elite guards — the Hoko Whitu A Tu — had quietly slipped into every vantage point around the pa, and several had drifted nonchalantly onto the marae well within defensive distance of their High Priest.

Glaring hate, with many whisperings and mutterings the crowd tried to comfort those who were to die.

'Listen everyone! Listen to what I have to say!' Motu, the warrior chief and the commander of the elite guards attracted attention; tattooed from head to foot and wearing the brief maro of the fighting man he shouted at the incensed crowd.

'You have heard the orders of our High Priest, that Tama I Waho demands a sacrifice for victory — blood of every Ngaitai! Are we to do the bidding of our God or as cowards flinch from death!'

Hearing this awful question, the crowd filled with weeping — knowing there could only be one answer.

Motu knelt on one knee beside his High Priest gripping his taiaha and ready to spring forward as he faced the people.

Slowly the High Priest surveyed the crowded marae. He smiled inwardly as a huge man had risen amongst them to speak.

This was his friend Taupoto, the mightly warrior from Pakowhai, the big pa at the junction of the two rivers on the Opotiki plain.

Taupoto's speech was brief.

'Let the wishes of Tama I Waho be obeyed at once!'

Stark naked Motu, and Taupoto, led several detachments of warriors in a compelling war dance.

Their penises erect in violent simulation of deflowering the enemy, the warriors' absolute contempt gripped madly at the hearts of the massed onlookers and their intended victims, as the wailing cry for the dead broke from the women.

This was the signal for death! Many weapons raised and fell. Thus died Ngaitai just as the Sacred Flame spluttered to extinction.

The sacrifice to Tama I Waho was fulfilled.

With victory assured, Punahamoa was seen to smile for the first time.

Many memories flooded his mind as he looked with obvious satisfaction at the slaughtered offerings.

He remembered especially the mighty pa at Tirohanga, and how Ngaitai using treachery gained admittance to this almost impregnable fortress. No treacherous Ngaitai would be allowed to remain in Hurumua except as sacrifices to the tribal War God.

Punahamoa vowed that Tirohanga would be avenged in the name of the Panenehu people who died when this stronghold fell with heavy slaughter.

He was very soon to realise his wishes.

His smile of vengeance grew broader.

But wait.

Their High Priest was again preparing to address the crowd.

'Tama I Waho has sent me a sign! He is pleased with your dedication — but demands one further test for the quality of your belief!'

Like a clever conjuror holding attention of the crowd the High Priest waited as he assessed turmoil before him.

'This great pa — Hurumua — is tapu with blood of our offerings. Tama I Waho cries for the ritual fires to burn again for the ultimate tapu cleansing!'

Suddenly the High Priest sprang into a violent haka screaming a frightening chant of instant instructions.

Even the mightly Taupoto and Motu and their warriors looked askance as they listened spellbound.

'Pull down the palisades
of Hurumua,
Great palisades,
All palisades
Must be levelled to the earth,
To be heaped up
On banks of Waiaua River,
And burned with
Ritual fire
For this is the wish
Of Tama I Waho!
Oh dreaded god
Guardian of our people,
Conqueror of all foes,
It is Tama I Waho for life!
Tama I Waho for glory!
Tama I Waho for victory!'

At first light the following morning the whole hilltop fortress seethed with activity.

As the big carved palisade post guarding the main gateway was pulled from the ground, Motu in full view of many people hit the post a sharp blow with his whalebone mere shouting for all to hear:

'On the morrow will fall the first fish to my mere!'

Thus prepared Punahamoa to meet the onslaught from the combined forces of Ngaitai, Whanau Apanui and Ngati Porou who fought under their great war leader the redoubtable Tu Te Rangikurei.

Needless to say Tama I Waho respected the obeisance of Punahamoa and rewarded with great victory the Whakatohea tribe who slaughtered the enemy in droves.

Tu Te Rangikurei fell in battle. His head was cut off and on orders of Punahamoa smoke-dried as a tribal symbol of victory.

A Prophecy Fulfilled (Extract)

Raumoko and Rangipai were still asleep when the old priest shook them awake just before sunrise. Sleepily they followed him out into the cold morning air. They went out the main gates and down to a small stream. Here Rangipai handed Tipu Tapeka the kawakawa leaf. He chanted a prayer as he dipped the leaf in the crystal-clear water and held it up to the sun rising over the distant hills.

Strangely a small rainbow seemed to weave around the leaf as the old priest prayed. He placed his right thumb in the water and sprinkled droplets over Rangipai and Raumoko. Then he threw the leaf into the stream where it disappeared in a little whirlpool which suddenly appeared where the leaf had fallen into the water.

Slowly the old priest turned and addressed Rangipai. 'You will have one son and a daughter. Your son will be born first; two years later a daughter will be born.

When the last of your children arrives, the power of the gods will turn upon me, and I will die — like that leaf you saw disappearing in the whirlpool. So shall I be plucked from this life.'

They all stood for long minutes in silence. At last the old man said, 'Come, we must return to the pa.'

Both deep in wonder at the ritual they had witnessed and the meaning of the words they had heard, Rangipai and Raumoko followed Tipu Tapeka.

Suddenly a call from the guards arrested their attention.

'Look! Look! A strange white bird with huge wings is coming over the sea!'

Almost rooted to the spot, Rangipai and Raumoko watched as the strange apparition drew steadily nearer.

Rangipai had a strange inexplicable presentiment and felt a chill shiver run up her spine. She clutched Raumoko, holding him close. 'What is it, dearest?'

He remained silent, at last saying, 'It's some kind of very large canoe.'

Deep in thought they returned to Te Hairini and joined the crowds of silent people gathered on the cliffs overlooking the sea.

Tipu Tapeka now made what was to prove one of the most startling prophecies. Looking hard at Raumoko, he said, 'You will remember my words, now I am going to give you the key to the future. It is spoken of by the old people and it is most appropriate for today.

'Kei muri i te awe kapara he tangata ke, mana te ao, he ma!'

'Behind the tattooed face a stranger stands. He will inherit this world — he is without tattoo!'

'I cannot believe that day will ever come,' said the young chief.

'It will,' replied the priest.

'You mean we will see people with no tattoo — on their faces?'

'Are they our people?' asked Rangipai in wonder.

'Yes,' said the old man, to both their questions.

'And our land?' asked Raumoko.

'A tribe of strangers will control it.'

'What about us?'

'Those of our tribe who live into that future will know the answer, for then our people would even so be strangers to us, who live now,' concluded the seer, adding, 'We must join the people or they will think we are evading them. I know they are all waiting to ask questions about that thing down there,' and his arm jabbed, pointing towards the sea.

He need not have worried as most of the tribe were much too busy watching the 'huge white bird' coming nearer with each breath they took.

Standing and watching arm in arm, Rangipai and Raumoko, with the old priest beside them and their people gathered around in hundreds, tried to understand the strange visitor. The War Chief, Haukino, with Awanui on his arm and his son at his side, watched from the observation platform. He was smiling and longingly fingering his taiaha. He had made his own interpretation as he gripped his taiaha tighter than ever.

'Stay here and look after our son. I am going down to have a look.'

'Be careful!' Awanui yelled after her husband as he raced out the main gates, calling to his men to follow.

The old priest was right in his prophecy.

It was really the beginning of the end to a long, long age of tribal power, and as it appeared they stood in wonder at the entrance of a strange new world.

It was October 1769.

Captain James Cook had anchored his Endeavour just beyond the breakers, in the wide expanse of the bay in the sea of the smoking island.

'Prepare the longboat, Mr Mate. Take a dozen armed men with you but don't use your firearms unless you have to defend yourselves. Those people coming down to the beach don't look too friendly to me. . . . But you can never tell with these natives.'

Orders rang out along the decks of the Endeavour. 'Shorten sail!' Then came, 'Furl mainsails!' intermingled with the call of the seaman sounding the lead.

'Twenty fathoms!'

'Fifteen fathoms!'

'Ten fathoms!'

'She's shoaling rapidly, sir; steady at the helm, capstan on anchors, slow away — she's holding, sir, seems like a good sandy bottom.'

Many of the seamen looked shoreward.

'Look at those black bastards on the beach. What an ugly-looking whore that one is. Shit! I wouldn't like to be among that lot. Man, they'd have your balls for a necklace and your arse for a flapjack.'

'Silence!' It was the captain speaking again.

'Be very careful, and don't get into any arguments. Offer them these bolts of coloured material and these trinkets. It always seems to work. Remember we want to try to make friends with them. Best of luck, Mr Mate.'

'Lower away longboat!'

'Lower away longboat!' repeated the bosun and the heavily-laden vessel was gradually eased from its cradle on the Endeavour to the ocean.

The longboat shot away from the side of the ship and with the dozen or so seamen was soon sweeping in towards the shore.

'Hokowhitu a Tu!'

The command rang out from the cliff top.

'Assemble! Assemble! Let us assemble together!' yelled the warriors as they all raced down to the beach behind their chief.

Seeing the warriors going down the path, everyone else at the pa wanted to follow — that is all those except the guards who were on watch and could not vacate their posts.

A large group led by Rangipai and Raumoko walked down the path to take their positions near the sandhills but well back from the beach.

Here Rangipai knew she could see everything that was going on.

'Look, the strangers have reached the shore,' said Raumoko pointing them to Rangipai. 'It's not far from the Big Rock where I am going to catch crayfish at low tide this afternoon.'

'And Haukino's down there too,' she replied. 'I do hope he is careful.'

'Don't worry about Haukino,' replied Raumoko. 'It's the strangers who will have to watch out.'

Suddenly the Hokowhitu a Tu could be seen swirling round the strangers and there were excited shouts as some of the warriors came racing back towards where Rangipai and Raumoko stood, with strange gaily coloured coverings in their hands.

Haukino Te Onewa was first to reach the longboat as it grounded gently on the shelving beach.

Only he perceived these strangers were men — but with white skins — and they were covered from head to foot in strange bark-like cloaks and wore thick coverings on their feet and legs.

A long glinting thing lay in the boat near one of the strangers who was

21

obviously the chief. Haukino picked it up by the handle and waved it around, giving the gunwale a sharp crack.

The weapon stuck deep in the wood and Haukino cut his finger trying to withdraw it. His blood dripped on to the weapon.

Haukino acted as a chief must in the circumstances. His blood was on the weapon and this made it tapu. He could not possibly give it back to the owner now. He had to take it away and bury it so misfortune would not come to the strangers. He had to protect them.

But what was this?

This chief of the strangers was trying to take it back. No! He couldn't give it back. It would be transgressing the law of tapu. Didn't the stranger understand that? Surely — why even a lowly slave knew of tapu!

'Get away, stranger!' he yelled, 'I am doing this for your own good!'

But the stranger grappled fiercely with him, yelling some unintelligible sentence again and again.

Haukino pushed the man away and he fell heavily on to the hard wet sand.

'Grab the canoe!' Haukino yelled at his men as he raced in to cut off the longboat from getting out to sea again.

But the man he had pushed into the sand had leaped up and sprung into the boat. Haukino lunged at him with the sword.

A sound of thunder echoed over the beach, and with it a flash like lightning.

By this time Raumoko himself had come to see what all the commotion was about.

He was followed by a great crowd of people from both tribes.

He was just in time to see Haukino stagger forward with a startled look on his face and sag heavily to his knees before falling face forward on to the sand, where he lay.

Many exclamations of surprise came from the warriors at the long magic flute that had knocked their great chief down, without even touching him.

The stranger snatched the long weapon that Haukino had in his hand and, shouting wildly, they all rowed furiously away from the shore.

Soon they had joined the Big Bird with the white wings that had remained just beyond the breakers.

With the rest of the tribe Raumoko watched in awe as the vessel moved slowly at first then much more rapidly, finally disappearing beyond the smoking island.

Freed at last as if from a magic spell, Raumoko bent down to assist Haukino to his feet. 'Come, Haukino, what are you lying there for?'

There was no reply.

He picked up the limp arm of the great War Chief and knew when he felt it that Haukino was dead.

The movement forced the body over on to its back. Right in the middle of the chest was a small round hole through which the blood trickled slowly on to the sand, staining the incoming tide.

Rangipai knelt before the fallen chief, pushing back the hair over his cold wet brow, silent in her thoughts.

She alone stood at the edge of the tide looking towards the sunset.

When Rangipai turned to go, her eyes filled with tears, but she gave the order and said simply to her warriors, 'Prepare for Haukino Te Onewa's tangi.'

The Hokowhitu a Tu constructed a litter of driftwood from the beach and picked up his body to take back to the marae.

Rangipai knew life would never be the same.

It was as if a fierce storm had blown itself out in the wake of the white-winged stranger.

Softly and quietly a deep stillness descended.

Even the waves and sea birds were hushed. No dogs barked. There was no wind. No one spoke, no one moved.

Slowly every head turned, and all eyes were focused intently on Rangipai and Raumoko as they stood clasping hands, facing their combined tribes, at the edge of the ocean.

First like a ripple, then as the rushing tide, echoing voices of their ancestors seemed to fill the hearts and minds of the people.

Led by their two young arikis, everyone was singing as they walked back to the pa.

HERETAUNGA PANANEHU PAT BAKER (1920; Whakatohea, Ngati Kahungunu) was born at Rakaia but grew up at Raukokore, Omarumutu, and Opotiki. Educated at Te Aute College he was the first Maori to gain a university bursary to study journalism which he did at the University of Canterbury. During World War II he was in the merchant navy and was involved in convoy battles in the North Atlantic, the Middle East and the Pacific. He also took part in the invasion of Europe. After working for the *Grey River Argus* and the *Star Sun* he farmed at Opotiki. Pat was secretary of Te Waipounamu District Maori Council (1965-1970) and the first chairman of the Canterbury Museum of Science and Industry. He has also been the District Council observer on the Maori Education Foundation for the University of Canterbury. When his business collapsed he was sentenced in 1973 to four years in prison on charges he denies. In 1975 he published *Behind the Tattooed Face*, the first historical novel by a Maori writer. 'Punahamoa' was written especially for this anthology. It describes one of the last great tribal battles fought prior to the advent of guns; it took place about the time Captain Cook reached New Zealand. The event is also described in *Behind the*

23

Tattooed Face, from which 'A Prophecy Fulfilled' has been taken.

Pat's second novel, *Cry For The People*, is at his publishers and a collection of poems and essays, *Priests of the Golden Summer*, is in preparation. He works as a clothing cutter in a factory in Christchurch.

Kingi M. Ihaka

Haka Taparahi

LEADER: Kia mau!
           A! ra! ra! Ko te Maori
ALL: Ka nukunuku!
LEADER: Ko nga iwi
ALL: Ka nekeneke!
LEADER: Ko te Maori
ALL: Ka nukunuku!
LEADER: Ko nga iwi
ALL: Ka nekeneke!
           A ka nekeneke nga iwi o te motu
           Ki runga o Whangarei-terenga-paraoa,
           Aue! Hei!
LEADER: A! ra! ra!
           Ko Tamaki e ngunguru nei
ALL: Au! Au! Aue! Ha! Hu!
LEADER: Ko Tamaki e rapu nei
ALL: Kei! Kei! Kei hea ra?
           A! Ha! Kei hea ra te ora?
           Kei hea ra te aroha?
           Korerotia ra mai nga tupuna
           Tuku iho, tuku iho,
           Kauwhautia ra mai Te Matenga
           Oatitia ra mai te Tiriti e!
LEADER: A! Ka ngaro ra! Ka ngaro ra!
ALL: Ka ngaro ra aku whenua
           Ka ngaro ra aku tika;
           Mataotao ana te aroha,
           Momona ana nga iwi whai rawa
           Tupuhi ana nga iwi rawakore:
LEADER: I! A! Ha! Ha!

ALL: Kua whati nga iwi te kimi te ora,
Marara noa ana ki ko, ki ko,
Kukume ai, rorona ai,
Nga whakararu ra o te ao,
Aue! Ka he te manawa.

LEADER: E, kia kaha e te iwi, e tu!

ALL: E tu, whititia ra nga hope te pono,
Kakahuria iho ko te tika hei pukupuku,
Herea te rongapai ra o te rangimarie
Hei hu ra mo nga waewae kia tu ai, takatu ai,
Te whakapono hei whakangungu rakau,
Hei tinei atu nga matia mumura te wairua kino,
Ka puta nga iwi ki te wheiao ki te ao marama ra e!

LEADER: Aue! Whitiwhiti!

ALL: Whitiwhiti ora! Hei!

Haka Taparahi

LEADER: Be ready!
It is the Maori

ALL: Who moves!

LEADER: It is the tribes

ALL: Which move!

LEADER: It is the Maori

ALL: Who moves!

LEADER: It is the tribes

ALL: Which move!
The tribes proceed to Whangarei-terenga-paraoa,
Aue! Hei!

LEADER: A! It is Tamaki which roars

ALL: Au . . .

LEADER: It is Tamaki which is fatigued

ALL: Hu . . .

LEADER: It is Tamaki which seeks

ALL: Where! Where! Where indeed?
Yes, where indeed is life,
Where indeed is the love
Proclaimed throughout by our forebears,
Preached since Marsden's time,
Promised since the signing of the Treaty?

25

LEADER:	A! It has gone! It has disappeared!
ALL:	My lands have gone
	My rights have disappeared;
	Love has become cold,
	The rich have become fatter
	While the poor have become leaner.
LEADER:	I! A! Ha! Ha!
ALL:	The people have fled in search of livelihood,
	And have scattered here, there and everywhere,
	Pulling here and pulling there,
	The problems of this world,
	Causing my heart to fail,
LEADER:	Oh, people be strong, and stand!
ALL:	Stand then and gird your loins with truth
	Put on the breast plate of righteousness.
	Your feet shod with peace
	That you may be able to withstand evil,
	And having done all, to stand,
	With the Faith as your shield
	To enable you to quench the fiery darts of the evil spirit,
	And the people to reach the light of day, the clear light!
LEADER:	Awake! Awake!
ALL:	Pass into life! Hei!

Poi

LEADER:	Kia mau!
	Titiro e nga iwi!
ALL:	Te kapu taku ringa
	He taonga tenei na nga tupuna;
	He poi, he poi, he poi, hei!
LEADER:	Poi puritia!
	Poi Takawiri!
	Taupatupatu, taupatupatu,
	Taupatupatu, ko te tau!
ALL:	Patupatu taku poi,
	Ka rere taku poi,
	Rere tika atu ana
	Ka tau ki Ngapuhi
	Kei reira te toka

Kei Rangihoua,
Kei Oihi ra,
Ko te toka tena
I poua iho ai
Te Rongopai ra e .... Ka mau!

LEADER: Hei whakakororia
ALL: Te Atua i runga rawa
Ka mau te rongo ki Aotearoa
Tena ano ra ko ana purapura
I ruiruia ra i roto nga iwi
Ka tupu ka hua e .... Hua nei!

LEADER: Whiti rawa atu koe
ALL: Ki a Raukawa
Ko Rota Waitoa
Hei mataamua,
Kei roto Wanganui
Ko Te Tauri
Ka tae nga rongo
Ki Ngati-Ruanui
Ko Manihera ra
Ko Kereopa hoki
I whakamatea nei
Mo te Whakapono e .... Ka tau!

LEADER: Ka rere taku poi
ALL: Ki te Tairawhiti
Kei reira e ngaki ana
Ko Taumata-a-kura
Kei Mataatua
Ko Ngakuku ra
Kei te Arawa
Ko Ihaia
Kei roto Kahungunu
Ko Te Wera ra e .... Te Wera!

LEADER: Tenei au ka huri
ALL: Te Tiriti o Waitangi
He pukapuka noa,
Whakaporearea,
Ka heke te mana
Murua iho te whenua
Ko te whakatauki
'Titiro ki te rangi
Tahuri rawa ake,

Kahore he whenua e .... Kua riro!'
LEADER: Ka tuhi, ka rarapa, ka uira
Te rangi e tu iho nei, e
ALL: Toia te waka,
Te utanga o runga
Ko te aroha;
Paiheretia mai
Te rangimarie,
Aue! Hei!

Poi

LEADER: Be ready!
Take a look all people
ALL: At what is in the cup of my hand,
For this is a treasure from our forebears;
A poi, a poi, poi, hei!
LEADER: Hold the poi!
Quiver the poi!
Twirl and strike,
And now the chant!
ALL: I strike my poi,
My poi flies,
And flies direct,
Landing in Ngapuhi country,
For there stands the rock,
At Rangihoua,
Even at Oihi,
That is the rock
On which was established
The Gospel .... and became fixed.
LEADER: To give glory
ALL: To God in the highest,
And peace was declared throughout New Zealand,
And its seeds
Have been broadcast among the tribes,
And have grown and borne fruit .... bears now.
LEADER: When you have crossed
ALL: To Raukawa country
It is Rota Waitoa
The very first Maori ever to be ordained
To the sacred ministry

And at Wanganui
There is Wiremu Te Tauri
The first person to introduce Christianity there
And the news has also reached
The Ngati-Ruanui people
Among whom were Manihera
And also Kereopa
The first Christian martyrs
For the Faith in New Zealand .... Indeed!

LEADER: My poi now flies
ALL: To the Eastern seas
And there strives
Piripi Taumata-a-kura
Who introduced Christianity to the Ngati Porou
While in Mataatua country
Is Ngakuku
And in Arawa country
Is Ihaia
And in Ngati-Kahungunu country
Is Te Wera .... Yes, Te Wera.

LEADER: I will now turn
ALL: To the Treaty of Waitangi
It is only but paper
Yet troublesome
Causing prestige to decline
And land to be confiscated
As a result was the saying
'We looked up to heaven
And before we knew where we were
There was no land left .... all gone!'

LEADER: The lightning glows and flashes
Well above the heavens
ALL: Drag the canoe
With its cargo
Of love
Bind it with peace,
Aue! Hei!

KINGI M. IHAKA (1921; Aupouri, Ngati Kahu, Rarawa, Ngapuhi, Waikato) was born at Te Kao and is presently Director of Maori Work in the Anglican Diocese of Auckland. Archdeacon Ihaka founded both the Aupouri Maori Club and the Putiki Maori Club and managed the Wellington Anglican Maori Club in 1965 when it toured North America, Great Britain and Hong Kong. He was a member of the Wellington Maori Arts Festival in 1967 and is currently the Chairman of both the New Zealand Polynesian Festival Committee and the Maori and South Pacific Arts Council. He was awarded the MBE in 1968. A noted composer, his publications include *Daily Prayers of the Week* and *The Service of Holy Communion,* both in Maori. The New Zealand National Band includes in its repertoire his composition 'Taku Toa' which is based on a Maori proverb dear to his heart: My prestige and mana are not limited to a single person, but to countless numbers.

Harry Dansey

Te Raukura: The Feathers Of The Albatross (Extract)

SCENE IV

THE MARAE AT PARIHAKA

Parihaka village is packed with people, men, women and children, seated on the ground. TOHU, TE WHITI'S *lieutenant, addresses them. Behind him the niu pole still stands, symbol of the Hauhau faith to which so many had turned in their desperation. Among the crowd sits* ROBERT PARRIS, *the Government Civil Commissioner, and his friend* JAMES FLEMING.

TOHU:　　Haere mai! Haere mai! Haere mai! Te Taihauauru, Parininihi ki Waitotara, haere mai! Te Tai-tokerau! Te Tai-rawhiti! Te Waipounamu! Wharekauri! Haere mai! Haere mai! Haere mai!

FLEMING:　What's he saying, Bob?

PARRIS:　　Oh, same old stuff, welcome, welcome, welcome. Mentions places and people, you know. When you've heard one, you've heard them all.

TOHU:　　Welcome to you all who come to learn, who come to worship. You bring with you gifts to sustain us all at this great gathering. We touch them in token of acceptance and

30

then they belong to all to share, one with another as our fathers have taught us, as Te Whiti has shown us, and as the faith in which we believe requires us. It may be there are some here who do not come to worship although they do come to learn, but to learn in a different way and for a different purpose. I have nothing to say to them, nothing, nothing, nothing. They come, they go, as the birds come and go. No one will harm them for this is the marae of peace. Enough! There comes that other, the good man, the wise man, the gentle man. I sit in the shadow of his greatness and his shadow is good. Enough, greetings to you all.

A murmur grows, runs round the crowd, heads turn and TE WHITI *enters quietly. A bearded man with kindly face and a gentle smile, he murmurs greetings as he passes to his mound, his speaking place on the marae.*

TE WHITI: Ma Te Atua koutou e manaaki! And God bless you too, Parris, and your friend whom I welcome.

PARRIS: Thank you, my good friend.

WI TATARA: Oh yes, God bless the Pakeha! It's his own God anyway. He brought it with him, like rabbits and blackberries.

There are angry cries from the crowd of 'Aue! Ka kino! Turituri!'. WI TATARA *acknowledges them, unrepentant, grins, waves, lowers his head and is silent.*

TE WHITI: I greet you, e Wi, oh yes, I greet you, and I grieve with you who holds still within the heart the memory of Hepanaia whom you loved. Ae ra hoki, ka tika to taua pouri, me tangi taua.

Murmurs of approval. WI *stands, bows his head.* TE WHITI *bows his. A low wail runs through the assembly. A pause.* WI *bows his head again, wipes his eyes with the back of his hand, sighs, and sits down.*

TE WHITI: Ka koa te hunga e tangi ana; ka whakamarietia hoki ratou.

31

FLEMING: What's he saying?

PARRIS: It's from the Good Book. Blessed are they that mourn for they shall be comforted.

TE WHITI: I have told you before and I tell you again that there is no victory save in peace. Yes, it is hard to believe this for we have been sorely tried and justice has been denied us. Yet still we carry with us so much that keeps our hearts from opening so that the message of peace can enter. Te Ua has gone I know not where. God rest him and give him peace. But behind him remains the shape and shadow of things which are better gone. The shadow of the niu which fell upon the land has been taken from the land. But there is another shadow. Oh yes, another shadow. The Pakeha is fair but his shadow is dark and his shadow is long and as it moves across the land, the land moves too, away from us, over to him. The Pakeha has taken the Waimate Plains south of the mountain. Confiscated land. But the Pakeha is not using it. Why are those who owned it not allowed back? Is this the way to ensure peace, Parris?

PARRIS: Te Whiti, I will tell you how you can be sure of peace. You must show by deeds that you are prepared to work for it. You must purify yourselves by work. Prove your good faith by building roads here, right here.

TE WHITI: Is it the road Parris wants or does he want a great deal more? You will take the people down the road and into your new towns and fill them with drink and when they come back the land will be quite gone. And again I ask, where are the reserves we have been promised? We are not allowed to go where we want to go and we are not told where you want us to go. What are we supposed to be, birds?

PARRIS: I don't think it will do any good to remain here. I think we had better leave.

TE WHITI: You may not be a bad man, Parris, but you have a bad master — and you serve him very well.

Exit PARRIS *and* FLEMING.

Oh my people gathered here from so far, I tell you that there will be a day of deliverance and on that day, when the Pakeha goes back to where he came from we will live before God, humbly and happily, each working for the common good, sharing what we make and what we grow in a land where men are equal and the wealth of the Pakeha means nothing. There will be no more fighting as you used to fight. Peace is our weapon. First man must be at peace with God. Then man must learn to love his neighbour and only God can teach him that. (TE WHITI *turns to the niu pole.*) We need that no more. I think it best we take it away. (*Murmurs of approval. The niu is removed.*) It has gone. If it ever had a purpose, that purpose is now fulfilled. Soon I will give you another sign so that all — Maori and Pakeha — may know. Soon I will give you a sign so that all may know that men and women, armed only with the power of the spirit, can fight and win. Behold I will show you a new way of prayer. E te iwi, Whakarongo! Again we gather in this place, here at Parihaka, on the marae of peace, to hear the word of God — we listen, we pray, we sing. And now we will dance. In the days of old the mighty men of God danced before the altar of their Lord, and we too will dance. We have no need to approach God in the manner of the Pakeha. He loves us and it is right that we praise him in our own way, in our own tongue and with the dances of our own people.

He puts out his hand and a woman gives him a poi.

Behold, I take the poi and I bless the poi and I say to you all in the sweep of the poi and the beat of the poi and the swinging and the thudding and the tapping of the poi will God be praised by his Maori people. Kororia ki te Atua!

TOHU: Amine!

ALL: Amine!

TE WHITI: I have chosen a company of our women to be the first to praise God with the poi. And I have said to them as St John said: 'Dress yourselves in white, for it is the colour of those chosen by the Lord who has said, "They shall walk with me in white: for they are worthy." ' Tama wahine ki mua!

Tama tane ki muri! E hine ma! Haere mai! Haere mai!
Haere mai koutou i waenganui i a tatou kia inoi hoki tatou i
te haruru o te poi!

Enter, singing, TWO LINES OF WOMEN *clothed from head to foot
in white. They wear the raukura, white feathers of the
albatross in plumes above their left ears.*

WOMEN:　Ka rere taku poi
　　　　E rite ki te toroa
　　　　Rere moana e,
　　　　He aha te tohu nei
　　　　Titia ki te mahunga?
　　　　Taku raukura,
　　　　Taku raukura e!

TE WHITI:　You hear the words, and you see the poi;
　　　　And in these words and with the poi
　　　　God is praised.

　　　　Look upon these garments, gleaming white.
　　　　They are God's own sign.

　　　　Now look upon the insignia above my brow: gleaming
　　　　　white above my brow.
　　　　This, too, is God's own sign.

　　　　Let us all wear this sign.
　　　　Let us all wear the raukura.

*He pauses while the people put on their head bands and their
three white feathers.*

　　　　Now, when you wear the raukura, remember what it
　　　　　means:

　　　　The first feather means: Glory to God in the highest;

Places feather in head band.

　　　　The second feather means: On earth, peace;

Places second feather in head band.

34

And the third feather means: Goodwill towards men.

Places third feather in head band.

Let us sing therefore, and in the words, and in the white
　　colour,
In the feathers of the raukura, and in the dance of the poi,

Let us remember:
Glory to God in the highest;
On earth, peace;
And goodwill towards men.

WOMEN:　Titiro mai ki te raukura
　　　　Ko te tohu tenei o Te Atua,
　　　　Titiro hoki ki nga Kakahu ma
　　　　Ko te tohu tenei o Te Atua,
　　　　Nana nei te kupu i nga ra o mua,
　　　　Na,

Tap, tap, tap of the poi.

E haereere tahi ratou me ahau
Ma hoki te kakahu,
No te mea e pai ana ratou e,

Tap, tap, tap of the poi.

Ka rere taku poi
E rite ki te toroa,
Rere moana e.
He aha te tohu nei
Titia ki te mahunga?
Taku raukura,
Taku raukura, e!
Ko te piki tuatahi o te raukura,
Kia whai kororia Te Atua i runga rawa;
Ko te piki tuarua o te raukura,
Kia mau te rongo ki runga ki te whenua:
Ko te piki tuatoru o te raukura,
Ko te whakaaro pai te tangata.

WOMEN *begin to move off stage.*

Ka rere taku poi
E rite ki te toroa
Rere moana e
He aha te tohu nei
Titia ki te mahunga?
Taku raukura,
Taku raukura, e!

Exit WOMEN

TE WHITI: Kia tau ki a tatou te atawhai a to tatou Ariki, a Ihu Karaiti, me te aroha o te Atua, me te Whiwhinga Tahitanga ki te Wairua Tapu, Ake, Ake, Amine.

ALL: Amine.

SCENE V

KOROHEKE: Confiscation and occupation of Maori lands continued — often of areas essential for Maori cultivation — so Te Whiti extended his policy of passive resistance. Repudiating all violence he sent his men all over Taranaki, to plough and fence land as a token of ownership and to destroy the liquor the Pakeha traders brought. The Maoris knew they would be arrested, but still went cheerfully to their tasks, determined to be arrested. Hundreds were arrested, and the jails at Auckland, Wellington and Lyttelton were full, until the Government was appalled at the cost of maintaining prisoners and policing the district. Maori prisoners were released from the jails, and more and more Maoris moved to Parihaka which became the largest Maori community in the country, and indeed a model community. But we must be fair, for not all the politicians joined in the clamour for removal of the Taranaki Maoris from their ancestral lands. For example, Robert Stout (who later became Prime Minister) declared: 'I call it murder, for we know that the Maoris are, as compared with us, helpless, and I am not aware of anything they have done to make us commence hostilities.' But Bryce and many of the settlers were determined to take decisive action; determined upon a show of real force. Refusing fresh negotiations. Bryce deliberately misinterpreted Te Whiti's figurative language and the Parihaka 'incident' began.

TAMATANE: So we come to the fifth of November, 1881. In camp close to Parihaka, the forces of the settlers set off at dawn on the nation's last armed land-grab. They were led by 'Honest' John Bryce, who had become Native Minister, and they came from Canterbury, Nelson, Marlborough, Wellington, the Wairarapa, and Taranaki. They had travelled by train and on horseback; they had marched the dusty roads of Taranaki and some had even come down the coast by surfboat. The rape of Parihaka — a peaceful, and almost unarmed, defenceless village — was to be carried out not by British Imperial forces but by true New Zealanders, and the invasion plans were hurried up because the Governor was out of the country. Bryce and the settlers were determined to disperse the Maoris, wreck the village, and take over the square miles of fertile, cultivated gardens.

KOROHEKE: You are becoming emotional, Tamatane. Let's be factual. There were about 800 men at Parihaka — that is, men of fighting age. Old men and women numbered about a thousand, and there were about 700 children. That makes 2,500. The Pakeha forces numbered about 2,500 armed men — so the odds were about even.

SCENE VI

EXHORTATION AND ARREST

TE WHITI, *and* TOHU *are with their people on the marae at Parihaka. The people are seated. None is armed. There is complete silence.*

TE WHITI: The day of the tempest approaches. The time for testing is at hand. The young men who have fenced and ploughed the land have done their work and now must all come back home — back to Parihaka, so that we may all be together... There will be no fighting. We will do nothing but glorify God, and bring peace to the land. ...Now let the glory of peace be upon the land; we abide calmly on the land, and the land — the land abides for ever.

37

Enter CONSTABULARY OFFICER. *There is silence. No one moves.*

OFFICER: On October the nineteenth, a proclamation was issued giving you, the people of Parihaka, fourteen days to accept the partition of the land, and submit to Her Majesty the Queen, or the land would be taken from you for ever. You were warned that failure to accept this would lead to disaster, in which the innocent would suffer with the guilty.

Silence and stillness. All watch TE WHITI.

TOHU: We faced imprisonment before — hundreds of us have been in prison for our peaceful resistance. This time we face death. This time we face the mouth of the guns and the point of the sword. To those who feel the call of the warrior, I say this: 'Let not the right hand, nor the left hand, do what the spirit of the warrior calls it to do. We do not hide. There is no place to hide. We stay on this marae, all together — in patience, unity and faith.'

Silence again.

OFFICER: You were told that all persons unlawfully, riotously and tumultuously assembled here must disperse, upon pain of receiving a sentence of up to imprisonment with hard labour for life. You have had one hour in which to disperse and have not done so. I have to tell you, Chief Te Whiti, that you will have to accept the consequences. (*Exits*)

TE WHITI: If any man thinks of his gun, or his horse, or goes to fetch it, he will die by it. Place your trust in forbearance and in peace. Let the booted feet trample where they will, the land abides for ever. And to the Pakeha I say this: I stand for peace. Imprison me again if you choose. Take me, for the sins of my people. I will not run. I will not run away. And even if you kill me, I will live in the peace that will follow. The future is mine, and little children when they are asked who brought the days of peace, shall answer: 'Te Whiti'. Kia Kaha! Kia manawanui.

TOHU: Kia kaha! Kia manawanui! Be still! Be peaceful! When the soldiers come, do nothing. Do not resist them! Even with a

38

bayonet to your breast, do not resist them! Our God is the God of peace!

Silence. TOHU *walks to and fro.*

TE WHITI: Be of good heart. Be firm. We are men of peace. The land abides.

Silence. TOHU *walks to and fro.*

Be strong. Be firm. This is the marae of peace. Even with the bayonet to your breast, resist them not.

Silence again. TOHU *walks. Bugle call.*

WI TATARA: Well, here they come!

Enter OFFICERS, SOLDIERS, CONSTABLES, CHAMBERS, PARRIS, COLONEL ROBERTS *and then* BRYCE *accompanied by* COLONEL MESSENGER.

MESSENGER: By Jove, Bryce, glad you've arrived. Never seen such a business. These people have been sitting here since midnight. Just waiting for us, doing nothing, just waiting. Youngsters packing the road down there, couldn't get through for a while without harming them. Girls — kids — skipping there, blocking our way with their skipping. And boys — offering us bread and food — offering us gifts and saying they were sorry for us! Scores of them, packing the road. I even had to lift one woman out of the way! Women and children! Well, now you're here, what do you want us to do?

BRYCE: Arrest Te Whiti and Tohu. Handcuff them. If any man as much as raises a tomahawk, shoot him.

ROBERTS (*to* CHAMBERS):
Arrest Te Whiti and Tohu, handcuff them.

CHAMBERS (*to* OFFICER):
Arrest Te Whiti. Handcuff him.

OFFICER *makes sign to* CORPORAL.

39

CORPORAL: Which one is Te Whiti, sir?

CHAMBERS: Oh stand aside man. Te Whiti, come forward.

TE WHITI: I will remain with my people. I make no trouble. It is you, the Pakeha, who is the troublemaker. If you have anything to say I will listen.

BRYCE: You there, some of you standing there, go in and arrest him.

Several soldiers and corporal rush forward. TE WHITI *fends them off and rises.*

ROBERTS: All right you constables. Let him walk if he will.

TE WHITI *and* TOHU *walk forward, their wives following.*

TE WHITI (*stopping to address the people*):
Oh my people. Live in peace. What you have seen today will pass away. I will return. I will be with you again.

A low moan passes through the people. An old woman rises and begins to chant. All join in, some at the back standing, swaying and weeping. The procession of prisoners and soldiers leaves.

MAORIS: Tangiaa taku ihu e whakamakuru nei
Ko au pea, e, te turia ki runga
He mahi whare koe ki miti mai te arero.
Maringi tohu au, e whaka, koia e tika
Taku takiritanga te kahu o te Kuini.
Ka piki nga rongo o Te Whiti kei runga
Hapainga atu au ki runga o Parihaka.
Kia whakarongo mai Moehau i reira
Hei panui atu ki te iwi o Titoko
Ki taku whakaaro he makau tupu koe
Ka mutu pea e, nga rangi hanihani
Tenei ano to raukura ka titia —
Ma te hau o waho e tiki mai e whawhati,
I weherua po i wake ai korua
He kai mutunga kore i taku tinana nei,
E nowhea nga mate e patu ra i aku hoa
Te karawhiu ai i te kino i ahau.
Kei noho au te ao hei kome au ma te ngutu i, i.

40

KOROHEKE: Having disposed of the leaders, the troops settled in. Parihaka was ringed with tents, but for nearly three weeks the Maoris sat, day after day, refusing to move, watching the soldiers at their work.

BRYCE: (*first to the people at Parihaka and then to the officers commanding constabulary and soldiers*): All of you, go home. Go back to your homes, or it will be the worse for you. You of the Waikato, go back home. You from Wanganui, go back home. Te Ati Awa, Ngati Ruanui, all of you here, go back to your homes immediately.

TAMATANE: But only a handful left; none would say where they came from.

BRYCE: Go into every house; turn out the people; break every cupboard, open every box. Get out on the plains. Raid every settlement, turn out every house; tear the houses down; burn them, scatter the contents on the maraes; tear down this great meeting-house here at Parihaka.

KOROHEKE: And the constabulary and the soldiers did exactly as they were told to do. A few muskets, powder horns, and tomahawks were found, and treasured greenstone and cash were stolen by the soldiers for themselves.

BRYCE: If they still won't go, line them up; divide them into groups; march them off. Get them away from here. (*Exits.*)

KOROHEKE: And they were lined up; they were divided into groups; they were marched off — 2,200 people, drafted like sheep, and 1,600 of them scattered over hundreds of miles of Pakeha-dominated countryside

TAMATANE: Kaati! Kaati! Enough. What more do you need to say?

KOROHEKE: Let one of them speak for the many...

A WOMAN: Upokokohua, Pakeha ma, kai a te kuri

41

TAMATANE: She says enough! And Te Whiti and Tohu...charged with inciting insurrection...committed to the Supreme Court where they were never brought to trial...subject to a special Act of Parliament whereby they could be imprisoned without trial, and finally taken into exile to the South Island, for two years until released in March 1883.

KOROHEKE: And so at last the exiles were brought home
And saw again the mountain of their dreams,
And stood upon the earth they loved so well.
Then loosening the ties on all their tears,
They wept for those beyond the sight of men.

TAMATANE: Across the years I hear the voices call;
I hear the widows' cry, the sickening crash
Of rafters falling in the burning homes;
The people driven out like drafted sheep.

The men who broke, and bent, and turned the law
Have done great evil, not alone to those
Of that far time, but also to our own.
And so I hold their sons to answer for
The fathers' sins, and thus I justify
What I may do in this my day and age.

KOROHEKE *and* TAMATANE *exit, and the crowd return on stage excited at the return of the exiles.*

SCENE VII

FINALE AT PARIHAKA

UIMANO: E te iwi, whakarongo! E hoki mai ano ki te wa kainga o tatou tumuaki o tatou poropiti. Oh, this is a happy day indeed and oh this is a sad day indeed. We will welcome them with tears and we will welcome them with song and then they shall tell us what we must do to be great and strong and how the land will come back to us again.

WI TATARA: E te iwi kua whakamine mai i tenei ra, tena koutou katoa. I too wait to hear from the lips of Te Whiti and Tohu what

42

they have planned for the future. I tell you that my ears are ready to hear them say: Enough of this talk of peace. We were wrong to counsel peace, peace, peace. We know the Pakeha now for what he is, deceitful, double-tongued, the very font of lies. We have known his gaols and his justice. Now is the time for action. Enough. Kati, kia ora koutou katoa.

Murmurs all round of approval and of dissent.

A VOICE OFF: Kua tae mai! Kua tae mai! Kua hoki mai ano a tatou poropiti!

Great excitement, hurryings to and fro, all face the direction from which the returning men will come.

WOMEN: (*waving green leaves in time with their chanting*): Haere mai! Haere mai! Haere mai! Haere mai o tatou poropiti, haere mai kia tangi ai tatou! Haere mai! Haere mai! Haere mai!

Enter TE WHITI *and* TOHU, *slowly,* TE WHITI *singing the old song of greeting to Taranaki Mountain which the Pakeha calls Egmont. His singing, the chanting of the women and the speech of welcome all may be simultaneous, now one rising above the other, then falling away.*

TE WHITI   (*sings*):
Whakawaiwai ai
Te tu a Taranaki
Okahu hukatere
I hurau ai koe ai

HARRY DANSEY (1920-1979; Ngati Tuwharetoa, Arawa, Ngati Raukawa) was born in Auckland. He died eighteen days after retiring from his position as Race Relations Conciliator. Brought up in Rotorua, Harry served in the Maori Battalion in World War II in Egypt and Italy. After the war he was a journalist with the *Hawera Star*, the *Taranaki Daily News* and the *Auckland Star*. He was awarded the Cowan Memorial Prize for journalism in 1968. In 1969 he was the NZPA representative on the Royal Society of New Zealand's Cook bi-centenary scientific expedition to Tonga and the Cook Islands. Harry was New Zealand's first Race Relations Conciliator. His publications included *How the Maoris Came to Aotearoa* (1947), *Cartoons* (1958), *The New Zealand Maori in Colour* (with K. & J. Bigwood,

1963), *Maori Custom Today* (1971) and *Te Raukura — The Feathers of the Albatross* (1974) — the first play by a Maori writer to be performed professionally and to be published.

The extract from *Te Raukura* centres on the man who preached peace, the remarkable Te Whiti o Rongomai, and the marae of Parihaka at the foot of sacred Taranaki Mountain.

Kohine Whakarua Ponika

Ka Haku Au

Ka haku au, ka mapu e
Ka riro ra i te ia e
E koro ma, te ao o nehera
Ka ngaro, ka ngaro
Ka ngaro e

Ka mokemoke nga mahara
Maturu noa nga roimata
Ma wai ra e kawe nga korero
Waiho, waiho
Waiho ra

Ma te wa, ma te wa
E takiri mai
Ma te Rangatahi
E whai hono e
Kia mau ai

E hika ma, me tautoko ra
Na te Atua te ao rere noa
Koi nei ra ka hiki te manawa
Ko koe, ko au
Hei waha e

Ka ngaro, ka ngaro, ka ngaro e
Waiho, waiho, waiho ra
Ko koe, ko au, hei waha e
I to taua
Maoritanga.

Ka Haku Au

I am so sad, my heart sighs
They are all gone with the tide
My loved ones, from the old world
Gone, gone on
But not forgotten

Loneliness clouds each day
Tears blind my eyes
Deep inside me I silently ask
Where is the strength, my strength
To carry on

Let the future
Bring what it may
Let the young ones
Tie the knot to hold
Securely hold

And let us all, with one voice
Fear not the dark, God made us all
My heart leaps high
My frail body
Trembles

I know and you know
This is your world and mine
And our heritage
It is
Maoritanga.

KOHINE WHAKARUA PONIKA (1920; Tuhoe, Ngati Porou) was born in
Ruatoki North and now lives in Turangi with her eight adopted children. She
began writing action songs when she was nineteen, having learned the art form
from her father, Wharetini Rangi. Her compositions have won many awards at
Maori cultural festivals and in 1966 her poi 'Toia Mai Ra' won a national award
sponsored by the NZBC. In 1969 she founded the Hei Tiki Maori Youth Club.
Two of her original compositions, 'Aku Mahi' and 'Karangatia Ra Pohiritia Ra',
created for Ngati Poneke, have become classic modern action songs. On both her
Tuhoe and Ngati Porou sides she is descended from famous composers, including
Te Rangiuia o Hauiti.

Hone Tuwhare

Reign rain

Neither juggernaut
man
nor crawling thing
with saintliness & ease

can bring
a mountain weeping
to its knees
quicker than rain:

that demure leveller
ocean-blessed
cloud-sent
maker of plains

Ron Mason

Time has pulled up a chair, dashed
a stinging litre from a jug of wine.
My memory is a sluggard,

I reject your death, but can't dismiss it.
For it was never an occasion for woman
sobs and keenings: your stoic-heart

would not permit it. And that calcium-covered
pump had become a sudden road-block bringing
heavy traffic to a tearing halt.

Your granite-words remain.
Austere fare, but nonetheless adequate for the
honest sustenance they give.

And for myself, a challenge.
A preoccupation now more intensely felt, to tilt
a broken taiaha inexpertly

to my old lady, Hine-nui-te-Po, bless the old
bitch: shrewd guardian of that infrequent *duende*
that you and Lorca knew about, playing hard-to-get.

Easy for you now, man. You've joined your literary
ancestors, whilst I have problems still in finding
mine, lost somewhere

in the confusing swirl, now thick now thin,
Victoriana-Missionary fog hiding legalized land-rape
and gentlemen thugs. Never mind, you've taught me

confidence and ease in dredging for my own bedraggled
myths, and you bet: weighing the China experience
yours and mine. They balance.

Your suit has not the right cut for me except around
the gut. I'll keep the jacket though: dry-cleaned
it'll absorb new armpit sweat.

Ad Dorotheum: She and I together found the poem
you'd left for her behind a photograph.

> *Lest you be a dead man's*
> > *slave*
> *Place a branch upon the*
> > *grave*
> *Nor allow your term of*
> > *grief*
> *To pass the fall of its*
> > *last leaf*

'Bloody Ron, making up to me,' she said, quickly:
too quickly.

But Time impatient, creaks a chair. And from the
jug I pour sour wine to wash away the only land
I own, and that between the toes.

A red libation to your good memory, friend. There's
work yet, for the living.

Drunk

When they hustled him out
at closing time he had
forty cents clutched in
his hands for another drink

Rain stabbed the streets
with long slivers of light
He picked his way
gingerly treading the golden
non-existent stairs
to the fried-fish shop

Whirling pin-points
of coloured lights confused
him: and when people appeared
to converge on him he swerved
to avoid them and collided
with a post

He sensed a sea of receding
faces picked himself up
and promptly emptied his guts
on the footpath fervently calling
for his bleeding mate Christ
who was nowhere to be seen

Later wearing a stiff mask
of indifference
he pissed himself in the bus

At work the next morning
he moved with effort in the hollow
silence of a self-built tomb:
unaware of the trapped mortal
crouching there

Owls Do Give A Hoot For Titokowaru
(to J. & J.E.)

Nearly always, and following each
raw and savage battle, it was you
who twitched the down-turned
corners of the lips to tired smiles,
set tired feet to rhythmic flexing;
the land, sky-bumping.

And now, utterly faceless, yourself
laid low, lowly, we lower you lower
than the breathy breathless note of
the mute bone flute placed in your
lifeless fingers

Of course, conditions permitting
and unmenaced by a friendly silence
deep in our hide-out, we chant your
songs with steely gusto, sometimes
stirring from a drunken thicket and
mist, a dark owl in sad voice
asking, asking. . .

The contours of your face, uneasily
we've forgotten.

Child Coming Home In The Rain From The Store

When I see you pause
make talk dawdle-walk
on the back road to your house
your house overlooking
the timber mill and timber yard
I know you stop only to talk
not to the cruel metalled road
but to a stone a solitary stone
sharp-edged with flat shiny
faces

Through your mind's eye know
the feel of washed leaves
made green again: tall rain-shafts
drifting: wind wincing
a water-filled pot-hole

And I child-delighting share
your long walk your talk
to things *and for things* along
the bent road to your house
where impatiently
others wait for the damp bread
you bring

Heemi

No point now my friend in telling
you my lady's name.
She wished us well: offered wheels
which spun my son and me like
comets through the lonely night.
You would have called her Aroha.

And when we picked up three young
people who'd hitched their way
from the Ninety Mile beach to be
with you, I thought: yes
your mana holds, Heemi. Your mana
is love. And suddenly the night
didn't seem lonely anymore.

The car never played up at all.
And after we'd given it a second
gargle at the all-night bowser
it just zoomed on on gulping
easily into the gear changes
up or down.

Because you've been over this road
many times before Heemi, you'd
know about the steady climb ahead

of us still. But once in the tricky
light, Tongariro lumbered briefly
out of the clouds to give us the old
'up you' sign. Which was real friendly.

When we levelled off a bit at the top
of the plateau, the engine heat couldn't
keep the cold from coming in: the fog
swamping thick and slushy, and pressing
whitely against tired eye-balls.

Finally, when we'd eased ourselves
over a couple of humps and down down
the winding metalled road to the river
and Jerusalem, I knew things would be
all right. Glad that others from the
Mainland were arrowing toward the dawn
like us.

Joy for the brother sun chesting over
the brim of the land, and for the three
young blokes flaked out in the back seat
who would make it now, knowing that they
were not called to witness
some mysterious phenomenon of birth on
a dung-littered floor of a stable

but come simply to call
on a tired old mate in a tent
laid out in a box
with no money in the pocket
no fancy halo, no thump left in the old
ticker.

Old Comrade
(to Jim Jamieson)

Like frightened girls, the years
ran in thickening to panic-stations:
the days ran out for Jim
as he walked past them, and beyond.

Why, only a few days ago, hatless,
immaculately tied and overcoated,
head-on, Jim shouldered his way out
of the Crown and into the wind
at the corner of Rattray Street: he
didn't hear me call out. Jim was
ghosting.

Shoulders hunched, tartan scarf whipping,
Jim leaned into the wind. The wind leaned
right back and then, pulled away. Jim fell.
He didn't feel the hard coldness
of the pavement, for, like an old friend
come back, the wind held him as he fell.

Well, there was no magic tolling of the bell,
and the skies never opened up. But the ground
did... At the graveside,
no one wanted to add or subtract. No one,
except the capitalist, who never even looked
up from counting his worthless paper-money.
But, you know

I reckon old Marx would make room for him;
Lenin, throw another log on the fire; and
Mao, like a full moon rising, pour a bowl
of tea, offer Jim a cigarette. Bet on it...

Haiku

Stop
your snivelling
creek-bed:

come rain hail
and flood-water

laugh again

Taniwha
(for Syneve)

I'm nine years old. I am called Tame Grey — coz of my father whose name is Tom. I don't know whether I got a true Mum or not. I never seen her.

I want to talk about my great granddad who was ninety years old. He's more than that. But I can't skite about him coz my great-great grandmother is still going strong. She smokes a pipe and can still push the lawn-mower. My father reckons she's nearly two axe-handles across the arse. Hang. But I never meshua her. I might get a smack.

My great-great grandmother's name is Te Haruru: Big Thunder. But I just call her Crabby for short. Hang, they say she's one hundred and twenty years old. But I can't skite about her either coz she's not even a Princess. I mean — I never seen her wear a Crown. Aw, I'm forgetting...

My great grand-dad was called Hawry Cray. He was named after the Right Honrable Sir Hori Kerei, the pakeha gavaner who helped to steal the lands. But nevermind that.

Hawry Cray and Te Haruru — we all live in the old place up on the hill looking out over the shops at Wheke. The proper name for the village is Eight Pussy. You can buy some meat and flour, some nails and mouse-traps and blackball lollies with white stripes all in the one shop there. There's the Grarge what sells meat pies. The Pub sells lemonade and potato chips and the Dairy sells white bread all cut up.

The School is over on the other side of the shops with the flag-mast sticking up and the onion jack waving. There's no Picture House, but there's the Church where we sing the same old songs over and over again. I know them all off by heart now.

My father, Tom — he doesn't live with us. He works in the Big Town forty miles the other way. He comes around once a month with a truck-load of cut-up wood and tips it all out in front of the gate. We have to climb through the wire to get out.

My father comes around just on kai-time. Never misses. Hang, he can eat. Mmmm, dough-boys. Mmmm, Puha. Mmmm, brisket-on-the-bone. Tino reka. Swallow-swallow. Kapai. That's all I hear. Then he pushes the chair back, belches, whacks his belly and gives me a ten cent piece.

Away he goes. 'Horray, son,' he says and rattles off on his truck brmmm — brmmm — brmmm. Smart double-shuffle on the foot-peddles away screaming, up and over the hill. And out of sight.

I'm not sorry. I scrape the dishes and wash up. It takes me two days to carry all the wood into the shed at the back next to the dunny. I make the job last until old Crabby feels sorry for me and forks out a fifty cent piece. You see what I mean, ay?

53

Hawry Cray, my great grand-dad, he never worried if I miss my School. He taught me how to swing a axe without cutting my foot. One day in the bush he told me to open up a rotten log with it and pick out some fat hu-hu grubs for bait. He taught me how to slide the hook through them, and how to tie the lot together with cotton so that the eel can't slip the hu-hu off easy. We caught a lot of eels that way. Then he showed me how to get the eel high up on the bank before clubbing it on the head without bruzing any other part of the body. We never going to starve.

The best of all, Hawry Cray taught me how to set some sticky lumps of honey in the mouse-traps. He taught me how to place the mouse-traps very careful among the branches of taraire tree. When I climb down we move away then and sit quiet in the sun and wait for the pigeon and the kaka to come and fight over the honey. Hah! Big surprise for them. One day a man with a shiny badge come along instead. Hang. Big surprise for us.

'Hey, what are you falluhs sitting here for, Hawry Cray?' he said. But my great grand-dad he's not a dum-dum.

'Well, you see this rotten log, ay?' said Hawry Cray. 'Plenty of hu-hu. Good for the eel, and good for me, too—'

'This is a private bush, Hawry — ' 'I know, I know. But does the hu-hu know that? Here, you try some, ay?' Then he pop a fat hu-hu in his mouth pinching off the black nippers. The juice roll down the corner of his mouth just like lolly-water. The man looked away. He left us alone after that.

Another time, a man in a neat suit brought a blue paper with a lot of words on it. It was a Cort Summuns.

'Just remember the date, Mr Cray. I'm only doing my job. You have to appear at the Cort.' He went away so that Hawry and Crabby could have a better look at the blue paper.

'You in big troubles again Hawry, ay?' said Crabby. 'Jingoes, you keep Tame away from School for too long —' My great grand-dad didn't hear her. He just walked over to the big open chimney where a small fire was going.

'Hah! What can *they* do to me,' he said. 'This is what I think.' The next thing I saw the blue paper curl up lazy in a flame floating up like a butterfly past the eels hanging there all opened out golden and juicy and smoked. Lovely.

When Hawry Cray died, everybody popped up like toast from nowhere. The men restled with the long poles and put up a big tent. There was a tangi going on with not much crying except from the womans. I give it a try, though. It didn't work. And then two old falluhs started to swear hard at each other and waving their walking sticks around like swords. Hang. Their eyes was shining like hot coals when you blow on it. But Big

Thunder — I mean, Crabby, she got very angry with them and put a stopper on it. After that, the two old falluhs sang some old Maori songs one after the other all night. I don't know who won. I fell asleep.

The next day they shot Hanky Pancake because she wasn't giving much milk. They shot her with the big gun my father owns. She just fell down kicking and rolling her big cow eyes just like a cat when you tickle it on the belly. Blood was coming out of her mouth and Hanky Pancake was licking it up just like runny chocolate. My father said a loud swear-word. He grabbed the gun and shot her again. Hanky Pancake stopped licking.

After that we roasted the part of her guts what look like sossiges. They was beautiful. Then the men stuck the hay-forks into the pieces of meat and toasted them over the fire to bring out the taste. They placed the pieces of meat in a long hangi — just like a trench — and covered it up with the sheets and the sacks. They heaped dirt over it, patting it here — patting it there, to stop the steam from coming out.

When everything was cooked, they carted the meat, the water-cress, the spuds and the pumkin over to the long tables where there was a lot of Maori bread and trifle and lemonade and lollies on top. Everybody ate until they was busting. Well, nearly everybody. My great grand-dad never got to the Cort . . . Aw, they can't teach him nothing.

When they took Hawry Cray to the Maori Cemetry, I got up beside him on the back of the truck. The Maori Cemetry is two miles past Eight Pussy. A lot of people followed us in the cars. The ride got bumpy when we left the main road and I had to hang on to the coffin to stop it from sliding around. Hawry Cray never even noticed me coz if he did he would have knocked.

They lowered Hawry Cray into the hole with the long ropes and a lot of Maori prayers. They filled the hole up with dirt until it was level with the top. They jumped up and down on top of him to stop him from coming up. Then they shovel some more dirt on him to make a nice smooth heap. Somebody put a marmite jar on top full of violets from Crabby's garden, but I didn't see. . . Goodbye Hawry Cray—

'What the hell you crying for?' my father said, putting a arm around me.
'He died good. No pain.' But I wasn't listening.
'Look, Tame, Hawry Cray was eighty years old. That's a good score —' I pulled away from him. My father's a big liar. Hawry Cray was over ninety years old. I just know that.

I walked home by myself. I didn't climb up on the back of the truck like the other kids. I kicked some stones along the main road and bruzed the toe of the new boots old Crabby bought for me out of her old age penshin. A lot of cars stopped to pick me up. I didn't feel like it.

I hopped the fence and shot across the Pakeha farm to the big pool where

Hawry Cray had set a eel-trap. It took me three goes to pull the eel-trap clear of the water. I nearly fell in. But I got very strong when I saw what was in it. Hang, I never seen a head as big as that on a eel before. There was two small ones in there too. They was dead.

The big eel had two little horns on his head. True. I thought, I'll fix you. I loosen the anchor rope and rolled the eel-trap away from the pool over to some flat ground. I found a heavy piece of willow first — before I opened the trap-door.

I got back to the old place just on dark dragging the huge eel behind me. My fingers was nearly cut to the bone by the loop of flax that I'd poked through the ear and out of the mouth of the eel and tied. I was tired.

There was a party going on in the tent: flat out. My boots was all muddy. My clothes was stiff with the slime from the eel — and my nose kept crying. 'This is a present from Hawry Cray,' I said, looking around like I wanted to fight. Everybody began to crowd around me.

'Wiiii. . .' said Crabby. 'E, Tame, that's a big taniwha you got. Kapai.' Then old Crabby took the eel away from me and started out to clean it. Somebody brought me a bar of chocalate.

'You wash up now, Tame. Change your clothes,' said Crabby, cutting here scraping there. 'You grab some bottle of lemonade before they all gone, ay?' Scrape, scrape. 'Aunty Mei is coming here to live with us.'

Aw, Aunty Mei? Hang! She won't even let me dip my bread in my tea. But I don't want to think about that just now. This is not her story.

HONE TUWHARE (1922; Ngapuhi hapus, Ngati Korokoro, Ngati Tautahi, Te Popote, Uri-o-Hau) was born in Kaikohe, educated at Beresford Street School (Auckland) and then apprenticed to the boilermaking trade. He was the president of the Te Mahoe Local of the New Zealand Workers' Union in the early 1960s. In 1964 he published a first collection of poems, *No Ordinary Sun,* the first book to be produced by a contemporary Maori writer. A recording of the poems was made in the same year. In 1969 he was the Robert Burns Fellow at the University of Otago (and again in 1974) and a year later he released his second collection, *Come Rain Hail.* In 1972 he published *Sapwood and Milk* and in 1973 (with Taura Eruera, Rowley Habib, Para Matchitt and Witi Ihimaera) he founded the Maori Artists' and Writers' Society. In 1974 his fourth volume of poetry, *Something Nothing,* appeared and the following year saw a second LP, *Wind Song and Rain. Making a Fist of It* (poems and stories) was published in 1978.

Hone's work has appeared is the following anthologies: *An Anthology of Twentieth-Century New Zealand Poetry* (1970), *Pacific and Other Verse* (1970), *Modern Verse For You* (1968), *My New Zealand* (1973), *NZ Listener Short Stories* (1977), *Ten Modern New Zealand Poets* (1974), *New Zealand Love Poems* (1977), *New Zealand Poetry in the Sixties* (1973), *Timber, Tussock and Rushing Rivers* (1973) and *Contemporary Maori Writing* (1970). He has read at conferences in a number of Pacific countries (see other contributors' notes) and made several tours of New

Zealand reading his work. He remains constantly in demand with schools through the Writers in Schools scheme.

At present Hone lives in Dunedin and has recently written, but not yet workshopped, a play *On Ilka Moor B'aht 'at*. The selection in this anthology, taken from the last ten years, only begins to suggest the range of his work over the four decades he has been a writer.

Kumeroa Ngoingoi Pewhairangi

Maunga Marotiri

E hara tenei i te maunga nekeneke.
He maunga tu tonu, a maunga e Marotiri e,
Ko te toka tenei, o aku tipuna,
He toka ahuru, he toka whakairo,
Kia tu tonu mai koe.

Hei karanga i to iwi,
E kanapa atu ra, o tini rirena,
Ki te Taitokerau, ki te Hauauru,
Ka ruruku atu ra, ki te Waipounamu,
Kia Tahu Potiki e,
E. . . . . . .Aue,

Taku tu whakahorahora, ka tuku te mania,
Ka tiaho te huainawa,
Hei aha e. . . . .Uhi tai, uhi tai Hei.

KUMEROA NGOINGOI PEWHAIRANGI (1922; Ngati Porou) was born at Tokomaru Bay on the East Coast where she still lives. Educated at Hukarere Maori Girls' College she has been closely associated with the work of Te Whanau-a-Ruataupare ki Tokomaru. She is a leader of Hokowhitu-a-Tu, and many of her compositions have helped to form a bridge between traditional composition and contemporary protest songs: her 'Maunga Marotiri' was written for Nga Tamatoa. Ngoi has been deeply involved, through the Tauira Trust, in a local self-help community development programme and, since 1978, she has been the Maori and Pacific Islander Continuing Education Officer for the National Council of Adult Education in Gisborne. She has been honoured by the Queen for this work. In 1980 she represented New Zealand at the South Pacific Arts Festival in Papua New Guinea, with Hone Tuwhare, Katerina Mataira and Wiremu Kerekere.

Te Aomuhurangi-Temamaaka

Te Hunga Kua Riro Ki Te Po

E koropiko
Whakahonore noa
Whakamoemiti
Ki te Matua
Nga tumanako
O taku Hinengaro
Kia hoki mai
Nga tau aroha
Moe mai e te tini raukura
I te wahangutanga
Mo te hunga katoa
Takoto mai, takoto mai.

Tenei te whanau
A-Ngai-tauira e
E mihi nei
E whakanui nei
Mauria te toki a manaha
Te manaha-nui-a-Tane
Tu mai te toki! haumi e!
Taiki e!

E Tō E Te Rā I Waho O Mōtu

E tō e te rā i waho o Mōtu i te pae raro o Whakaari
Pumau ana tō heke i tō heke raro e hika e — e
Kore rawa koe te tatari noa ki te huringa muri e
Engari mā ro ana tō tū ki te poroporoaki mai e
Ki te Ao mā rama ki te Ao tangata, ki te Ao hurihuri
Tiahoaho ana te murara mai o tō u kā nohi
Whakakoi ana koe i ā u hoari hei aha e e

Tera pea kei tua o te pae-raro o Whakaari tā u e hiahia nei. Ahakoa a
Ranginui i whakapekapeka i tō huarahi ki nga taura kapua kore rawa koe
mō te tō muri e.

Pohēhē ana koe ka whai atu āu e, i au mahi maminga! Aha! ha! Taotū ana i
a koe te paeraro o Whakaari. Kākari mai ana kōrua — riro atu ana koe i te

58

paeraro. Tōtohe ana koe ki te haere i tau haere ā, toromi ana koe. Nanati ana te wheke a Tangaroa i tō kakī — Whakatahataha ana to haere, whakatakataka ana o moata i muri tonu mai i to whakaahuatanga i a koe i runga i te kare o te wai o te Moana-nui-a-kiwa. Piata ana te moana i a koe, engari kua timata kē a Hine-ahiahi ki te toha i tana huru. Kai hiwa ra! Kai kiwa ra!

Mokemoke ana te tū a Whakaari i waho o te moana. Ā no he whenua mahue. Ko te kare anake o te ia o te moana e papaki kau ana i te akau e rongonā atu ana.

Rere pōpoto noa, te rere a te kawau i runga i ngā wai popokura — he kai rā mā taku noho puku e. E to e te rā, E moe e te rā i tekau-am-rua e. Hei tō hokinga mai ka ao, ka ao ka awatea!

TE AOMUHURANGI-TEMAMAAKA (1927; Te Whanau-a-Apanui, Kati Tahu, Te-Aitanga-a-Mahaki, Ngati Porou) was born at Omaio. She was educated at Turakina Maori Girls' College, Christchurch Teachers' College, the University of Canterbury and Victoria University. Formerly an itinerant teacher of Maori she is currently a Maori language teacher for the Correspondence School.

Her waiata and stories have appeared in *Koru, Te Ao Hou*, and *Te Kaea*. Many of her compositions have been broadcast by Radio New Zealand. Her work has also been released on record and has taken first place in competitions at Gisborne, Hamilton, Ngaruawahia, Rotorua, Christchurch and Blenheim and has been performed by groups such as Te Wahi-Pounamu and Tairawhaiti (in Rotorua). She helped write the Ringatu Prayer Books in the 1960s and is at present writing a biography of Paora Delamere, her father, who is the head of the Ringatu Church.

Alistair Te Ariki Campbell

Walk The Black Path

Walk the black path
Walk the black path at noon
Walk the tilting earth
Between dream and nightmare

Bright orange are the shadows
Under the awnings
The eyes of the parking meters
Weep tears of blood

The rapist in the doorway
Leaps out with his long knife
Clouds of chloroform
Roll off his tongue

He slashes to the bone
With his teeth of stainless steel
And grips in his paws
Buttocks of crimson

The cranes on the skyline
Fish from dry canyons
The lost dreams of typists
And cries of battered babies

The young lawyer hangs himself
In the courtroom lavatory
In female underwear
And surgical gloves

The executives swop wives
In the padded penthouse
Their turned-on daughters skid
On multiple rape

Walk the black path
Walk the black path at midnight
Walk the tilting earth
From nightmare to nightmare

Waiting For The Pakeha

Here we are assembled on the bank,
a hundred souls — the remnant of our tribe —
decked out in mats and bearing greenery
to welcome to the pa our Pakeha.

And there's our chief, his club held ready
to give the signal for the show to start,
a sudden blink as of the moon through cloud
the only sign of life on his carved face.

Behind him, with bowed head, her pointed breasts
parting her long black hair, stands his daughter —
an offering to the Pakeha. Surely
such loveliness will fetch a crate of muskets.

The scouts we sent to meet the Pakeha
grin at us from the opposite bank,
their heads impaled on stakes. Our enemies
grow bolder every day, and they have guns.

But where is he? Where is the Pakeha?
The elders in their fly-blown dog-skin mats
yearn for their smoky whares — the womb
of Mother Night. Dogs whimper, and the children

dream fearfully of ovens as they burrow
into the warmth of their mothers' bodies...
The enemy guns are growing more insistent:
we shall not wait again for the Pakeha.

The Manner Is To Be Deplored

The manner is to be deplored.
When the sky split open like a melon
and yawned with glory,
the creek beds frothed with blood
and the dogs on the valley floor
lifted their golden muzzles.

You were on the far side of the lake
dancing among the tall grasses,
smiling at your hands
weaving before your face like moths,
like white moths.

I was Odysseus
strapped to a ram's underside,
my legs about his rump
like a lover's.
I have escaped Time's blinded eye.

When you came to me,
you wore a white slip —
nothing else.
You were cold and wet
from the lake.

The manner is to be deplored.
When they came in,
we were still embracing
and you were still
shivering.

They came across the frosted grass
in their great policeman's boots
cracking the moon
in the iced puddles.

I had to empty out my pockets
like a common criminal.
How could I explain the flowers
you gave me — the wild flowers —
the shells, the mermaid's beads,
the birds' cries, the love words
worn smooth as pebbles?

My mother curls up beside me,
small as a dead bee in a match box.
It is a blessed secret
I hug to my chest
like these hospital blankets.

The manner is to be deplored.
I have worn ratskin gloves
for the last time.
I have worn my father's rage —
his mad red eye glaring at me
through the spy-hole —
absolutely for the last time.

Caesar and Napoleon
have paid me their respects.
They bow deeply over my hands.
They back out, still bowing,

and collect their hats
as they leave.

Flowering Apple

It is a long lost waterfall
Perpetually covered in spray.

A rose tree grows by the wall
Where an old man digs the clay.

He leans on his spade and spits
And squints side-long into the sun.

A dark wind rises in fits
And the apple tree dances in foam

Like a branch in a waterfall
When the white air is alive.

A rose tree grows by the wall
Where an old man digs his grave.

A Woman In Love

An Angel has entered my womb,
flooding my veins
with a resurrection of sunlight...
I embrace you with my hands, my feet,
my everything.

Your nearness tumbles over me —
an avalanche of all my wishes
crazily come true.

I rejoice in your hands, strong
and yet so gentle,
deliberate and surprising too.
Your fingers talk to my body —
will it never stop trembling?

For you I have endured many deaths —
loving you least
when most I hated life,
loving you most
when most I hated death.

Don't you remember me?
You were there —
the white light pouring through the bars,
the tenderness stroking my hair
when I was locked up
in the cellar of my mind.

Your hand unlocked the door
and set me free —
free to wander the streets,
free to love, free even to hate.

Do you remember me now?

Grandfather Bosini

About him I know next to nothing.
I would like to think
that he was fierce and proud,
with the fierce proud blood
of his ancestors beating
in his veins — his ancestors and mine
who ate human flesh.
All I know is that he was small
and never left the Islands.
He was probably gentle.
If he had violent thoughts
he kept them to himself.
But when he came to die
he wept fiercely for my brother
killed many years before in Italy.
He called out many times
for his Maireriki, 'Little Flower',
and then he died.
He was ninety-nine.

Burning Rubbish

On this wild wet Sunday morning
I am burning the week's rubbish
In the oil drum by the red hut
While the dogs graze in the spring grass
Under the ngaio tree. I hear
A thrush sing somewhere above me,
In the sodden foliage, a song
Out of key with what the storm wind
Has been singing all weekend.
I look up but I can see nothing
But plunging branches and a gull
Back-pedalling across the sky.
Above the whitened bay, pigeons
Hang in a shimmering curtain
As they check and turn in their flight
And vanish, beautiful as our love.
I would like to believe the thrush
When he asserts that there is room
In this world for the two of us,
But the wind is more persuasive,
And not even the rain can douse
The flames that are consuming
Our dreams with the week's rubbish.

To My Grandson Maireriki Aged One Day

Fierce little warrior,
What are you dreaming of
In your pre-dawn sleep?
The ancestral carver
Who jealously preserves
The stern family likeness
Has carved your small face
From obsidian, denting
The bridge of the nose
So that you grimly frown
As if bracing yourself
To wake up in a world
Far removed from the warm

Maternal waters of Tongareva
Where you had waited
All these years to be born,
Moulded in the spirit
Of the last anointed ariki
Whose proud name you bear.
Dearest blood of the land,
The wonder of your parents
Elizabeth and Gregory
Through whom our ancestors
Express their brooding care,
What more can I wish you than
The fulfilment of your dreams,
Love and peace of mind
And the world to enjoy?

Friend:

This is the dearest of my wishes,
The last leaf shaken from the tree —
Sow the South Wind with my ashes
To fall in tears on Kapiti

ALISTAIR TE ARIKI CAMPBELL (1925; Cook Island Maori) was born in Rarotonga. His father was a New Zealand Scot, John Archibald Campbell, and his mother, Teu, was a daughter of Bosini of Tongareva (Penrhyn Island) of the Northern Cook Islands group. On the death of his parents, he came to New Zealand in 1933, and was educated at Otago Boys' High School and Victoria University of Wellington. After training as a teacher, he joined the Department of Education where he edited the *School Journal* for 17 years before being appointed to the New Zealand Council for Educational Research as senior editor. He lives with his family at Pukerua Bay, 20 miles north of Wellington.

The range of Alistair's poetry is conveyed in his collections, *Mine Eyes Dazzle* (1950, 1951, 1956), *Sanctuary of Spirits* (1963), *Wild Honey* (1964), *Blue Rain* (1967), *Kapiti: Selected Poems* (1972, 1973), *Dreams, Yellow Lions* (1975) and *The Dark Lord of Savaiki* (1980). As well he has written a children's story, *The Happy Summer* (1961); numerous radio plays (one of which, *The Suicide*, was published in *Landfall* 112) and a stage play, *When the Bough Breaks* (1974).

Alistair has participated in the production of two television documentaries: *Island of Spirits* (1973), which was awarded a Gold Medal at the International Film Festival at La Spezia in 1975, and *Like You I'm Trapped* (1975), a study of his personal poetry. Two of his poems, 'The Return' and 'Elegy', with settings by the New Zealand composer Douglas Lilburn, can be heard on an LP record under the title of the poems. His *Collected Poems* were published in 1981 by Alister Taylor.

In 1974, he conducted a poetry workshop for Pacific writers at the University of the South Pacific in Suva and, again, in 1980 in Lautoka. In 1976 he went on a concert tour of New Zealand small towns with the pianist Barry Margan. This was followed by an invitiation to participate in the 1978 Adelaide Arts Festival where he presented a paper and read a selection of his poems. In 1979 he was one of The Four New Zealand Poets who went on a six-week tour of New Zealand.

Long associated with the activities of PEN International, he was president of the centre from 1976-79. In this capacity he was instrumental in setting up the 1979 New Zealand Writers' Conference in Wellington.

Alistair's work has been represented in numerous anthologies including: *An Anthology of New Zealand Verse* (1956), *The Penguin Book of New Zealand Verse* (1960), *Recent Poetry in New Zealand* (1965), *An Oxford Anthology of Twentieth Century New Zealand Poetry* (1970), and *Ten Modern New Zealand Poets* (1974).

Merimeri Penfold

Marituu

Haanguu te poo! Whango te poo!
Teenei te hau kei te tiirengirengi,
Kei te tangi aawhiowhio i te poo
I runga o te tai o Paarengarenga,
O te waahi tapu nei a Maarituu.
E whai ana i ngaa maatua kua ngaro
I te iwi noo raatou eenei
E takoto ake nei, e anga ake nei
Ki ngaa whetuu i te poo, te raa i te ao!
Kei teeraa nuku ko Ngaa Kapua, Te Mingi.
Kei teeraa neke ko Taumata-roa, Te Pokere.
Kei teeraa wehenga ko Waioomio, Te Mira,
Ponataura, Paapaarei, Te Waharua, Maarituu —
Naa raatou nei eenei taunaha,
Koia raa ngaa koopikonga
A raatou, a raatou, raatou ee
Kua riro, kua riro ki te poo, ki te poo,
E takoto wahanguu nei
I runga o Maarituu e pae nei.

Marituu

The night is still, the night is silent.
But now the wind comes restlessly,
Lamenting as it goes about in the night
Over the sea at Paarengarenga,
And Maarituu, the sacred place.
It is seeking the elders who are gone
From those whose kin
Lie here, facing
The stars by night, the sun by day.
Over there, Ngaa Kapua and Te Mingi —
Over here, Taumata-roa and Te Pokere —
Yonder, Waioomio and Te Mira,
Ponataura, Paapaarei, Te Waharua, Maarituu —
It is they who named them.
Here are the places where they wandered —
Those who have gone, gone to darkness, darkness,
And lie silent,
Resting on Maarituu hill.

translated by Margaret Orbell

Ngaa Ture Whenua

E tuki, e tuki, e tuki ee, ngaa ture, ture whenua ee, te tauiwi ee!
    Hei aha, hei aha raa, e Tauiwi ee?
    Naau te kii, te kii mai, 'E nuku, e nuku ki Rohe Taaone ee, te utu he moni tekihana ee! Nuku mai i te rohe kaainga ee, whenua tuku iho, kaahore e utu ee!
    Rangirua ana ngaa mahara, e tirotiro kau ana te tangata ee! Kaahore he mana, kaahore he marae, e ngaro ana te wairua Maaori! E tuu ngohengohe kau ana, e tuu mokemoke ana te tangata ee, i ngaa ture aki a Tauiwi ee, ture tukituki tangata, ture hamapaka, koia anake! Uukuia naa!

The Land Laws

Men are beaten, beaten, beaten down by the laws, the land laws, the strangers *ee*!
    O strangers, why, why?

68

It was you who said, said to us, 'Move, move to the towns, earn money for sections! Move from your homes, the land you inherited, and don't have to buy!'

Our thoughts are confused, men stare about in vain! There is no mana, no marae! The soul of the Maori is lost! Men are helpless, men are lonely, because of the harsh laws of the strangers, the laws that beat men down, the humbug laws, only humbug! Wipe the shit away!

translated by Margaret Orbell

MERIMERI PENFOLD (1924, Aupouri) was born at Te Hapua, Northland. She is a lecturer in Maori Studies at the University of Auckland. She is a member of the Maori Language Advisory Committee to the Department of Education and is a member of the Maori section of the New Zealand Council for Educational Research. She is a member of the Te Hapua Incorporation Management Committee and was a member of the editorial committee responsible for the preparation of the latest edition of H.W. Williams' *A Dictionary of the Maori Language.*

MARGARET ORBELL (1934) lectures in Maori at the University of Canterbury and was educated at the University of Auckland where she later lectured in Maori Studies. A former editor of *Te Ao Hou* she is married to the painter Gordon Walters. Her first book was *Maori Folktales in Maori and English* (1968) and in the 1970s she published three books which profoundly altered how we view both traditional and contemporary Maori oral and written literature: *Contemporary Maori Writing* (1970); *Traditional Songs of the Maori* (1975) with Mervyn McLean; *Maori Poetry — An Introductory Anthology* (1978). These books together with Barry Mitcalfe's *Maori Poetry - The Singing Word* (1974) and the present volume, provide an insight to the immense richness of traditional oral Maori literature and its successor, contemporary Maori writing. It is not without significance that the first of these five volumes was published in 1970 and the last at the opening of the next decade.

J.C. Sturm

First Native And Pink Pig

Mrs Harrison sat patiently at the kitchen table, pen poised above the last invitation, and looked across at her small son.

'Come on,' she urged, 'can't you make up your mind? Who's the last one going to be and I wish you'd stop reading till we've finished this.' George flopped his comic on the table with a sigh, folded his arms across it and reluctantly turned his attention on his mother.

'Can't I have both?'

'No, you can't,' Mrs Harrison answered firmly, 'we've been over all that before and the answer's still no.' George screwed up his face.

'Well, I don't care which one I have. It doesn't matter much, does it?'

'As far as I'm concerned,' said his mother, raising her eyebrows, 'it doesn't matter at all, but I need a name to write on this. Which one is it going to be?'

'I don't know.' Mrs Harrison put her pen down carefully and leaned back in her chair.

'Look, George, I've been sitting here for the last fifteen minutes waiting for you to make up your mind. Why can't you? What's holding you up? Can't you just say, I like Peter better than Michael — I'll have him, or Michael's good fun at a party — I'll have him? I can't see why you're finding it so difficult.' George wriggled in his chair and fingered the comic.

'Well, I *do* like Peter better than Michael, but he gets asked to all the parties and Michael doesn't get asked to any.'

'I see,' Mrs Harrison said slowly. 'Still, that doesn't mean you should ask Michael if you really don't want to. Any idea why he doesn't get asked?' George shrugged his shoulders.

'No, except that he's a bit rough with the little kids and gives a lot of cheek.'

'Mmm, I don't like the sound of that. Anything else about him?' There was a long pause while George hunched himself over his comic.

'Yes,' he muttered at last, 'yes, there is. He doesn't like us.' His mother frowned in bewilderment and sat up straight in her chair.

'What do you mean, he doesn't like us? I've never met the child. How can he not like us if he doesn't even know us?' George crouched lower over the comic till his nose was nearly touching it.

'I don't mean just *us*. I mean he doesn't like Maoris.' He raised his head cautiously and looked at this mother, but she had picked up her pen again and was doodling on the cover of her pad. She'd felt all along there was something behind this invitation business, but she hadn't expected this, and here she was taken unawares with a mind like a cheap department store. She wondered, with a sudden sense of having failed somewhere, how long it had been going on without her noticing something was wrong, and why hadn't George told her? She'd have to get to the bottom of it now.

'Tell me Georgie,' she said carefully, 'have you been having trouble at school over this?' and she glanced up from her doodling. George nodded.

'Yes, I have, a bit. Some of the boys don't like Maoris.'

'And this Michael — what's his name?'

70

'Caine.'

'This Michael Caine is one of them?' George nodded again.

'You know that play I told you about, the one where me and Albert were first and second natives?'

'Yes, I remember, it was a good play,' Mrs Harrison replied, watching his face. He didn't look uncomfortable any more, now that he'd started talking. 'Go on.'

'Well, ever since then, Michael and a few of the boys, but mostly Michael, keep on calling us first and second natives...'

'Do you mind being called a native?' put in his mother quickly. George shook his head.

'No, of course not, not in the way you mean,' and his mother looked down at her doodling hurriedly. He was so sharp, she'd have to be careful. 'They aren't calling us *real* natives, like the ones you said belong to the land and all that, and they aren't just remembering the play or joking either. They say it — well — ' he screwed his face up again and scratched an ear, 'well — as though we're dirty, or got something the matter with us,' he finished lamely.

'A term of abuse,' Mrs Harrison murmured to herself. 'And what does Albert do? He's much darker than you.'

'Oh, he cheeks them back, calls them pink and white pigs and things like that. And he's a much better fighter than I am,' he added thoughtfully. Mrs Harrison's grip on her pen tightened and she jabbed at the doodle. 'But I know he doesn't like it even though he says it's only cheek,' went on George in the same thoughtful voice, 'and when he told his mother — gee, she went nearly raving mad. The trouble with them is,' he said, smoothing his comic out with a frown, 'I don't think they'd like to be called any kind of natives — not even real ones.' Mrs Harrison nodded understandingly.

'Yes, I know what you mean. I've noticed that about Albert. It's a pity.' She laid the pen down and propped her elbows on the table. 'But listen, George, if this Michael Caine is so nasty, and silly — and he *is* being silly, you know,' she said pointedly, 'because he doesn't know what he's talking about — why on earth do you want to ask him to your birthday party?' George's face brightened and he propped himself on his elbows too.

'Well, I read in a comic once, Mum, about a chap who had an enemy, and he invited this enemy to stay with him for the holidays, and after that they weren't enemies any more because they'd got to know each other properly.' Mrs Harrison watched him with slow misgivings as he went on eagerly. 'And I thought if Michael could come to the party and have a good time and see what we're like and all that, he'd stop being such a — so silly. I think it might work, Mum. You know all the boys want to get invited to my parties. They say they're beaut fun and you're so good at making pies and things.'

71

'Well, that's something,' smiled his mother feeling ridiculously pleased with herself, 'but there's one thing, George, about your plan. Because it worked in the comic doesn't mean it's going to work here. And what if it doesn't, what will you do then?'

'I know,' he muttered, his face clouding over again. 'I've thought of that. That's why I couldn't make up my mind.' They looked at each other for a moment.

'But I'd like to give it a go all the same,' he said finally, 'and if it doesn't work, I'll never ask him again.'

'Okay,' nodded his mother, picking up the pen, 'Michael Caine it is. Now if you can be in bed by the time I've done this, you can finish reading that story.'

The Saturday of the party was fine, which was something, thought Mrs Harrison, as she went over in her mind the twelve hours that lay ahead, but the promising morning rapidly developed into a series of last minute hitches and disappointments. George opened his presents from the family straight after breakfast, and the windjacket with the fur collar from his grandmother, which he knew he was getting and had counted on wearing that afternoon, was too small and had to be wrapped up again for taking back to the shop. The book his grandfather sent him was one he already had, and the pocket microscope from his father proved to be much more difficult to manipulate than it had seemed in the shop. Only his mother's gift, a blue and yellow plastic glider with a marvellous wing span of eighteen inches, was un unqualified success. Then the telephone began ringing. One boy couldn't come and another wasn't sure. His favourite Aunt, who had promised to be at the birthday tea and bring a surprise with her, was sorry she couldn't possibly manage it, but if she came on Sunday instead would he save her a piece of cake? And worst of all, in the middle of lunch his father was called away urgently and had no idea when he would be back, though probably not till late that night. George had grown quieter and quieter as the long morning dragged on, and after his father had gone, he buried himself in a comic as though he had forgotten it was his birthday and there was to be a party and a plan to carry out. His mother left him alone till half past one before she jollied him into clean clothes and his best jersey and gave him some of his father's brylcream, and then she sent him off with enough money to shout the other boys at the local cinema. 'Have a good time,' she called after him as he went down the path, 'tea will be ready when you all come back.' By four o'clock everything was prepared — cheerios in a pot on the stove, little meat pies keeping warm in the oven, bowls of fruit salad on the bench, the table crowded with sandwiches, chocolate rice bubbles, fancy biscuits, chippies, lollies, bottles of fizz and the big cake with Happy Birthday George in silver letters

72

encircled by ten red candles. She checked the number of plates and straws, put some paper serviettes handy in case they wanted to take home what they couldn't eat, and made herself a cup of tea. She felt nervous and on edge. It's ridiculous she told herself as she changed into the dress George liked best and·did her face and hair, after all, who is this wretched Michael Caine? Just a cheeky little boy who needs to be taught a thing or two. And if George's plan doesn't work — so much the worse for Caine. It would be his loss, not theirs. But the nervousness persisted, grew worse if anything, and she was almost glad when she heard voices coming up the path. Once things got under way she'd be all right.

Albert burst through the back door, slammed it behind him and flung himself into a chair.

'First up,' he panted, and ran an experienced eye over the table of food. 'Gee — I love those chocolate rice bubble things.'

'Good,' Mrs Harrison smiled, straining the cheerios over the sink, 'there are plenty more.'

'Hullo!' called George from the back porch, and the others bundled into the kitchen and stood staring at the table.

'Mum, you know Dan and Graham, don't you?' and the two boys jostled each other and grinned sheepishly at Mrs Harrison. 'Andrew didn't turn up, and this is Michael Caine.'

'Ah,' said Mrs Harrison, smiling carefully, 'I've heard quite a lot about you, Michael, I'm glad you could come to George's party.' Michael didn't seem interested in the food like the others and stood staring about the kitchen at the gleaming floor, gaily painted cupboards, stainless steel bench, flowers in the window, and now he glanced sharply up at Mrs Harrison. Big for his age or older than the rest, she thought, still smiling at the straight fair hair and blue eyes, and he's sharp — too sharp and cocky.

'Well, thanks for asking me, Mrs Harrison,' he answered, and looked past her at the shining bench. 'You know,' he said, nodding towards it, 'my mother's got a bench just like that. You've got a nice place here, Mrs Harrison.'

'Yes, haven't we?' she beamed at him. 'Now come along and sit up, the cheerios are getting cold. Michael, will you sit over there next to George—'

'Can I sit next to George too?' Albert asked quickly.

'Of course. You sit on this side, and Graham, you're next to Michael, and Dan next to Albert. Right? Now — two four six eight —'

'Bog in, don't wait!' shouted the boys, and grabbed at the food.

'What was the film like?' asked Mrs Harrison, moving round the table and taking the tops off the bottles.

'A real beaut,' Albert exclaimed through a mouthful of cheerios. 'You see, these settlers wanted to buy some land from the Indians, but the Indians wanted to keep it for themselves, so —'

'— the settlers shot the Indians — pow! pow!' interrupted Michael.

'Shut up, Caine,' Albert growled, 'who's telling this story?'

'Anyway, a lot of the settlers got shot too,' said George, shaking his bottle to make it fizz.

'But the settlers won,' Michael persisted, helping himself to the last pie. Albert glared at him.

'Nobody won. They just made a sort of agreement —'

'— so the settlers could have the land,' finished Michael. 'That's what really happened, didn't it, Mrs Harrison?'

'I'm afraid I don't know much about early American history, Michael,' she replied, not looking at George and Albert, 'but it must have been something like that. Now, who'd like another pie?' and she took a fresh tray out of the oven. 'What about you, Graham? You're being very quiet over there, and you too, Dan.' Dan and Graham had been methodically working their way round the table while the others wasted time arguing, but they barely glanced at the assortments already on their plates before reaching up for the tray Mrs Harrison lowered over their heads. Somehow, Michael's bottle of fizz was sent flying, and a good half of the drink gurgled over his plate and splashed down the front of him. He righted it quickly and half rose to his feet, holding a clenched fist over Graham's head.

'You clumsy clot, I'll get you for that,' he threatened, and Graham shrank back in his chair giggling nervously.

'Never mind, Michael,' Mrs Harrison said quickly, 'I've got an extra bottle you can have. Would you like to come to the bathroom and wipe that off?'

'Yes, I suppose I'd better,' he muttered, looking down at his dripping clothes, and followed her out of the room. George and Albert exchanged glances.

'Here,' Mrs Harrison handed him a dampened towel, 'rub it with this and it mightn't stain.' Michael looked at it dubiously. What had his mother said about not using the towels? He shook his head.

'It's all right, thanks, I'll use my handkerchief,' and he pulled one out of his pocket, passed it hastily over the wet patches and hurried back to the kitchen. All the pies and cheerios and most of the sandwiches had gone. Albert was monopolising the chocolate rice bubbles and Dan and Graham were busy cleaning up the biscuits. George emptied the last of the chippies on to his plate and called out to his mother.

'Mum, what about the fruit salad? We're still hungry.'

'Good heavens,' she exclaimed, 'I forgot all about it,' and she handed the bowls round the table. Michael didn't want any.

'Are you sure? Well, how about a chocolate rice bubble?' and she removed the plate from under Albert's nose and held it out.

74

'No thanks. I don't like the smell of them,' he replied looking hard at Albert. Albert stopped munching and looked back.

'Perhaps you'd like a white bread sandwich instead,' Mrs Harrison said crisply, in spite of herself, and turned away to the bench. Michael glanced at her back and dug an elbow in Graham's ribs.

'That's right,' he whispered loudly, 'eat up like a good boy. Here, let me help you,' and he tipped the bowl of fruit salad into Graham's lap.

'I'm sorry, Mrs Harrison,' Graham stammered nervously, 'but my fruit salad — I didn't —' Mrs Harrison swung round and caught Michael's grin.

'That's all right, Graham,' she soothed, 'Scoop up what you can with your spoon and then go to the bathroom. George, I think it's time you lit the candles.' She handed him a box of matches. 'Ready? Happy birthday to you — happy birthday to you —' The others joined in, Michael roaring like a bull, and George pretended he was shy and hid under the table.

'Come on first and second natives,' Michael shouted over the smoking candles, 'how about a haka? The one that's got whaka something in it,' and he grinned knowingly at Dan who choked on a mouthful and started to laugh and thought better of it. Albert was on his feet, leaning across the table and glaring at Michael under straight black brows.

'Shut your face, Caine,' he shouted back, 'or I'll shut it for you, you pink pig!' George looked at his mother.

'Sit down, boys,' she said firmly, 'while George cuts the cake and makes his wish.' George plunged the knife in recklessly. 'And Michael, if you want to hear some Maori — whakarongo mai, fermez la bouche!' She looked at him steadily.

'Gee — listen to that,' breathed Michael, opening his eyes wide. 'What's it mean Mrs Harrison?'

'It means the pig is in the pig-sty,' she said lightly and laughed. 'Now off you all go into the sitting-room and look at the presents while I wrap up a piece of cake for each of you to take home.'

When she went through to the front room with the cake, Michael was standing by the windows examining the glider and the others were trying to work the microscope.

'Here you are boys,' she said, 'and I think it's time to go now.'

'Can't we have a game, Mum,' George pleaded, 'just one. We always do.' His mother made a show of looking at her watch. She'd had enough, and it didn't matter what the real time was, it was still time for them to go. And then she remembered the plan.

'Well, I suppose, just one,' she gave in reluctantly, 'but only for five minutes, so let's have something short and simple. How about Simon Says, and I'll give the winner sixpence. How's that?'

'Yippee!'

'Spread yourselves out so you won't hit each other. Dan, you might put an arm through the window if you stand there. That's better. Now, are you all ready? Simon says — do *this*, Simon says — do this — do *this*!' Dan went out almost straight away and Graham followed suit soon after. But George and Michael and Albert copied her movements like three well-drilled soldiers moving as one man, and no matter what she did she couldn't trick them into a wrong move.

'I give up,' she said at last, 'I'll never get you three out.'

'Please, Mum,' George pleaded once more, 'You can't have three winners. Just one more go.'

'All right, I'll try to make it harder,' sighed his mother. 'The last man's out. Ready? Simon says — ' and that time George was a split second behind the others. He sat down without a word and concentrated on Albert.

'You two don't want to go on, do you?' Mrs Harrison asked hopefully. They nodded without taking their eyes off her and she looked at their strained faces and tense bodies and wished she hadn't been such a fool to suggest a competitive game — she might have known this would happen. It didn't matter who won, there was bound to be trouble whichever one it was. She looked at her watch and pretended surprise.

'Do you know we've been playing for fifteen minutes instead of five? I declare myself beaten and you two the winners,' she smiled, 'and I owe you sixpence each.' Michael and Albert glanced at each other, but took their money without a word. 'Now it really is time to go. Don't forget your cake,' and she ushered them out the front door and watched them troop down the steps. George picked up his glider and followed them.

'I'll see them down to the road,' he told his mother, 'and then I might give her a try-out on the back lawn.' She nodded understandingly. After the performance at the tea table, who'd want to share a new glider with that lot.

George stopped before he got to the gate and watched his friends disappear round the other side of the hedge.

'Bye! See you on Monday,' he called out, and turned back up the path. He wasn't sorry to see them go. It had been a good party, but next year perhaps he'd just have Albert, and his mother might let him stay the night and they could pack some food and go for a tramp over the hills or something. Suddenly something struck him between the shoulder blades and he wheeled round with a gasp to find Michael on the step behind him.

'Got you,' he grinned, 'time you had your ears cleaned out, Harrison.'

'Oh, I heard you all right,' George lied, trying not to show that he'd got a fright, 'but I wanted to see what you'd do. What do you want? Forgot something?'

'Nope.' He moved up beside George and looked at the glider. 'I heard

76

you say you were going to give her a try-out and I thought I'd have a go too.' George shook his head and backed slowly up the next step. The sneak — creeping up on him like that.

'I've changed my mind. Too many trees around here. It needs plenty of space like a park —'

'Aw — come on,' Michael cut in impatiently, 'you're just trying to put me off,' and he twitched the glider out of George's grasp, poised it in one hand at shoulder level while he fended George off with the other, and then launched it down the path. George held his breath as he watched it swoop straighten out rise again curve suddenly with a flash of yellow wings like some tropical bird, watched it crash high against a tree and fall to the ground in two pieces. He let out a cry and bounded down the steps to where it lay. Michael followed slowly with a worried frown. He'd only wanted to have a go — hadn't meant to break it. How was he to know it would turn like a boomerang? It had been a good party, almost as good as the chaps at school said it would be, and he was glad he'd come in spite of his mother's warnings. And now this had to happen. Not much chance of being asked again.

'Look what you've done, Caine,' George cried, his voice shrill with anger and the desire to weep, 'you've wrecked it — wrecked it.' Michael peered at the broken pieces George was trying to fit together with trembling fingers, and mumbled something, but George wasn't listening.

'I wish I'd never asked you to my party. I wish I'd asked Peter instead.' His voice broke. 'Look at it — finished. I've got a good mind to tell my mother who did it, you clumsy clot.' Michael coloured angrily and clenched his fists.

'Who wants to come to your lousy parties anyway? Simon Says and all that kids' stuff!' He hunched his shoulders and brought his face close to George's. 'And you can tell your mother something else too. Tell her I said she's a dirty stinking brown cow of a Maori, and see what she can do about it.' George lashed out at him blindly, missed, and stumbled to his knees as Michael dodged back.

'Yaa —' he jeered, retreating down the steps, 'missed — first native missed. What are you on your knees for? Better go and see mammy, and don't forget what I said.' And then he was gone.

George picked himself up, collected the pieces of glider and made his way slowly up the path, but the steps seemed too high and his knees shook and his chest didn't want to go on breathing. He sniffed once and wiped his nose along his sleeve. What could he tell her, what was he going to say? She was running water and clattering dishes in the sink and didn't hear him come in the door behind her. He put the broken glider on the table and slumped in a chair, waiting, and suddenly she looked round startled, as though he had called out.

'Hello George, I didn't hear you come in. How long have you been there?' Her eyes narrowed and she came across to the table wiping her hands on her apron. 'What's the matter?' and then she saw the glider and frowned. She'd gone to some trouble choosing it, discussing wingspan and flexibility and weight and heavens knows what else, until the shop assistant had left her talking to herself and gone away to serve another customer. And after all that it hadn't lasted him a day.

'How did that happen? I didn't think you'd break it so soon What a pity.' She couldn't keep annoyance out of her voice. George looked at her present.

'It was Caine,' he said dully, 'he crept up behind me and grabbed it and threw it against a tree.' His mother's frown deepened and she made a noise in her throat.

'The clumsy clot. What did he want to do that for?' She looked up when George didn't answer and saw his face. Exhausted, she thought and no wonder. 'Well, never mind, I'll see if I can get another next time I go to town. How's that?' Still no answer. 'George did you hear what I said? I'll get you another —' He moved restlessly in his chair and looked out the window.

'It's not just the glider, it's the plan — it didn't work.' His mother sat down opposite him and pushed the broken toy to one side.

'How do you know? Did he say something?'

'He said it was a lousy party, just kids' stuff, and he didn't want to come to any more.' Mrs Harrison sniffed and straightened the crumpled tablecloth.

'That suits me just fine, and I couldn't care less what he thinks about the party. But that doesn't spoil your plan, does it? I mean, it's not what we were talking about when I was doing the invitations.' George looked at her miserably. Her hair had got messed up when she was playing Simon Says and most of her make-up had worn off leaving her forehead and nose shiny and slightly greasy and her lips pale inside what was left of her lipstick. Tiredness deepened the lines and hollows of her face and she looked old.

'He called me first native again, and then —' He turned away to the window once more, 'and then he said I was a dirty stinking brown Maori.' His mother watched him closely for a minute. He was shaken and she'd have to do something about it, restore his confidence in what he was, even if it meant taking a leaf out of Albert's book.

'George, tell me, what is Michael Caine?'

'A pig,' he replied flatly without hesitation, 'just a pig.'

'That's right, and he doesn't know any more than a pig, and when he calls you or Albert or anyone else names, he's only grunting. Do you see?' and she smiled at him inquiringly. George nodded and forced a lop-sided smile back. He was tired, so tired he wished it could be tomorrow — or yesterday. 'Now I'd better finish those dishes,' his mother said and stood up, 'and will you gather your presents in the sitting-room and see if you can find places for them in your bedroom?'

'Okaydoke, Mum,' he managed to sound cheerful, and did a sort of hop step and jump out of the room and down the passage. His mother watched him go with some surprise. That had been easier than she'd expected, or perhaps he hadn't been as upset as she thought, in which case she'd overdone the pig business. She moved over to the sink and turned on the tap. Oh, well, what did it matter as long as she'd helped him get things sorted out in his mind. George stood in the middle of the sitting-room and stared blindly at the pile of presents on the sofa. And then he scooped them up in his arms all higgledy-piggledy, string and paper too, and did his act down the passage again, and shut his bedroom door carefully with one shoulder, and leaned against it and wept.

Jerusalem, Jerusalem

If my date hadn't been late that Friday night I wouldn't be telling you this, because I wouldn't have met Olive instead and found out what I did. A brisk southerly had been hosing down the city all day, leaving it brighter and darker and taller and wider than it ever really is, and excited in a shivering jittery kind of way, like a dog that has just had a bath it didn't want. It certainly wasn't the night for a leisurely stroll down town or to be loitering in shop doorways, and yet a surprising number of the city's population were doing just that. There were the usual pub leftovers and the picture crowd and the ones who like eating late in Chinese restaurants and the others who would later take up residence in the coffee shops if they hadn't managed to gate-crash a party. And there were exhausted housewives, weighted down with the weekend shopping and drooping on tram stops, while bright young things, all eye-shadow and stiffened petticoats, clung to their Valentinos and hastened towards Romance. Some of the shops had closed already, hustling their customers and assistants outside where husbands waited with pale-faced children and boy-friends shuffled impatiently and dropped half-finished cigarettes and stood on them. And as though the natives weren't more than enough, two American ships had berthed that afternoon, and the pavements were awash with sailors and girls like gaudy tropical fish.

I was afraid of missing my date in that crowd, so worked my way round the traffic lights twice, just in case, hopping from one side of the road to the other whenever the greens gave me the chance, as a child jumps from rock to rock when the waves suck back and wait, and trying to gain a foothold on each corner was worse than landing on a slippery ledge with someone standing in the way. In the end I gave up, and elbowed myself into the doorway of Madame's exclusive gown salon. I wriggled into the black satin cocoon in the window and went to the party and had a fabulous time and came back on the stroke, like Cinderella, to find a little fox terrier man thumping a newspaper tail against his thigh and snapping at my legs, have a drink have a drink come and have a drink. The last corner, which was also the first, proved to be the best. I backed up against a wall of marcasite and New Zealand souvenirs, wondering how much pressure plate glass can take to the square inch, and then I saw Olive. I never know why some faces stand out in a crowd, but they do, and the shifting shapeless mass suddenly becomes a background to one small oval of meaning, and the shock of recognition is so great that you hail a mere acquaintance as though he were a beloved uncle, and then you have to turn away quickly to hide your excitement while you try to remember his name. Olive had such a face, and my heart leapt and flipped over and went through all the gymnastics hearts are supposed to be capable of, when I saw it. Not that she was a close friend of mine or ever had been, even in the old days, but she belonged to the brightest of my childhood, and who can stand on a street corner and not tremble as the past walks out of a crowd?

I don't know how long the Kellys had been at the Bay before I first saw them. A public works camp had come from nowhere and dug itself in on the outskirts of our small community, and it was hard to keep track of all the new faces. The 'permanent residents', as they called themselves, didn't like the invasion one bit. (I think they feared deep down it was the beginning of the End, and in a way, I suppose it was.) They used to go to the local store in twos and threes and pretend they couldn't think what they wanted and turn to the nearest stranger and say, I'm not in a hurry, you go first, and then stand back and watch while their victim blushed and stammered and the woman behind the counter who didn't want to lose any old custom on account of the new because you can't depend on PWCs, would go to the fridge at the other end of the room and call out, did you say *half* a pound of butter?

One of these sessions was in full swing the afternoon I found Billy and Ken sitting on the ground beside the store door with their backs against the wall. Now that tickled me. We local kids used to get up to all kinds like turning somersaults on the rail at the top of the steps and accidentally kicking people as they came out, and dressing up a dog and taking it for a walk in a borrowed pram, and leaving dead wetas beside the seat in the Ladies. But we never, not ever, sat on the ground outside the store and put our backs to the wall. So I sauntered past them and back again, humming carelessly to myself, and stopped to look at the view, and turned a somersault or two, and I liked them. I liked the way they sat and grinned and nudged each other and whispered in something like Maori, but it wasn't, and I even liked the way they soon lost interest and ignored me. And then the woman came out, and it was my turn to lose interest in them. She was tall and dark and thin, and had a thing like a bright cotton curtain wrapped around her somehow and hanging right down to her large bare feet — I looked again, *bare feet* — and her toes sort of spread out and flapped a bit as she walked away. I was goggling after her open-mouthed, and wondering if she really walked differently from us or if it was only because of the curtain thing round her legs, when Billy and Ken scrambled up and raced after her, laughing and shoving each other as they went. Inside the store the post-mortem had already begun, and everyone was fairly clamouring to get her knife in. *What a get up have you ever never in my whole life they say he's white can you imagine what next.* And the woman behind the counter who had her shoes specially made (glacé kid, you know) because of her bunions, and always wore corsets for her weak back (you could see where they stuck into her middle when she bent over), fanned the air in front of her as though some one had made a bad smell, and vowed she had never *never*, had such a...such a *creature* inside her shop before.

When Billy and Ken came to school, and that was some time after the store, they brought two sisters with them. Mary was olive and pink and very shy and had her mother's straight blue-black hair. Judy was brown and round and curly and her teeth were appalling. The four of them had enormous black eyes and could use them like gimlets when they wanted to. Our school was one room with a porch for coats and two teachers and a paddock with pine trees at the far end, and whatever we did, we all did it together, because there weren't enough of us to split up into gangs. So when some brought bags of marbles, they'd be shared out, and at playtime the whole school would play, and the little ones who were too young, like Mary and Judy, would yell and jump about and get in the way.

Billy and Ken were very good at marbles. They would crouch in the dust like cats and open their eyes wide and let fly, and whenever they scored a hit and they nearly always did, you'd wonder the glass could stand it. But our favourite game was rounders. Every lunchtime, unless it rained and sometimes even then, the man teacher, who was young and liked to keep fit, would come out swinging the round bat and divide us into teams and toss for it and scatter the fielders round the paddock. Then he would tuck his trousers into his socks, like plus-fours, and lead the batting side and tear round the field roaring like a bull, out of my way out of my way, and we'd fall over ourselves laughing and roll in the grass and laugh and laugh because we loved it and he looked so funny. And on very wet days, after we'd finished our sandwiches, we'd sit round the old stove in the corner and have a community sing, and the woman teacher would warble, 'D'ye ken John Peel', and if we didn't, she'd shout the words at us, stamping on the beat till she was red in the face and her fronts flopped up and down.

There were a few lunchtimes when both teachers were too busy to keep an eye on us, and we'd sneak down to the out-of-bounds pine-trees and play apes, and Billy and Ken would swing the farthest and hang the longest and make the worst faces, till someone thought they heard the bell, and then it was *slither* and torn clothes and hands and a race across the paddock not to be the last one in. I don't know how those two teachers stood that job, because, in the classroom, even more than in the playground, whatever we did, we *had* to do it together. There wasn't anywhere else to do it. But they stood it, all right, and if the new ones, and there were several besides the Kellys, had hopes that they wouldn't be noticed in the confusion that was us working, they didn't have them for long. Mary and Judy had practically no English and the boys were loath to use what little they had preferring expressive grunts instead, but they were all extremely quick in the uptake, only didn't let on. If that teacher had realised what was going on behind the grunts and solemn eyes, she might have saved herself many patient painstaking hours, or taught them more than she did. On the other hand, she might have given up the job altogether. I was on the other side of the room and didn't see much of them during classes, but every afternoon I found out what they had absorbed during the day, because as soon as we were clear of the school gate they started to chant it, finding the rhythm in it and stamping it all the way down the hill to the beach. And Ken, who was a wicked mimic, would caper before us, and *be* that poor teacher.

Although Tom Kelly had a public works job like most of the newcomers to the Bay, the family lived down on the beach instead of up at the camp. It might have been that there weren't enough army huts to go round, or it might have had something to do with what happened at the store. Or perhaps he was just trying to make his wife and children feel at home in their new country, though I shouldn't imagine that the Bay, even the beach part of it, would have much in common with Apia. Anyway, whatever the reason, he had taken a house at the foot of the big hill, and Mrs Kelly had used all she had to make it into a home. The all consisted of several finely plaited mats, a few beautifully polished coconut bowls, a table and chairs, some crockery and cooking utensils, nearly enough beds and bedding to go round, and the old gramophone. After these had been arranged in the living room facing the sea and the three bedrooms and the dummy kitchen, there was still plenty of room to move about. No matter what time of day I went to that house, and I practically lived there, Mrs Kelly was nearly always out the back preparing food. The kitchen was a dummy one because it didn't have any of the things you'd expect to find in it, like a stove and sink and water and cupboards, so she had made herself a cook-house with some corrugated iron and a fireplace of stones from the beach, and if we couldn't find her inside when we came in from school, she was bound to be out there in the space between the side of the house and the tin fence, sitting on her haunches and poking and stirring and wiping her eyes with the back of her hand when the fire smoked. She could sit like that, on her haunches with the long skirt wrapped around her thighs, for hours.

I don't know what she did for company when we weren't there because she never went out, not even to the store after the first time, and didn't have any visitors because her English wasn't good enough. But she had plenty to keep her busy. There were the mats to shake and water to fetch and clothes to wash and driftwood to be gathered. We used to do what we could to help, like going messages and sweeping the path with a manuka broom, but it wasn't much, and Olive, who was much older than us, had to leave first thing in the morning for the factory in town and didn't get back till late. We hardly saw her except at the weekends, and then if she was in a good mood, she would call us to her bedroom and rub coconut oil into our scalps and whack them with a brush till it hurt, and let us play with her nail polish and powder till we got silly and made a mess, and then we were bundled out and the door closed. And sometimes, when we were tired of the beach or it was raining and we didn't know what to do with ourselves, Mrs Kelly would line us up in the living room and show us how to do the siva, gliding and turning and dipping before us like a bird, and her hands were flowers folding and unfolding and folding again. We used to giggle at first and push each other and pretend we were shy, but the bird and the flowers went on beckoning beckoning, and slowly, one by one, we would follow, gliding and turning and dipping and folding, till we weren't us any more, only birds and flowers. Then Mrs Kelly would snap her fingers and stop and smile at us, and the boys would whoop and fall on their backs and kick their legs in the air while we thumped them and thumped them.

But of all things we did in that house, the boys liked playing the old gramophone best. They would pull it out from the corner and crank the handle and put on 'Jerusalem, Jerusalem', and while it was playing, they'd sit cross-legged on the floor like stone images and gaze out the window with wide darkening eyes. And when it was finished, they'd crank again and put on the 'Hawaiian War Chant' and leap about the room and shake themselves as though they wanted to get rid of their arms and legs. Then they'd go back to 'Jerusalem'. I used to feel uncomfortable about this at first. Hymns meant standing up in church in your hat and gloves, and not knowing the meaning of the words half the time, and watching the choir move their mouths about as though they had toffee sticking to their back teeth. Or they could be your mother trilling in the kitchen like a canary as she prepared breakfast on the mornings she felt good. But they didn't have anything to do with cranky old gramophones and Hawaiian war chants and sitting cross-legged on the floor and listening. Nothing at all. It took me quite a while to get the hang of it.

We played in the house, but we lived on the beach. And we did the kinds of things all children do on beaches, like playing french cricket with a bit of old fruit-case for a bat, and writing our names and the date in the damp sand with a stick, and skimming flat stones on the water and counting the hops, and throwing seaweed and old fish heads at one another. But we used to get tired of these, and then we'd really *do* something, like making a Map or a Plan and going on a Hunt. We often went on a Hunt, because if we were lucky, it would end up being a Feast. There were small purple crabs under the rocks nearest the house and big red ones in the deep channels further out and paua at low tide and sea-eggs if you knew where to look. The biggest crab we ever caught was a real red whopper, like a small cray, but we didn't eat him. We had been hunting all afternoon and made a good haul and taken it up to the cook-house, and Mrs Kelly poked our prize catch among the glowing embers and we squatted behind her and smelled the lovely smell and hugged our knees against our chests and grinned at one another. She had raked him out to one side to cool and we were saying who'd have which part, when Tom Kelly looked round the corner of the house. He hardly ever came home till well after our bed-time, but there he was, looking at us without a word, and then he walked over to our Feast and picked him up and took off the back and crammed it all into his mouth at once. And the red legs dangled below his yellow moustache and wiggled up and down as he munched and munched. So we had the sea-eggs instead, and I bolted seven, because of the crab, and was sick all that night.

But he never found out about our Plan. The Bay was really three small bays, and we had explored every rock and pool of it except the ones we couldn't reach, and sometimes we would sit in the sand and screw up our eyes against the sea glare and gaze at the part we didn't know and wonder what it was like, out there. And one day we couldn't stand it any longer and that's when we made our canoe. We built it with corrugated iron and the ends of fruit-cases and bits of old sacking, and Mary and Judy kept a look-out for grown-ups because they were bound to say I don't think that's a very good idea, and we used to be careful about hiding it under branches and clumps of seaweed, though no grown-up who was really grown up would have guessed it was any kind of a boat. Early one good calm morning when we had the beach to ourselves, we launched her, and she floated away from our proud hands like a log. She could take only one of us at a time, so our Plan was for the first one to sail out the first bay and round into the second, and the second one to sail out the second bay and round into the third, and to come back the same way and do it again, till each one of us had sailed round all the bays. And that's what we did, only we didn't sail, we paddled. The one whose turn it was would get in gingerly and the others steadied her and handed him the fruit-case paddles and gave him a bit of a push in the right direction and clambered over the rocks trying to keep level with him, just in case, and shouted look out mind the seaweed, while he paddled like mad to get round before she filled up.. So we found out what it was like, out there, and the Great Octopus who lived in the Deep Water beyond the Last Rock, jerked and writhed and bulged his eyes with rage, as we slopped and wobbled by.

That was Summer. Winter brought the bulldozers and the rain and the mud, in that order, and then a repeat of the same. One afternoon when I came home from the Kellys, I found the first of the bulldozers had removed a bank that just happened to be in its way, and half our front lawn and path that just happened to be on top of the bank, had gone too. A slab of concrete was still hanging on and jutted out from the new cliff edge like a diving-board, but the next morning it wasn't hanging on any longer, and slab by slab our path was turned into diving-boards that slipped away and lay like tumbled tombstones in the ruined clay below. And the bulldozers moved on. The Ladies went in a morning and the tennis courts that afternoon. The store was picked up and dumped down in the manuka a hundred yards off the road, and the woman behind the counter vowed she had never, *never* been handled so roughly by *anyone* before. Some of the 'permanent residents' had left already, shutting windows and locking doors and making sure the power was turned off, after it had dawned on them that the new road was going to be put through their privacy and not over the hills behind.

The shrewdest of the PWCs who had no memories to muddle them like us, and found it easier to imagine what the new Bay would be like when the road was finished and the bulldozers carted away, said, good riddance, to the 'permanent residents' backs, and left their army huts smartly and moved into the vacant houses. But they made some bad mistakes, for all their shrewdness, and had to pay for them. There was the bloke who went nosing in the gully that was supposed to be an old Maori burial ground, because someone had told him there was so much greenstone down there you couldn't help tripping over it. Well, he tripped over all right, and

85

broke his leg and couldn't climb out, and when they found him two days later he was gone in the head and had to be taken away. And there was the drunk who got lost the night of the storm and went down the hill instead of up and passed out on the second zig-zag and was dead of exposure by morning. That was the night our canoe disappeared. And up at the camp some one's baby died of diphtheria before they realised what it was.

But while the 'permanent residents' who were trying to stick it out, worried about compensation, and the PWCs were busy getting themselves into trouble, we kids had the time of our lives, at least in the beginning. The bulldozers were hard at it when we went to school and we used to crowd round the big shovel, watching the polished teeth bite into a bank and jerk and strain till the clay cracked and gave at last, and was caught up by the grab and dropped into the trays of the waiting trucks. And if we went too close, the drivers would shout and wave us back and you could tell they were swearing, though on-one could make himself heard above the roar and growling of the machines. We were late for school more often than not but it didn't matter, we could always say the road was blocked, and the teachers were so afraid one of us would get bulldozed along with everything else, they never said a word. At three o'clock it was a race to be first through the new cutting, and the smooth clay was all pale blues and greens and golds running into one another and thick and quiet under our feet like A1 linoleum, and you could walk over it and look back and not see a mark anywhere. Then one of the big boys who did geography, said they found diamonds in pale blue stuff, and we used to clamber up the terraced banks and dig with sticks till they snapped and claw with fingers instead and lift the lumps above our heads and dash them open on the ground in case the diamonds were hidden inside, and our nails were always pale blue. Sometimes a machine broke down and was left behind by the others, and we would perch all over it like seagulls and boys narrowed their eyes and moved their hands about and made the noises just right, only not so loud.

But the bulldozers moved on, and we were left with the rain and the lorries churning our A1 linoleum into grey porridge, and there weren't any diamonds, and we didn't like the mess that used to be the Bay, any more than the grown-ups did. It was *change* when you got there and *change* when you got back and having to go the long way round, and those of us who had gumboots and slippers were always getting them mixed up in the school porch and going home with two lefts or none at all and not being able to explain why. And some of the mothers made the boys come to school with their heads wrapped in newspaper, like cabbages, because they were sick and tired of buying a new sou'wester every week. By the time the 'flu came, the grown-ups were so fed-up with everything, they couldn't crawl into bed fast enough and turn their faces to the wall, and didn't we kids have to get off our tails then! If we weren't fetching and carrying and trying to cook for our own family, we were doing it for someone else's and no one bothered to say *change* or cared if we lost all our clothes.

What with the diving boards slipping faster than ever and my mother in bed, the Kellys had been away from school several days before I had a chance to go down to the beach. And when I did go, I almost wished I hadn't, it was so awful. Olive was staying in town and came home only at the weekend because the new road made it harder to get to the factory on time, and Tom Kelly had moved on with the bulldozers, but Mrs Kelly and the four children were there and even I could see they were very sick indeed. They had dragged their beds into the corners to try and keep dry, because the roof didn't leak, it simply let the rain in, and the water was up to my ankles in the dummy kitchen. I couldn't get round to the cook-house because the bank behind the house had slipped and blocked the back door, but even if there had been some food out there it probably wouldn't have been the right kind for 'flu. I sat on the end of Mrs Kelly's bed and talked about the weather, but I wasn't sure she understood, her eyes were so bright and strange. And the children didn't want to play even being-sick-in-bed games, like I Spy. They just shivered and shivered and put their heads under the thin damp blankets. My mother was too sick herself to do anything, but she gave me lemons and honey and aspirins and cooked food to take down every day. And they recovered slowly, like everyone else, but most of the mats were ruined and the cook-house was a shambles. Before the children were well enough to go back to school, I went down with chicken-pox and complications, and by the time I could be wrapped in a chair and put out in the pale Spring sunshine, the diving-boards had slipped away right up to our front door and my mother said it was time to go. So we left the Bay, and the Kellys, and moved north.

'How many years is it? asked Olive. I smiled down at the two little girls sharing the handle of her shopping basket, because they were very like Mary and Judy.

'I'm not sure,' I replied, pretending to count them, 'but too many, anyway.' We had stumbled over the awkward preliminaries, the crowds pressing about us and the noise of the traffic, making them even more awkward, and now there was nothing left to talk about except the memories we had in common.

'And how is your mother?' The question had been waiting impatiently on the tip of my tongue all the time. Olive looked at me sharply with surprise, and away again.

'She's dead. It's a wonder you didn't hear about it.'

'Oh,' I said, and it was my turn to look away, 'I'm so sorry,' as though I had just trodden on her toe. And my date could have whistled in my ear then, and I wouldn't have known.

'Yes, she died soon after we left the Bay. We moved not long after you, and went north too. But she never really recovered from the 'flu and that house, especially that house.' She made a small grimace at me, and I nodded. 'They pulled it down as soon as they got rid of us, and about time too. It was condemned, you know, even before we took it, but Dad was prepared to pay the rent they wanted, so they stretched a point.' I leaned against my plate glass, hardly hearing what she said. People had a habit of dying, they were doing it all the time, and it didn't do to forget it.

'And the children' I asked, looking down at the two little girls, 'how are the children?' She smiled and put her arms round them.

'You're getting mixed up, aren't you? They aren't like this any more. Judy's got a baby, and Mary,' she hesitated, and the smile faded, 'well, Mary's been in the San for a while, but she'll be out soon.' The children had been listening and watching us with bright dark eyes, and the one like Judy suddenly piped up.

'And Uncle Billy knows all about gaol and tells us, and so does Uncle Ken, but he's only been there once.' Olive shook the child by the shoulder and frowned, and she looked up at her mother, bewildered. 'That's right, Mummy, Uncle Ken's ...'

'That's *enough*,' snapped Olive, and nearly jerked her off her feet. There was a long pause, and Olive tilted her chin away from me and watched the sailors and the girls on the other side of the street. The traffic lights blinked and blurred, blinked and blurred.

'What could I do?' she suddenly burst out, facing me furiously though I hadn't said a word, 'what would you expect me to do? Dad went back on the public works, and I had my life to live too, didn't I? And a good job at the factory at last.'

'Of course,' I managed to put in, but she hadn't finished.

'And I used to go out and see them at the orphanage every week, and when they left there I thought they were old enough to look after themselves. And I married a Yank,' she fumbled among the parcels in her basket and looked across the street again, 'I married a Yank, and he didn't come back.' She lifted her shoulders with a deep breath and let it out quickly. 'And by that time it was too late. So there's just the three of us,' and she looked down at her children. They had been watching us uncertainly since something had gone wrong with the conversation, but now they brightened up again and smiled at their mother hopefully, and Olive smiled at me in spite of herself, and I smiled at the three of them. And one or two people glanced at us curiously as they pushed past, we all looked so happy.

'Well, bed-time at the zoo,' said Olive briskly, and the two little girls shook her arm and jigged up and down, crying no, no.

'Yes, I'd better be off too,' I said, forgetting all about my date, 'it's not the night for hanging around, is it?' And Olive smiled again as she turned away from me for the last time, and half waved before she crossed with the green. And the little girls went hopping and skipping on either side of her, like children on a beach.

J.C. STURM (1927; Taranaki) was born at Opunake. For the past eleven years she has been a library assistant at the Wellington Public Library. Her first published story, 'The Old Coat' appeared in the first issue of *Numbers* in 1954, beside Alistair Campbell's poem 'Aunt Lucrezia: A Portrait'. A year later her story 'For all the Saints' became the first story written in English by a Maori writer to be published in *Te Ao Hou*. In the process a new direction for contemporary Maori writing was established. In 1966 'For all the Saints' appeared in *New Zealand Short Stories* (vol. Two) and was thus one of the first stories by a Maori writer to appear in an anthology of New Zealand writing. It has since been broadcast in West Germany.

In the 1940s, a number of her poems had appeared in various student newspapers and in *Review*. In the 1950s she wrote book reviews for *Te Aou Hou* and *Numbers*. But it was not until 1980, on the occasion of the opening of the Women's Gallery in Wellington, that she undertook her first public reading (with, among others, Keri Hulme and Patricia Grace). As a result of that reading a publisher is currently considering a collection of her stories set in New Zealand and India (where she lived in 1958) to be called *The House of the Talking Cat*.

Saana Murray

My Decree

To the House of Parliament
I come from Te Rerenga Wairua
Cape Reinga and Spirits Bay
My Land Grievances I bring
As recorded before today
A Judge of the Land Court
By your so-called democratic policies
Claimed for himself our land and wealth
King of the North was he
While the Maori died landless
And in sheer poverty

So I've come to the battle grounds of your creeds and deeds
That betrayed our Ancestors in the Treaty of Waitangi
Thousands were slaughtered and slaved
Now condemned to extinction by the White Man's pen

I climb your steps today
Guarded by the Lion Symbol of past decades
Wide gaping mouths that devoured Treaty Vows
At your cold grey feet
I read our Youth's plea: ·
You've stolen our Lands
You cannot legislate our Souls
Europeanisation is our deadly foe
We defy and oppose

Tangata, Man, is most precious of all
Maoriness is the seed of Youth
The very heart and soul of Aotearoa

We leave your fate to the unknown
The fighting spirit of the Maori Warrior lives on
I must preserve my seed
I refuse to be Europeanised by 1973

This is my decree:
I will remain a Maori

SAANA MURRAY (1925; Te Aupouri) was born at Te Hapua, in Te Hiku o Te
Ika, and is a teacher of Maori Studies at Hillary College. 'My Decree' forms part of
the prelude to her collection *Te Karanga a Te Kotuku* which documents the agony
she felt during the struggle to have her ancestral lands placed back in Maori hands.
Her work featured in a film on the 1975 Land March from Te Hapua, in the 49th
ANZAAS Congress abstracts (vol. 1, 1979) and in *Haribol*. Her second collection,
The Hard Road Back To Our Marae Pa, is in preparation.

Arapera Hineira Blank

He Kōingo

A Yearning

I reira ahau	I was there
Tūtaki tāua	We met
Haurangi ana	Drunk
Ka kite ahau	And I saw
i a koe	you
Me te mea nei	As if
he taniwha	a magic bringer
Ka minamina	Then I wanted
kia piri.	to be close.
Hei konei rā	That was all
Te marama	The moon
ka huri	Turned to
He maramara	bits and pieces
Marama rākau	Became lean
Huri noa	Was
Marama nui	Swollen
Ahakoa rā	No matter what
Mau tonu.	It was there.
Kakai ana	Eating
Kongakonga a	bits and pieces
Kikokiko	Then flesh
Kore he	As if there
Tīmatanga	were no beginning
Kore he	And
Mutunga	no end
'Ka mate ka mate	'From darkness
Ka ora, ka ora'!	into light'
Ināianei kua	Now I
kite ahau	have seen
Ki te minamina	if you desire
koe	or want
Ki te pirangi	whether only
koe	a dream
Ahakoa wawata noa	Satisfy

Mē kai kia kī
Engari kia tika te
Haere!

Your hunger
But be
true in spirit!

Waiata Mō Te Tāne

For My Husband On The Occasion Of His Birthday

I puta mai koe he tangata
O tapuwae
he whai mana,
O ringaringa,
he whai hua,
To manawa kī tonu i
te aroha,
To ūpoko
he tapu,
whai kai.

You were created a man,
Your footsteps
given power,
Your hands
given creativity,
Your heart filled
with love,
Your head
sacred,
having the gift of understanding.

Kia mirimiri koe
i tō wahine,
Pēnei tonu koe
ko Tū, ko Tāne
nāna nei i
waihanga mai tana wahine
a Hine-ahu-one.
Mē aroha hoki te tāne
kātahi anō ka whānau mai
He puāwai putiputi,
i ōna ringa.

When you caress
your woman,
You are like
the War God, the Creator
who fashioned
his woman
from earth.
For a man must love
before he can bring forth
the bloom of flowers
with his hands.

Ko
Whai-uri koe, ko
Whai-mata koe.
'Papā te whatitiri!
Hikuhiku te uira!
Ka kanapa ki te rangi!'

You are
Father-of-children
You are
Substance.
'Thunder crashes!
Lightning streaks!
Across the heavens!'

Hurihia to kanohi
ki te Tairāwhiti

Turn your face
eastwards,

92

Nō reira nei
Te tūmanako
O ngā tāngata katoa.
Kia pēnei tonu koe,
Ake! Ake!

Where all men
gather hope.
Be like this
forever.

Rongokako

My left foot looks
like my Aunty Lena,
Slim when I squeeze
my toes together.
My right foot looks
like me whenever
I squeeze or expand
them in or out.

Whatever they look like
What they feel like
Matters most to me.

Walking a street
irritates, they drag
sweat, feel my weight
pinch, uncomfortable
in leather or plastic
until I

Walk barefooted on
soft velvety green upon
brown grass and crackle
with pleasure of traditional
earth to earth-bound
ritual.

Like feeling that
My feet melt with many feet
The throb of rhythmic
Thudding and rising and falling
Waking, sleeping, dreaming
of satisfying things.

Like
What it is to have
a love of life
of laughter and dancing
and yet knowing
that beneath me there is
substance.

ARAPERA HINEIRA BLANK (1932; Ngati Porou, Ngati Kahungunu, Rongowhakaata, Te Aitanga-a-Mahaki) was born at Rangitukia. She was educated at Hukarere College, Wellington Teachers' College and the University of Auckland. A teacher for twenty-five years she is at present teaching Maori and social studies at Glenfield College in Auckland.

Arapera's stories and poems have appeared in *Te Ao Hou, Education, Pacific Quarterly Moana* and *Ocarina* (India). Her stories can be found in two anthologies: *Contemporary Maori Writing* and *My New Zealand*, and have been broadcast by Radio New Zealand. In 1959 she won a special prize in the Katherine Mansfield Memorial Awards. Her essay on 'The Role and Status of Maori Women' recently appeared in *Women in New Zealand Society*.

Patricia Bell

Kuia

She sits on a low stool
Beside the glowing range
Feeding it ti-tree
From a box on the hearth.
Old woman with sepia skin
Carved lines down her cheeks,
With iron-grey hair
Pinned in knot behind.
From an oblong tin worn smooth
She takes strands of tobacco
And rolls thin cigarettes;
And cares for a husband
Irascible with stones.
He sits in his chair
Behind the curtained window
Smoking, watching the street,
Watching the street.

And the wooden clock
Its pendulum silently swinging
Ticks their lives away.

Maungapōhatu

Weatherboard huts lichen-grizzled
Straggling together at road's end
Above the bush filled ravine.
From a rusting hinge
A sagging door yawns;
Inside, the sickly smell of ashes
From a long dead fire.
Yellowed newsprint hangs
Mouldering from the wall.
In late afternoon the rising wind,
And a solitary fantail chittering
In erratic flight, hawking.

PATRICIA BELL (1932 Arawa, Waikato) was born in Auckland and began
writing in 1977 after living in Zambia and travelling extensively in the countries of
southern Africa where many of her poems and stories are set. Educated at Hamilton
Technical College she now lives in Carterton. Her work has only recently started to
appear in print: six of her poems have been published in *Landfall* and *Monthly
Review*. More are soon to appear in other anthologies and school texts. A volume of
poems *African Images and Other Places* is in preparation as is *The Arrivals*, a novel.
She attended writers' schools at the University of Zambia (1971) and the University
of Cape Town (1972).

Hinauri Strongman Tribole

The Offering

'When tomorrow comes, will we be going fishing, Grandpa?' Rererangi
asked.

'Too right,' said the old man, 'but first we get some bait. Why don't you
fetch our spears and a kit and we'll catch a few of those rock crabs. Then

95

we'll get some pipis and some of that snapper your Auntie Ani didn't cook last night.'

'Beaut! What a feast those fish are going to have,' shouted Rererangi.

'Aye,' said the old man. 'Fish like a change, too, so I put a cooked pipi on one hook; I bait another hook with a piece of raw crab; then as an extra bonus I sometimes add a bit of fish to the third hook. I call this 'fish stew' and the fish go for it, too! You wait and see.'

Before Auntie Ani had finished her first cup of tea of the morning Grandpa Pita and Rererangi were rowing across the glassy, early morning harbour to one of the many fishing spots the old man knew. Taking his bearings from his old chimney pot to the west and lining up this marking with the solitary cabbage tree which grew on top of the old fortifications to the east, he dropped anchor.

The dinghy rocked gently as a light swell came in with the tide. A gull called and dropped into the sea. The boy watched another follow and he knew it would be a good day for fishing.

Suddenly his line gave a sharp tug.

'Give it a jerk! Give it a jerk!' shouted the old man. 'That will set the hook. Good-oh! Now more line. More! You've got him. Oh-oh, give him a little more line. Let him run with it! It's a beauty. Look at him break surface. That's a kingfish. Get him round to the side of the boat. That's it.'

Rererangi's fingers were bleeding but he kept pulling in the handline, coiling it around a bit of tanekaha until the old man was able to lift the fish into the boat. It was a big one all right: a kingi as big as one of Grandpa Pita's arms. Rererangi was beside himself with excitement and pride as he looked at the gleaming, flapping blue and silver fish.

The old man carefully worked the hook from the kingi's mouth. 'I reckon this is the biggest fish you've ever caught, eh?' he said without taking his eyes off the loosening hook.

'Too right, Grandpa,' Rererangi grinned proudly.

'Good on you.' Then the old man looked again at the kingi fighting for air on the damp planking. Its silver scales gleamed brightly in the morning sunlight. A darkening eye hung in the shadows of the bottom of the boat like the moon caught in the sky after the sun had come up. 'This is the first catch. . .the first of Tangaroa's children.'

Sensing the note of seriousness in his grandfather's voice Rererangi also watched the fish sucking at the air, pulling at the air like someone standing up on the marae for the first time to speak, touching the air as if it were touching a friend, for courage. The boy knew what was expected. He turned. 'We better not keep Tangaroa waiting too much longer for this fish, Grandpa.'

Heaving the fish up on its tail, the boy slid it overboard. The kingi hung in the water for a moment but when Rererangi blinked and looked again it wasn't there. It might never have been there. Even the bottom of the boat was steaming in the hot sun, the dampness from the fish drying like tears before they could be wiped away.

'So long, kingi,' Rererangi shouted. 'Tell Tangaroa thanks for letting me have you for a little while, anyway.'

In an effort to hide his emotions, Rererangi looked back at his grandfather and in a voice that ran like a little wave trying not to break he said, 'What will we do now? I'm getting hungry. Can I eat this pipi?'

'If you eat the bait, you ruin the catch. Your Auntie Ani's going to be a bit wild when she looks for that fruitcake for her morning tea. Here, we better eat all the evidence before she thinks it might have been us.' The old man and the boy divided the fruitcake between them.

The boy was exhausted by the time they got home. Auntie Ani started to say something but then she saw his hands and instead she took him over to the tap.

'You go get me some of those kawakawa leaves,' she said to the old man. 'We've got to fix these hands. What have you been doing to your mokopuna?'

Then she stood holding the boy while the old man went out back in the dying light. 'You should have let that old man carry all that fish up the road. How you two catch so many fish, anyway? Which of youse are going to help me clean all these fish now?' she laughed.

The boy looked over into the darkness in the window. He could just see a gull hanging motionless in the evening sky, like a pale star. The first star of the night.

HINAURI STRONGMAN TRIBOLE (1926: Ngapuhi, Ngatihau, Ngatiwai) was born at Whakapara but grew up in Whangaruru South. She has retired from teaching and lives in Bountiful, Utah. Her work has appeared in *Te Ao Hou, New Zealand Home Journal,* and the *CBS Times* (Canada). 'An Apple For The Teacher' was published by the New Zealand Department of Education. In 1980 she presented three papers to the World Conference on Records in Salt Lake City and they are to appear in a subsequent conference volume. In the 1960s she attended three creative writing workshops at the University of Utah where she was a student. Hinauri has three volumes in manuscript: *About Face* (a novel), a collection of short stories and *Reflections* (poems). She has been heard on radio in both New Zealand and Canada.

Katerina Te Hei Koko Mataira

Te Ātea

Te Pakanga

Ko tēnei te wā...
O te pakanga nui

Haruru ana te ao

Ko tēnei te wā ...
O te pakanga roa

Uira ana te ao.

Ko tēnei te wā ...
O te pakanga wehi
Murara ana te ao
Ee...i...
Taukuri e!
Murara ana te ao.

He wā kino
He wā piro
He wā wetiweti

Ko tēnei te wā ...
O te pakanga nui
Haruru ana te ao

He wā tino kino
He wā tino piro
He wā tino wetiweti

Ko tēnei te wā ...
O te pakanga roa
Uira ana te ao

He wā patu tāne
He wā patu wāhine
He wā patu tamariki

Ko tēnei te wā . . .
O te pakanga nui
Uira ana te ao

He wā patu manu
He wā patu ika
He wā patu kararehe

Ko tēnei te wā . . .
O te pakanga wehi
Murara ana te ao

Ee. . .i. . .i
Taukuri e!
Murara ana te ao

Kua hinga ngā whare
Kua hinga ngā kāinga
Kua hinga ngā tāone nui

Ko tēnei te wā . . .
O te pakanga roa
Haruru ana te ao

He wā kino
He wā piro
He wā wetiweti

Ko tēnei te wā . . .
O te pakanga nui
Uira ana te ao

Kua mate ngā manu
Kua mate ngā ika
Kua mate ngā kararehe

Ko tēnei te wā. . .
O te pakanga wehi
Kua mate ngā kararehe

Ee. . .i. . .i
Taukuri e!
Kua mate ngā kararehe

He wā tino kino
He wā tino piro
He wā tino wetiweti

Ko tēnei te wā . . .
O te pakanga nui
He wā tino wetiweti

Kua kurehe ngā rākau
Kua kurehe ngā pātītī
Kua kurehe ngā putiputi

Ko tēnei te wā. . .
O te pakanga nui
Kurehe ana te ao

Ee. . .i. . .i
Taukuri e!
Kurehe ana te ao

Ka hinga ngā tāne
Ka hinga ngā wāhine
Ka hinga ngā tamariki

Ko tēnei te wā . . .
O te pakanga roa
Kurehe ana te ao

Ee. . .i. . .i
Taukuri e!
Kurehe ana te ao

Ka hinga ngā toa
Ka hinga ngā iwi
Ka hinga ngā tāngata

Ko tēnei te wā . . .
O te pakanga roa
Murarara ana te ao

Ee. . .i. . .i
Taukuri e!
Murara ana te ao

Kua piro ngā whenua
Kua piro ngā moana
Kua piro ngā mea katoa

Ko tēnei te wā...
O te pakanga nui
Piro ana te ao

Ee...i...i
Taukuri e!
Piro ana te ao

Ka mate ngā toa
Ka mate ngā iwi
Ka mate ngā tāngata

Ko tēnei te wā...
O te pakanga wehi
Mate ana te ao

Aue!
Taukuri e!
Mate ana te ao!

Untitled

Tirohia a Tama-te-rā
E haehae ana te kahu o te pō e
Whāwhai ana ia te tīhore atu
Te kahu pouri e

Horomia kai-horo
Nga pūkohukohu te piki nei e
Huhutia te rehutai
Tāpapa mai rāi te moana

Whātero mai rā te arero
Te miti te kiri e
Tērā ko Papa-tū-ā-nuku
Pūhanahana e

Ēngari au
Mā wai e tīhore atu
Tōku pouri e
Kua riro ngā whenua
Kau hinga ngātōtara
O te wao-nui

He tauhou tēnei
Te tū nei e
Mē tana toki e
Aue...he kiritea

Me taku reo
He waha huia
E tangi maiangi mai rā
I te wao-nui ngarongaro e

KATERINA TE HEI KOKO MATAIRA (1932: Ngati Porou) was born at
Waipiro Bay, Ruatoria. A former research fellow at the Centre for Maori Studies
and Research at the University of Waikato she is now a freelance writer in
Hamilton and is a member of the editorial board of *Pacific Moana Quarterly*.
Mataira's work has appeared in *Te Ao Hou, Te Tautoko* and *Te Wharekura*. She has
also contributed essays on Maori culture to *The Maori in the 1960s* and *Polynesian
and Pakeha in New Zealand Education*. Her essay on Maori song-poetry in vol 2 of
the latter journal remains one of the most important commentaries on the subject.
She is the author of *Maui and the Big Fish* (1972), *Maori Legends for Young New
Zealanders* (1975) and the *Oxford Maori Picture Dictionary*, and illustrates much of
her own work. In 1979 she was awarded the second Choysa Bursary for Children's
Writers to enable her to complete four children's picture books based on Maori
legends (two books are to be produced for each legend — one in Maori and the
other in English).
The extract included here is from *Te Ātea*.

Rowley Habib (Nga Pitiroirangi)

Orakau

Again the storming of the troops of the palisades.
Again the repulse.

Again the storming.
And yet again the repulse. Wave upon wave.
Through a day and a night and another day.

And now the numbers of the defenders lessen.
And now their ammunition runs pitifully low.
They weaken from lack of rest and food
And sleep is a thing of the past.

Again the women and children in battle.
Again the use of sticks for bullets.
And still the invaders come
Their numbers seem limitless.
For every man who falls two move up to take his place.
They seem indestructible.
The spirit of the defenders fails.

Yet through the ordeal, the sinking morale
These words still able to be uttered.
'Friend, this is the word of the Maori.
Ka whawhai tonu, ake, ake, ake.'
We will fight for ever and ever and ever.

Ancestors

Where once my ancestors grubbed for the fern's root
They build their hygienic houses now.
And where the wild pig roamed and rooted
They've measured the land into precise sections
Worth 3 000 dollars (or to sound better
For the prospective buyer, 1 500 pounds).

And here where once on an excursion up the back
Jacky pissed on a scrub
And thought no more of it
A house stands worth 10 000 (quid that is).
And where Tamati did something worse
There stands yet another house
Even more expensive than the first.

Jacko

After many months, awe-struck the new wealth
my old home town seeing. One day driving out
into the newest most affluent suburb
a curious sight. A man on a pushbike
scouring the fenceline of the new prosperity
looking for Christ knows what.

Drawing alongside

I recognised an old school crony.

'Jacko' Potai

bewhiskered and in rags. A relic from the past.

I did not greet him, instead eased the '64 Holden
quickly away with a sense of uneasiness.

For I

recall his ancestors once owned the land around here
for as far as the eye could see.

A Coloured Man Addresses A White Protester Against Apartheid

That you bared your skull to be bottle-battered
on that festival day for me.

O how you must

have annoyed that crowd for daring to spoil their fun.

I cannot yet grasp the motivation of your action though
— for you see in my own way
I am brainwashed too.

For you seem to me

to be like a man cutting his own throat.

God, may I remember,
if ever the boot is on the other foot,
that fair head with the blood-streamed face.

Wail O Black-Clad Women

Wail O black-clad black handkerchief headed women of my race.
With the willow-twisted wreaths on the crown

cry out as you did of old
for those of high ranking; the rangatira.

Spring forward challenger with your wero
the flashing taiaha, the pukana
— prance and leap, spear the tongue in and out
like the lizard.
                    Grimace.
Protrude the eye-balls till the whites show
— lay down the ceremonial twig and move back;
waiting, as you did of old.

Cry out in chant O women.

Not now though for the high-born sons
inheriting the chieftainship.
                            But of the new breed,
the new leaders in a new world.
Those who earn their ranking through the sweat of their brow
though they come from the humblest beginnings.

Go Home Maori

At first the words washed harmlessly off her
— the kids chanting on their way home from school
— but when persisted began to hurt.
In the end they were like spear-thrusts.

She could not quite put into words
the feelings that sometimes swelled in her
in indignation; sometimes twisted her mouth to wry smile.
For to her she *was* home.

It was true
she was born up country; even raised there.
                    But
she was aware (as was no one else in that affluent
                                    neighbourhood)
that her ancestors, three generations removed
once inhabited that land; perhaps had done for centuries.
They were dispossessed by the musket that time.

Now
it was the jibes that drove her away.
Finally they became too much
                    And she left

Moment Of Truth
(Maori Land Protest Sit-in)

They said a while ago that the fuzz were coming to take us away.
Someone said they were massing outside the Town Hall
and that there were a lot of them. Someone cracked a joke
and a nervous giggle rippled through the crowd.

Your mind, not wanting to believe, searches around for an explanation.
It might be a brawl in a hotel or a gang of bikies.
But you have to face the truth. It's you they're after all right.
Shit, what do I do? (It's not just a saying then that your feet turn cold.)

I've never been to prison before and the only confrontation
I've had with the fuzz was when one handed me a summons
for a driving offence, years ago. And I'm forty now.
And what about my wife? And what about my kids?

How will they get on? And will I be branded criminal
for the rest of my life? There is little comfort
in someone saying that we will be political prisoners.
And even less when he assures us that thousands will side with us.

I think to myself, 'Brother, there might just be you'
And someone else, trying to persuade us to leave
tells us we could get up to thirty years for what we're doing.
We would have laughed at him before. But there is only silence now.

When will they be arriving, the fuzz? I'm a layman to this sort of thing.
What will I do? Do I stretch out stiff and make myself
as awkward as possible to carry? Or make myself all floppy —
or is that just what the girls do? Or worst of all, will I chicken-out and
        run?

And will they bash my head with batons in the dark
because one of the others called them pigs the other day?

106

And how long will this go on? Will this be just another false alarm?
Like the one the other night? I mean, I want to get on with other
     things.

I wish they'd hurry up and come, the fuzz and get it over with.
This waiting is getting me down. My nerves are packing up.

Another Kind Of Wilderness
(Mount Eden: summit and prison)

                              Up here
                              I find it hard to steer
                              my attention
                              clear
                              of that other institution
                              so inappropriately
                              called after a hill
                              that rises so beautifully.

And the Obelisk
four-sided keeps mentioning
the deeds of the Pakeha
— refers to '. . . the memory
of the Pioneer Surveyors Who. . .'
(no need to mention priorities,
for the last three words are headed with capitals).
'. . . the Pioneer Surveyors Who
played so worthy a part in the transformation
of a wilderness into the smiling land
which lies before you!'
                    Amen!
I suppose the Maori was a part of that so-called wilderness.

Look out all sides on fog-filled air
and then if you can bear
— indeed if you dare
look at that austere
stark grey stone-cold barbed-wired building
— I mean *really* look at it
and think on it
and not merely flit

107

across it
at someone trying to draw
your attention to it
and say 'Oh that's the prison; an eyesore'
and hastily look elsewhere
and remark on the beautiful view from up here.

— I mean really look at it
and still pat ourselves on the back
about a wilderness transformed into a smiling land.
A wilderness
transformed into another kind of wilderness.
And there is no question
that the Maori is very much a part of this one.

Memorial Day

In beautiful sunshine, a hundred people
(descendents of the old chief) gather
around the cloth-draped plaque on the
neat-clipped lawn to the Pakeha house
waiting...

... And

towards the end of the afternoon-long whaikorero
steps forward a man, tall even in age
addresses he the gathering.

Then, for those who do not understand the tongue
these words only in English.
But first, turns he south, east, north, west
describes slow circle back to the gathering
'For as far as the eye could see'
Said barely above a whisper. 'For as far as the eye could see'
all this was once his. And now eyes lower to the tiny plaque.
Unveiled it stands two feet high embedded
in a square foot of land. 'Only this.'
No need for further explanation
he faces back into the gathering.

Motu

A small stir of restlessness ran through the class. They had not quite settled down yet. Sitting at her desk, Miss McKewen was engrossed in marking the attendance book. After a time she lifted her head and looked off to the back of the room, searching out one of the children.

'Where's Thomas today, Motu?' she asked.

Motu stood up at the back of the room. 'Please Miss, he's got a crook guts,' he replied.

'I beg your pardon!' Miss McKewen said.

'Please Miss, he's got a crook guts, and Mum told him to stay home.'

Miss McKewen flushed a deep red. The rest of the class looked around at Motu. The boy stood bolt upright at his desk, shoulders pressed well back and hands clasped behind his back, as the children were taught to do. Some of the class began to titter.

'You mean sore stomach, don't you?' Miss McKewen said.

'Yes Miss, a crook guts. He couldn't get out of bed this morning.' A perplexed look came over the boy's face. He couldn't understand what all the sudden attention was about. He put his hand to his stomach, indicating the region of the pain.

'We usually say sore stomach, Motu,' Miss McKewen said. 'It's considered rude to use the expression you just used. Didn't you know that?'

'No Miss,' the boy replied. 'That's what the old man and lady said.'

Miss McKewen looked as if she would choke, but not entirely from shock, for beneath it all she was as much amused by the whole thing as were the children. She was silent for a moment, seeming to catch her breath; then she swallowed and heaved a deep sigh. 'And you don't use those words either,' she said. 'Good heavens, you don't go calling your parents by those names, do you?' And her voice went up incredulously at the end. She turned to the rest of the class. 'How many of you call your father and mother that?' she asked. 'What Motu just called his parents.'

'Me, Miss — Yes Miss,' came some replies quickly, without thought.

And the more 'civilised' were quick to add, 'No, Miss — I don't Miss — Not me, Miss. We don't call *our* mother and father that.'

'What do you call them then?' Miss McKewen asked.

'Mummy and Daddy.'

'Or Mum and Dad, Miss.'

'Or your mother and father,' Miss McKewen added. 'Is that right?'

'Yes, Miss, our mother and father.'

Calling his parents 'mother and father' seemed so strange to Motu. But it was the way he heard some of the Pakeha kids referring to their parents, and some of the more 'advanced' Maori families. So odd and cold sounding. Motu hated it and knew that he could never get around to calling his parents this.

'Well now, Motu,' Miss McKewen said, turning back to him. (And she called him 'Mow-to' although his name was really 'Maw-to'.) 'You know what we call our parents don't you?'

'Yes, Miss.'

'Well, what do we call them?' she asked.

'Mum and Dad,' the boy replied. He was very nervous and was starting to move about, fidgetingly, behind his desk; ducking his shoulders self-consciously. And he knew he could never get around to calling them those other names even if it killed him.

'Or your mother and father,' Miss McKewen reminded him.

'Yes, Miss.'

Thankfully Miss McKewen didn't pursue this any further. 'Good,' she said, cheering up a little. 'Now don't let me hear you ever referring to them again as the "old man and old lady".' (She seemed to take a delight in saying this last phrase for she said it a little louder than the rest.) 'Do you understand?'

'Yes, Miss.'

'And don't let me hear you ever saying those other horrible words again either. It's rude, vulgar. Why, you're swearing, didn't you know that?'

'No, Miss.' The boy blushed.

'Well you are, you know, almost.'

'Ye-e-es, Mi-i-iss,' some of the others chorused in.

'All right, now settle down,' she said. She was wanting to bring the subject to a close so she could get on with marking the attendance book. This unexpected diversion had already cut into quite a bit of her time. But she wanted to make sure this sort of thing never happened again. Good lord, you never knew who might be in the room when one of them came out with such a remark. So she gave them one final warning.

'Now remember *all* of you, I don't want to hear any of you ever using those expressions that Motu just used, do you understand?' And she added, 'Just because you hear other people using them' (and she meant of course their parents or the grown-ups), 'it doesn't mean to say that you have to use them too.' With those last words her lips shut tight in a way that told the children she wanted to get on with something else.

So they were expressions, some of the children thought.

At the back of the room Motu was still standing, his face dark with frustration. He looked about bewildered. The rest of the class shifted about and faced the front again, still tittering a little.

'All right,' Miss McKewen said. 'You can sit down now, Motu.' And

110

her head lowered to her work again. If any of the children had been watching her closely they would have seen a faint smile touch at the corners of her mouth for just an instant, as the quaintness of the boy's expressions still ran through her mind. For really, despite everything, she had enjoyed it, just as much as she was sure the rest of the class had.

Then she was again seriously absorbed in marking the attendance book.

Strife In The Family

Sometimes the children would be left to the father's care, their mother having gone off on the booze with some friends after having had an argument with their father. The children would never hear these arguments. They always seemed to happen when they were not around, or else their parents broke off as soon as the children came into the house. But once or twice the children heard their father's voice raised and angry coming from the bedroom where he and their mother were. He never hit their mother or at least never in front of the children. But the children could tell when their parents had had a row or were angry with one another. Their mother's face would be flushed dark and set like stone. And red weals would stand out just below her eyes, as though she had had her face over the stove for some while and was very hot. And their father would be very silent and would get about with quick nervous steps coughing all the time. A small grating cough, as though he could not quite clear his throat of some irritation. And the children could almost feel the heat coming off him, so stored up was his anger and so hard was he trying to contain it. And it made them feel as though he would blow up any minute.

The children would sense the tension between their parents almost immediately. Even if no harsh words were passed in their presence. Their parents used to try hard for the children's sake, sometimes trying to speak civilly with one another but the children sensed the strain between the two, and in these times they would be a little afraid and would only talk in whispers. It was as though a wet blanket were cast over them.

Those evenings when their mother would go off on a binge with some friends or relations from down the road, the children's father would feed them on bread and cold water and the children would be resentful of their father for the bare and unsavoury meal he dished up to them. They used to chew away at the dry tasteless bread and were forced to drink their cups of water only to wash the bread down, so dry was it. And they were a little afraid their father would be angry if they did not drink it. Yet they would also feel tender towards their father in these moments and a little sorry for him and they would be all against their mother. Motu would often wonder if she would feel this wall of antagonism against her, her husband and her children against her? But when they sat down to a good cooked nourishing meal in the morning laid out by their mother (she must have come back some time during the night, but the children never heard her) before they went off to school they were so grateful that they had to forgive her. And everything would be back to normal again. Although they tried to maintain a little of the coolness towards her, hoping she would notice it, and repent and promise never to do it again. The children would come home from school to a normally run household in the afternoon. Their mother and father would be on talking terms again and everything was back to normal. A great relief used to come over the children and they would be happy.

These occasions didn't happen often, but they *did* happen, and when they did the children couldn't understand why or how their mother could leave them. They loved her and they felt that she loved them. But in these moments they felt the bondage and the strength of her love weaken and doubt entered their minds horribly. They never questioned their mother about last night. Most times they were just too glad to have her back to care for them and they would feel their security surging back into them as they sat about in the kitchen watching their mother diligently ironing their clothes.

Then one day Mrs Joseph packed the younger children off and went and lived in an old family house (on her side) about four miles away; away down on the fringe of some cut-out bush. The children only suspected the reason for this sudden shift and afterwards they found out for sure. Their mother had had a row with their father. They realised that it must have been much worse than the others for their mother to leave like this. But somehow they felt that this had been brewing for a long time.

The children were a bit annoyed at having to move because they had to leave their friends. They were thrown into an entirely different environment and for a while they were lonely and begrudged Luke and Arthur, their two older brothers, being able to remain behind with their father.

The children used to have to walk half a mile to the main road to catch the school bus and they did this first with mixed feelings of bewilderment and belligerence. But it was a novelty to them and after a while they got to enjoy the walk to the road. Walking the narrow roadway that was only two tracks cut into the ground the width of a car's wheels apart and that had grass growing in the middle on a raised piece of ground. And they got to quite like the place in general. For one thing it was good to be away from the dust of the roadway that their old homestead suffered from badly. And the air was so clean and fresh at their new place, and they would smell the sweet odour of the bush on the hills behind the house, and for a change it was good to have no one else around you. And of course if they wanted to, they could cut across the paddocks and through a bit of cut-out bush to the Ormsby's place about two miles away or else in the other direction to their cousins the Whetus' place.

The house was cosy and big enough and it had three bedrooms in it that they could have used but the children preferred to all pile into the one room using the two beds in there. When they had first moved in they used the two separate rooms that their mother allocated for them. Aroha and Louise slept in one and Motu and Marylin in the other. They did it partly because of the strangeness of everything and partly because the idea thrilled them a bit. But afterwards they preferred each other's company and they used to lie there in bed discussing amongst themselves.

And the pepes used to come down from the bush and hit against the windows attracted by the light in their room. Big ones. The children had not seen pepes as big as them before and they used to sit up a little afraid in bed: at first exclaiming loudly because of the sizes of the things and calling for their mother and once or twice one would find its way into the room and fly about furiously, hitting against the wall and sometimes almost putting the candle out as it passed through the naked flame. There would be a great din and heads would go under the blankets and pop out again to see what had happened to the creature, only to see it crawling up the wall and there would be squeals and screams until their mother came in and knocked it down with a towel. She would pick the thing up by the back, between her fingers and go and throw it into the fire. And there would be 'Oooohs!' from the children, and 'Mum how can you do such a thing', all watching their mother with big eyes as she carried the fearsome creature between her fingers. But after a while they got used to the knockings of the pepes against their windows at night.

And the house was clean and smelt of bare wood scrubbed a thousand times with warm water and soap. And the rooms were bare but cosy.

And their mother used to make fried bread and she and the children used to sit around after tea eating great heaps of it and drinking tea. It was the one thing they really shared during their stay there. It was a highlight to their day, sitting around joyfully eating their bread and sharing the happiness with their mother.

Their mother never made this bread very often back at the old homestead but now at the insistence of the children she made it every day. She did a lot of things that she never normally did back home and the children felt she was enjoying the liberty of it. The Maori in her came out more, living here, and she seemed to enjoy doing all the old things she used to do when she was a child. And on the weekends sometimes, she

113

would go for a walk with the children in the bush, climbing the ridge of the hill behind the house gathering puha in a kit and resting and lighting a cigarette and looking back down over the flats below, and she used to tell them stories and old tales about the place. She had grown up there. There was another old homestead not far away. It belonged to one of their mother's older brothers. It was a much larger house that was surrounded by a picket fence. The house was in decay and unlivable in. Parts of it were beginning to fall away. There were many fruit trees growing around the house, both at the front and back; apples, peaches, plums and greengages. The grass was growing long and wild, nearly claiming the whole of the ground surrounding the house.

At the back against the tall fence grew some raspberries and it was these that the children enjoyed most. But they always went there with a feeling that old Pita their uncle would suddenly appear from the house and catch them in the act of stealing his raspberries, so they used to approach the raspberry canes stealthily from the side of the house, climbing through the hole in the fence and then treading light-footedly around between the house and the greengage trees, and then into the long grass that surrounded the raspberries. They were well hidden in this tall grass while they plundered the raspberries. They did this elaborate manoeuvre also partly because it was fun.

Sometimes at the week-ends Arthur used to come down on his horse and stay there a while, cutting a big heap of firewood and doing odd jobs about the house. And it seemed strange Arthur leaving them later on; getting on to Goldie his horse and saying goodbye and waving to them. It seemed odd, their brother Arthur whom they had lived with all their lives, getting on his horse and riding away from them and saying goodbye when all the time he shouldn't have to be saying that. And it was these times that the children felt nostalgia for their old home and wished for a reunion of the whole family.

And sometimes, after they had been there for about two months, their father used to come visiting their mother. He used to come down at nights, walking all the way, about four miles. The children used to know when their father was coming. They would be sitting at the tea table after the meal or sometimes even during meals (they used to have their meals quite late and it would be dark most times before they were finished) and they would see the light of a torch flickering on and off coming down the roadway. At first they wondered what it could be but even before he got to the house the children knew that it was their father. They recognised the peculiar way he held the torch. He would walk with it in his hand swinging backwards and forwards with the motion of his walking. It used to appear as though the torch was being switched on and off. But it wasn't and it was this peculiar way of his that the children recognised that first

114

night. Their mother must have known long before then that it was her husband but she did not let on, for when the children exclaimed excitedly that it was their father, she was unmoved.

The father came in rather awkwardly that first night. The children were glad to see him and fussed about him and Motu smelled his father's peculiar man's smell and it made him a little nostalgic for the man. And at once, in that moment, he loved his father and felt sorry for him.

The man came into the room taking off his cap, an uncertain smile touching his mouth. He stood inside the door wringing his hands together nervously. 'Hullo Mary,' he said.

'Hullo Peter,' the mother said and she sat there watching him and there was no expression on her face.

'I just thought I'd — a — come over and see how you were getting on,' their father said.

'Thank you, Peter,' the mother said. 'I'm very well. And yourself?'

'No good, Mary,' the father said. 'Why don't you come home. It's no good like this. The boys aren't getting fed properly and the place is in a bit of a mess.'

The mother did not answer. She looked away from her husband into the light of the lamp, her eyes fixed and wide as though she were hypnotised.

'I couldn't, Peter,' she said, 'not just now.'

'Why?' the man asked.

The children's mother straightened and she almost flared up then. They saw it teetering at the brim, her anger nearly overflowing, then she slumped back into the chair again.

'You know why, Peter. Do I have to go on telling you.'

'But think of the boys!' her husband implored. 'They miss you. They want you. Think of these children. It's no life for them stuck away down here in the bush. Think of the children, woman!'

'The children are happy here,' the woman said. 'They'll tell you.'

The father turned to them and said, 'Are you?'

The reply was a mixture of agreement and disagreement. Some shaking their heads and others nodding. Motu felt it was all right to stay there for a little while longer at least but apparently Louise felt it was time they were going home and now was her chance to express it.

'I thought you all said you like it here,' the mother said.

'Yes — No.'

'You see,' the father said.

The mother looked away from them tiredly yet with a certain amount of defiance on her face still. She wasn't going to give in so easily.

'I suppose you would like a cup of tea,' she said. 'Sit down.' Her husband was still standing in the middle of the room.

'Yes, if you wouldn't mind, please, Mary. I would.'

He sat himself down at the table opposite her. The children's mother got up and went to the stove and poured a cup of tea. She placed it before her husband and all the while the man was watching her. She took no notice of him.

'Thank you. Thank you very much, Mary,' he said, and he sipped gratefully at the tea. There was silence for a while in the room. No one knew what to say. Then their mother said, 'You children better go off to bed, go on and have your wash now, you must be tired after playing all afternoon.'

Once in their room they lay there listening to the muffled voices of their parents talking in the kitchen.

'I hope we go home,' Louise said. 'No,' Aroha said. 'You don't know,' Louise said, 'I hope we go home.'

'Back to that old dump,' Aroha said. 'I hope he stays the night,' Marylin said.

'Yes,' Motu chimed in. 'Me too,' Louise said. 'Yes it would be all right if he came and lived here,' Aroha agreed. 'If Luke and Arthur and dog and cat all came and stayed here. That would be different.' And they all lay there wishing that their father would stay the night. After a while they fell asleep and in the morning their father was gone and they were very disappointed.

Their father visited them often after that, every Tuesday night, about eight o'clock. They would see the torch flickering on and off, coming nearer and nearer along the narrow roadway towards the house — winding a little to the north and then curving back on to the house again — and they would all become excited and speculate among themselves.

Their mother wasn't so hostile towards him now, and always had a hot cup of tea ready for him as soon as he came in the door. And she began to greet him with a smile now also. At first a reserved one and then gradually it became more open and unrestrained.

The children used to have to go off to bed (not until they fussed about their father for a while though and all had a turn at being nursed by him. But it was the same story, he ended up by nursing and fondling Louise in the finish while the mother bustled the rest of them off to bed.).

In the bedroom while their mother was tucking them in they would ask, 'Well Mum?' and their mother would smile and reply, 'I don't know. I don't know. But don't go asking questions like that. You just get to sleep.' And she would try to become stern and the children would say, 'Aw come on Mum, what eh!'

But she would not give anything away and would tell them to hurry up and get to sleep.

So the children would lie there and listen to the muffled voices of their parents talking in the kitchen till they fell asleep again and they never once

116

heard their father leaving, but in the mornings he would be gone.

They began to ask their mother quite regularly after that as to what was going to happen. But their mother would not commit herself.

Then one day when the children arrived home from school their mother had some of their things packed and at their insistence she finally told them they were going home the next day.

This was met with great jubilation, and the next day Luke, Arthur and their father came down in the old Buick and the shift back to the old homestead began.

A Young Man Feeling His Oats

When Motu got a little older they shifted him into the 'outside room' with Arthur. The 'outside room' had been attached to one end of the front verandah some time after the house had been built, as the family had grown.

Motu used to love sleeping in the same room with his brother. They had beds in opposite corners and he would watch his brother lying with his arms under his head, smoking a cigarette and looking at the ceiling. And he would see the muscles of his brother's biceps bulging because he always wore only a singlet. Arthur always smoked a cigarette before he went to sleep. Sometimes he smoked two, lying there and looking at the ceiling. And Motu used to wonder what he was thinking of. He used to suppose it was of some girl or perhaps girls. And his brother had that peculiar smell about him. A smell the boy loved; of sweat from beneath the arms. And his brother had a peculiar cough also. It was a small soft cough. He was always doing it as though it were a habit. Because there never seemed to be any phlegm with it.

Motu used to say his prayers in those days, every night before he went to bed. He would kneel down beside his bed on the mat and say — 'Our Father Who art in heaven. . . .' And he used to pray that God would look after his family. And he said a special prayer for Arthur. He thought he could feel his brother's eyes on him, watching him, while he knelt there praying. And he felt good. He wished that he could convert Arthur and get him to say his prayers also. Because he loved his brother and wanted him to go to heaven too.

Arthur had just finished school and was working on their father's pine plantation, with their cousin Jack Brown (who was the same age as Arthur), clearing the fire-breaks. Their father used to pay them. Arthur was the wild one of the boys. He got around with the crowd who liked fighting and drinking and pig-hunting and chasing girls. But he was the most lovable of the two brothers, as far as the children were concerned. He could do nothing wrong in their eyes.

Motu had heard rumours that Arthur had been in one or two fights. Real fights that is, not the fights that boys have at school, but men's fights. But they were only rumours and he was not sure. But Arthur got about with his cousin Jack and his family and the rest of his relatives on his mother's side and they were a pretty wild mob and were always in fights and drinking and chasing women and going out pig-hunting or chasing brumbies. So Motu wouldn't have been surprised if his brother had been in one or two fights. Luke was different to Arthur somehow. He could not (or didn't wish to) mix with the other young men around the settlement. And anyway he had gone straight off to college as soon as he left school.

Arthur's parents had wanted him to go off to college too. Arnold Booth, their uncle in Taupo, had said it was the best thing to do now days if a chap wanted to get on. But Arthur had put up so much opposition that in the end his parents had given up the idea. And anyway they couldn't imagine Arthur doing well at a college, for although he was fairly clever, he just didn't seem to be cut out for that sort of life. He was too wild and loved the outdoors and doing physical things. As far as Arthur was concerned he wanted to be out working as soon as possible. He couldn't get out working quick enough. He wanted to be a man amongst men. His cousins and them, and the chaps who worked in the mill and the bush.

One night, a wild stormy night, Motu was awakened from a deep sleep by someone thumping upon the front door to the house. He lay there in the dark, still groggy with sleep, trying to clear his brain. The wind lashed the heavy rain against the house and for a while he thought he must have dreamt it. But no, he was sure he had heard a man's voice cut off abruptly by the noise of the storm. Through the wall he heard his father's voice, but he could not catch what he was saying above the din of the storm. The thumping on the front door grew louder and louder and the voice could be distinguished. It was Willy Hagg. The boy could tell he was drunk, very drunk. He knew that his brother was awake and listening although there was a deep silence from that corner of the room. And he knew that his brother had stopped breathing and was holding his breath to hear better.

'Pete!' Willy was calling in a thick heavily slurred voice from the verandah. 'Pete. Open up. I want some liquor.' Mr and Mrs Joseph didn't answer, hoping that the man would go away. The knocking kept up incessantly, the voice growing more and more demanding. He began using obscene words. At last the boy heard his father's voice calling above the noise of the wind and rain. 'Go away Willy, I've got no liquor. It's late. Go home. You'll wake the whole house.'

'Don't bloody-well lie to me Pete,' Willy shouted back, his voice thick and slurred with his drinking. 'I know you've got some beer there somewhere. Come on open this door before I kick the bloody thing in and wake the whole house.'

'Go away Willy. It's late. I'm not getting up,' the boy's father called. 'Come back tomorrow. Go home and sober up.'

But the banging and shouting grew stronger and more demanding, and the man began to kick at the door with his foot.

Motu heard his brother curse in the dark, then he was silent again. But when Willy wouldn't go away and kept up his persistent noise he heard his brother curse again and he heard the blankets being thrown back and then his brother was at the window with one knee on the boy's bed and he opened the window and said, 'Go away Willy or you'll wake the whole house up.' The rain blew a little through the window.

Willy immediately turned his abuse onto Arthur and the boy heard him say, 'Go back to bed. You're too young to be interfering. You keep your nose out of this. You're just a kid yet. Still shitt'n yellow. You go and tuck yourself up in bed.'

Willy should not have said that for the next thing Motu knew was the door being flung open, and Arthur was out on the verandah. There was the sound of quick footsteps across the verandah and then scuffling and grunting noises. Then there was a loud sound, like someone being slapped, only it didn't sound like the usual noise. It was a sound that Motu had never heard before. He heard Willy cry out loudly and there was a great noise as though someone had fallen off the verandah. The boy flew to the window and in the light from his parents' room (for his parents were up now hearing the scuffle), he saw Willy lying flat on his back on the wet gravel of the front yard and Arthur standing there hunched over on the edge of the verandah holding his right hand.

The boy's parents were at the door. His father had a torch.

'Is he all right?' they were enquiring and Motu could detect a note of anxiety in their voices. Arthur was looking over at the fallen man a little apprehensively.

'You shouldn't have hit him,' Mrs Joseph said. 'It was none of your business.'

'But the man's a nuisance,' Arthur said. 'He can't come around here swearing like that.'

'I don't care,' his mother said. 'You shouldn't have hit him. The man was drunk. You know what Willy's like.'

'But he asked for it,' Arthur said. He was still keyed up and talking quickly, the words coming thickly because of his excitement.

Willy stirred and pushed himself up slowly into a sitting position. The rain poured down onto him soaking him through to the skin. Blood was streaming down his face from a cut in his cheek.

Mr Joseph hurried down the steps to him and attempted to help him up.

119

But Willy shrugged him off, flailing his arms about wildly.

'Leave me alone,' he growled. 'Take your hands off me.' He got unsteadily to his feet by himself and began adjusting his coat which was up over his shoulders. He was soaking wet. He stood there shakily, and then he looked up at Arthur who was still standing hunched on the verandah.

'Think you're tough don't ya,' he said. 'Think you're good hitting a man when he's drunk. You wait till I'm sober boy. We'll see then. I'll kick the shit out of you.' He ran his hand over his face smearing the blood and making his wound look much worse than it really was. He turned and staggered towards the gate mumbling to himself all the while. At the gate he turned and looking straight at Arthur and said, with a sneer on his face, 'You're just a kid yet. You'll see. I'll kick you to death.'

Arthur gave a small cry and made a lurch towards him but his father rushed across and caught him. Just then Willy scooped up a handful of gravel and flung it at them and quickly ducked out the gate. It was intended for Arthur but it hit his father as well. They were too far away however for it to do any harm.

Mr Joseph cursed. Arthur was all for going after Willy but his father restrained him.

'I only wanted to get rid of him,' Arthur said. He was still breathing heavily.

'You shouldn't have hit him,' Mrs Joseph said again. 'Not the way he is. You never know what might happen.'

Motu didn't know what his mother was referring to at the time but found out later that Willy's face bled easily especially the left side which was twisted up (pulling his mouth up on that side) from the stroke he had suffered when he was a small boy. It was this side of the face that Arthur had struck him on and that was why there was so much blood.

Outside, beyond the hedge, they heard Willy's voice calling back, 'You wait Pete. I'll get you. I'll put the bloody cops onto your tail. They'll shake you along.'

'Don't take any notice of him,' Mr Joseph said, 'He's drunk.' He was turning to go inside now.

'You'd better get on back to bed,' Mrs Joseph said. Speaking to Arthur. 'And don't you go doing that sort of thing again. You just keep your nose to your own business.'

'But Mum!' Arthur said passionately. 'I'm not going to go have anyone speak in front of you like that. Not in front of you.'

'I don't know about that,' the mother said. 'Willy's all right. He would have gone away. I hope you just didn't hit him for the love of it my boy. There's worse people around than Willy. Because if you did you'd better keep your fists to yourself. Otherwise you'll get into serious trouble one of these days. Picking on a drunk man. And Willy too. Don't use us for your excuses.'

Arthur fell silent and turned towards his room, his shoulders still hunched. Motu remained motionless to the side of the door. When his brother came in he brushed quite close to the boy, and the boy smelled the oil from his brother's body and the rain on him. Motu jumped quickly back into bed then.

'Did he hit you?' Motu asked his brother.

'No,' Arthur replied. 'We just scuffled around for awhile, then I pushed him off and got a clean hit at his face. I felt the skin of his face give when I hit him.' He lit the candle and Motu could see he was still shaking a little from the excitement. 'Old Willy bleeds easy. I should have known not to hit him, especially on his left side. But he made me so wild.' He broke off and fell silent for a while, looking into the flame of the candle. Then he said, half to himself, 'I was stronger than him. I could feel it. I lifted him off his feet once there, clean off his feet. He was thrashing with his legs trying to kick me.' And Motu could detect the thrill in his brother's voice. And he felt an immense pride for his brother. Arthur took his towel and began drying himself, his face and hair and then his shoulders and arms. He looked at his right hand. The knuckles were a little skinned, and he rubbed them.

'Call me a kid,' he said. Still more to himself, 'Gawd I caught him a beauty though. Smack on.'

He got into bed and lit a cigarette and smoked it for a while. Then he said good night to Motu and blew the candle out. And the boy saw the cigarette glowing in the dark. Growing bright as his brother drew on it, then dying down. And the boy saw the smoke drifting up in front of the glow.

Dole Day

Joe was woken by Kath's door opening. From the noise she made he guessed she was in another temper. He heard her go into the children's room and knew one of the kids must have been making a noise; Wiki crying or something. Then his door opened and Kath began rummaging around on top of the dresser.

'What're you after?' He felt lousy from a poor night's sleep.

'The throaties. Where are they?' Kath sounded irritable. She coughed. The hollow-chested cough that hit her often and scared him.

'They're not in here.' He racked his brain to recall where he had seen them last. He was anxious to appease her.

He remembered. 'They're on the bookshelf out there.' Why hadn't she looked there in the first place, he wondered irritably. Just her way of telling him she had been kept awake all night with a sore throat and then was expected to get up to the children as well.

She must think I deliberately ignored the children's crying, he thought. But he never heard the children because of the double wall with chimney and wardrobe between his bedroom and theirs. There was only a thin wall on Kath's side. He kept telling her this, but she either forgot or didn't believe him.

After she left he switched on the transistor to find out the time. It was only five thirty. He groaned. Another broken night. They were starting to mount up and were making both of them bad-tempered. He knew he wouldn't get back to sleep again, so he left the transistor going. He reached up and pushed in the button of the alarm clock.

At seven thirty, feeling as though he'd not had any sleep, he got up and went into Kath's room. She was awake and he could see she was angry.

'I'll get the kids off to school,' he said. 'You stay in bed.' He felt guilty about the earlier scene, and sorry for her too.

'Didn't you hear the children?' she asked.

'No.'

'Wiki was crying for about half an hour.' He knew that meant more like five minutes. 'She woke Huia up and the two of them started howling. Wiki fell out of bed, poor thing. It's a wonder she didn't hurt herself. She was freezing when I went in.' He knew this meant she was merely cold. 'You *must* have heard her. She hit the floor with a hell of a thump.'

She had a way of emphasising unpleasant words. Almost as if she relished them. This annoyed Joe intensely. But he said, 'I can't hear them very well from my room. You know there's a double wall there. I've told you that before.' He knew she didn't believe him. 'Do you want to swap rooms?' he asked.

'Well, leave your door open, or something.' She seemed not to hear his offer. 'God, you must be deaf, or don't want to hear.'

'I'll leave my door open tonight.'

'What time is it?'

'Half past seven.'

She made an effort to get up.

'You stay in bed,' he told her. 'I'll manage the kids all right. What do you give them for lunch?'

'Just give them twenty cents each. They can buy a dairy lunch.'

She slumped back into the bed. He could see she was exhausted. He'd never been able to overcome a feeling of being responsible for her sufferings. And there were times when he felt she set out to make him feel that way. But the guilt was there.

He had a hell of a rush to get the kids off in time to catch the school bus. Even then their hair wasn't combed properly. But he told them to tell their teacher that their daddy was responsible; their mummy was sick in bed.

He had breakfast, then took a plate of porridge up to Kath. She woke with a start as he crossed the room and flung herself on to her back, making a loud sucking noise as she took in breath. It was a way of hers. Mostly it irritated him but this time he felt a sudden tenderness towards her.

Only the top part of her head showed above the blankets. Her hair fell about her face. Her eyes were shut and they looked very weary. Yet somehow she looked beautiful lying there; soft and warm and desirable. He put the plate of porridge on the window-seat, sat on the edge of the bed and reached across and brushed her hair back from her face. He stroked her forehead and her hair and realised again, with some surprise, just how wavy it was.

It was the first thing about her that had caught his attention. It was thick — thick as rope, he used to think — and strong looking. And it was abundant and wavy. Until it started falling out after she had Huia, their first child. And then it got strangly and lost its lustre because she didn't have the time to care for it. And it began to smell of the kitchen; the cooking and the greasy washing-up water.

She wore her hair loose in the early days, so that it hung over and almost hid the left side of her face. She wore it long, like he preferred; well down past her shoulders. How soon we forget, he thought. How far away those days seem now.

He remembered, when they were making love in those days, how he used to spread her hair out over the pillow — it was so abundant that it almost covered the entire pillow — and bury his face in it, feeling the silkiness and thickness and smelling the fragrance that rose from it. Sometimes he would hold his head back to look at her hair. It didn't seem to matter how often he studied it, each time he would marvel at its pure chestnut colouring. And this heightened the sensuousness of the moment. He associated a lot of her sexuality with her hair. And her unusually shaped forehead, the dome protruding almost to the point of deformity. He supposed that others might not find it attractive, but for him it was one of her most alluring features.

As he stroked her forehead he knew that he was still very much in love with her — the tumbled hair, the high colouring of her complexion, the familiar odour rising from beneath the blankets. The startled movement and quick sucking intake of breath when she woke and flung herself on to her back; all this endeared her to him now. An urge to climb into bed with her almost overpowered him. But he checked himself. It would be unfair.

It had been *his* idea that they sleep in separate rooms, for he was such a bad sleeper and Kath was a light one. He'd never known anyone to fall asleep as quickly as she did; nor to wake as easily. Between his tossing and turning, trying to get to sleep and her waking with a start each time — he used to think her heart would stop one of these nights — sleeping in the same bed became an ordeal. And with Wiki being a bad night baby, neither of them were getting anywhere near the sleep they needed. It got so that he used to lie awake all tensed up, afraid to move in case he woke Kath. It became an agony. So finally he moved into the spare room. It's strange how difficult it was to do that. For there seemed to be some sort of stigma attached to couples who slept in separate rooms or even in separate beds. Well there was where he came from. It took him four years to overcome it. Yet it hadn't affected their sex life. Far from it. If anything it improved it. He supposed it had something to do with 'absence making the heart grow fonder'. Or something like that. Only in his case it was desire.

Kath insisted that she wouldn't mind if they still slept together. This was another case where he felt she was putting the responsibility unfairly on his shoulders. For he was sure she had been as miserable as he was in the same bed and equally relieved when he shifted.

'What was the trouble last night?' he asked now.

'I had colic again. Kept me awake all night.' *All night*, he repeated wearily in his head.

'Never mind,' he said. 'You rest. I'll get the house tidied up before I go. The kids are off to school now. You just rest.'

'Where are you going?' He could tell her mind wasn't ticking over.

'You know, I want to check out those jobs that were advertised in the paper on Saturday.'

She was silent. He wondered if she really knew the truth all along.

It was funny, he thought, how he could lie to her about some things, yet found it impossible to do so about others. A tiny voice in his head kept repeating — that will come later. It made him feel uneasy, for he recalled how he had started out, pledging that he would always tell her the truth, no matter how painful it might be to them. But he hadn't known about the long drawn-out pain of being married. In the end he had decided that what the heart didn't know it didn't grieve. He got up to leave.

'I'll get up in a minute,' she said. Her voice sounded distant. 'I'll be all right. I've got a lot to get through before Betty comes. She's coming for lunch.'

'Could I ring her and tell her to call it off till another day? Tell her you're not feeling well?'

A shadow of annoyance crossed her face.

'No. I've been looking forward to having lunch with her. One of the few things I've got to look forward to these days.' Something like a whine crept into her voice. It was a way of speaking she used increasingly these days.

'I'll be all right,' she said. 'Just leave me alone for a while.'

124

Betty was a good friend of theirs. A solo mother. Joe liked her, but didn't really like Kath mixing with all these solo mothers. He felt that their talk about what bastards their husbands had been and how they were better rid of them, must sooner or later have a demoralising effect. But he held his peace.

'What time's she coming?'

'We're having lunch together. Look! Just leave me alone now, will you?' A note of desperation crept into her voice.

He went to the door. 'Do you want me to take the phone off the hook?'

'Just go! Go!' Her voice had become shrill. But she nodded.

He closed the door quietly behind him as he left. He felt disgruntled at being dismissed like a truant schoolboy. He made his way downstairs. Other things were eating him also. Why couldn't she have at least given him some peace of mind by staying in bed? At least until it was nearly time for Betty's arrival. But it was always like this. Something always cropped up to cut her sleep short. So she went around half dead most of the time, as if to remind him that her life with him was one of continual hardship and suffering. And it wasn't any fun for him either; her being tired all the time. And he had a nagging suspicion that she was lying to him just now; that she was deliberately trying to throw him out of sorts. First it had been a sore throat that had kept her awake; now it was colic. But this was how their life had been for some time now. They both suspected ulterior motives to everything the other did. So there were constant scenes of recrimination that, up to now, had been resolved by heart-felt professions of their love for each other, either during sex or with it soon following. He told himself he'd climb into bed with her later in the morning. Once she'd had sufficient rest.

He tidied up as quietly as he could. Made his and the children's beds; tidied the lounge and washed the dishes. He went up to see if Kath wanted toast and coffee but found she hadn't touched her porridge. She was dozing, so he took the plate and quietly left the room.

It was hard to tell which came first; whether his being kind to Kath by bringing her breakfast in bed — something he had to admit he didn't do often — was his way of softening her up for sex later. Or whether the feeling of tenderness he felt for her earlier was the reason for his being kind to her now, with the idea of sex following. Perhaps it was a mixture of both. He didn't know. All he was sure of was that deep down he was still very much in love with Kath.

He decided against getting into bed with her later. Told himself that it was far too time consuming. He had done this sort of thing before. Perhaps too often. It was all right if you didn't have anything else to do. Otherwise it became frustrating in its own way.

He set the alarm for eleven fifteen and took it up to Kath's room in case she overslept. Then he snatched an apple and a couple of bananas from the dish on top of the 'fridge and stuffed them into his bag. And very courageously, for him, he felt, he left Kath and the house and made his way round to the bus stop.

He got off at the Hutt Park Raceway corner and walked all the way into Lower Hutt. He had come to enjoy these walks, especially if the sun was out. He found they helped clear his head and loosened him up from the tensions of home life. It was about a mile, just a good distance for him.

He walked the full length of the Lower Hutt shopping centre to get to the Labour Department. Going there was almost a formality now, because it was pretty unlikely, at this time of the year, that there would be job vacancies. It was almost the summer holidays. Yet he had to get a clearance from the Department before he could get the dole money.

He left his bag, with the handle of his tennis racquet sticking out, at the top of the stairs, out of sight of the counter. The usual woman attended to him. He knew her face well, for she was the one between him and the dole money. He, on the other hand, must be just another in a sea of faces. We must all look alike to her, he thought. She must know it off by heart, by now; the way we approach the counter with that unmistakable look.

He'd discovered that it paid to adopt a kind of cringing manner when applying for the dole. You had to try to look like humility itself. The relationship between you and the person behind the counter was that of a dog to its master. And like the dog, you had to wag your tail to show you were grateful when you got something. You bowed and scraped and made appreciative noises. But there was *some* compassion over the counter. And we both need each other, he thought. I need the money and they need to feel their life has some purpose. And it helped to have a wife and family back home somewhere.

Make them feel they are doing some good; make them feel important — like little tin gods. Give them a sense of power. So the more cringing you were the better your chances of getting something. And the less you were likely to be harassed by probing questions.

The woman shot him a quick glance and without a word took the application form and stamped it. Joe thanked her and beat a hasty retreat, in case she should suddenly change her mind. Out of sight, he picked up his bag and jogged down the stairs. He felt a little lighter in spirit already. Half the battle was won. Now for the next half.

He crossed the street and went quickly through the arcade into Queen's Drive and down to the Social Security Department. Again he made sure to leave his incriminating bag out of sight.

A half dozen people were already in the room. The three enclosed counters were occupied; two women and a man. They were involved in earnest conversation with the 'tin gods' behind the counters. It always surprised Joe to see how young some of these were. He didn't know why but it seemed odd that you had to rely on someone so young for your daily bread.

A woman with a baby in a pram was sitting on the only chair in the room, smoking. The baby was crying and she pushed the pram backwards and forwards with furious movements. She looked to be barely in her twenties. Another woman was standing, leaning against the wall. She was older and looked washed out. She was smoking also. A couple of children wandered about the room. Joe did not know who they belonged to. One of them wandered out the door and a woman at the counter turned and in a harsh voice called out a name. Joe looked through the glass panelling of the door and saw the child heading off down the stairs and went and retrieved her. He brought her back, kicking and squealing, holding her under her armpits.

'Yours,' he said. The woman thanked him without enthusiasm.

A woman and the man left the counter simultaneously. Joe could tell by the way they said 'thank you ' that they must have been successful.

'Next.' The two officers called together. Joe waited. The young woman with the pram got up and went to the middle counter. Joe looked across at the other woman leaning against the wall.

'I'm being fixed,' she said in a lowered voice and pointed to a glass partition through which he could see a passageway and closed doors.

Joe quickly stepped up to the vacant counter. A middle-aged woman confronted him. She looked hard-bitten. He hadn't dealt with her before. She snatched the form from him and looked at it.

'You're late, you know,' she snapped.

'I'm sorry.' Joe was about to make up an excuse but she never gave him the chance.

'You're supposed to be here by nine-thirty.' She went on, tight-lipped. 'It's written on the application form.' She paused as if to let this sink in. 'We'll let it go this time. But next time you might have to wait another week before you get your money.'

Bloody bitch! Joe thought. But to her he said, in a very mild voice, 'I'm sorry.' He knew he was supposed to be there by nine-thirty, but hadn't bothered up to now. And nothing had ever been said before.

The woman studied the form briefly then snatched up the rubber stamp and banged it vigorously. Joe watched her with sheer hate. He supposed she was thinking, 'Another bloody bludger' and was frustrated because she couldn't do anything about it. I wonder if someone's screwing her, he thought. Probably not. Probably what's wrong with her. And he wondered how many more times his application form would be stamped before it finally reached the person who made the decision on it.

The woman looked up and just for an instant their eyes met. Hard steel-cold eyes looked into his. Joe tried to shield his hatred. It was imperative that he kept in good with everyone. 'We'll forward the money to you — if everything is in order.' That was nasty, that last bit. Did she *really* have to say it? Joe wondered. But they always added that last piece — 'if everything is in order' — and it always left you with a feeling of anxiety. Right up until you received the money, you wouldn't be sure whether you were going to get it or not. He wasn't sure whether this was the effect it was meant to have but sometimes he thought it was. Yet he supposed they had to protect the System somehow. Otherwise people would think claiming the dole was a push-over and everyone would be bludging off it.

Once more he was out in the sun. He felt relaxed now. The ordeal was over for another week. The cheque usually arrived in the mail on Thursdays. All he had to do now, he told himself, was wait.

As he strolled back towards the arcade he thought, it's just as well they're not all like *her*. His mind dwelt on the hard-bitten woman at the counter. She gave him the creeps. Especially those cold fish eyes. They put the shits up him. He was surprised they didn't employ more people like her to run the office. There'd only be half the people applying for the dole if they did. For all taken into account, despite what he might think and say, they weren't a bad bunch really.

On his way back through the arcade he stopped at the newspaper stand and made as if he were taking change from his pocket. He went through the motion of putting coins into the slot and took a newspaper. He wasn't even sure if he'd get round to reading it. But that wasn't the point. The point was, he told himself, getting something for nothing. And anyway that huge organisation could afford it; had tons more money than he. And for what? They were the *real* bludgers.

He went up a flight of stairs into the coffee bar that bridged the arcade and ordered coffee. He usually went up there after his ordeal with the Social Security; it helped him unwind.

He spread the newspaper on the table, but found it dull reading. He noticed heaps of magazines stacked on the seats. He thumbed through these instead; *Time, Newsweek*; some women's magazines. They were far more readable. There were a number of *Playboys* too.

The young couple who were in the bar when he had come in got up and left. Now he had the place to himself. Before he left he went around gathering up the *Playboys* and stuffed them into his bag along with his tennis gear. There were five of them. He knew the owners wouldn't be able to trace their disappearance back to him. He left the bar feeling elated. There weren't many things he liked better than getting something for nothing, especially from people who had more than himself. It was quite a feat in this day and age. *Playboy*! Now there's a case in point, he mused.

Just look at what they get *their* money from. And they make *millions*. He wouldn't buy one on principle. But getting them for nothing was another matter. It was as if, in some small way, he was beating the System. All told, it wasn't too bad a morning, he assured himself.

He strolled leisurely back up High Street, window-shopping on the way, feeling the pleasant heaviness of the *Playboys* in his bag.

It always puzzled him why the railway station was so far from the shopping centre. It was about half a mile away. But there you are, he told himself, it's not ours to ask the whys and wherefores, it's ours to do. He crossed the bridge over the river and walked slowly up to the station.

The units ran only occasionally during the day and sometimes you had to wait a long time for one. Like now. For Joe had seen a unit pull in, then out again, heading for Wellington, after he had crossed the bridge. The idea of making a bolt for it had crossed his mind, but it was far too nice a day for rushing around. And he was in no hurry.

To pass the time he strolled about the station, looking in here and there at doors and windows and studying the notices and posters stuck on walls. He relieved himself in the toilet at the end of the platform, then came back and sat on the last seat. It was the only one in the sun. He stretched his legs out and tried to doze. May as well catch up on a bit of sleep, he thought, seeing I have such a long wait ahead of me. He began to feel voluptuously warm, stretched out there with the full force of the sun beating down on him. He dozed.

Occasionally someone came on to the platform. Joe would cock one eye open to see what they were like. Always, in the back of his mind, he hoped it would be an attractive female. Later, two young girls did come on to the platform. Joe knew well before they came into sight that they were young girls. He heard the brisk click-clock noise of their shoes. They were wearing those fashionable brogue-heeled shoes. He ogled them as they passed and one had not bad legs. And because he was feeling drowsy and warm, Joe felt a stirring in his loins. Otherwise it was good having the station all to himself.

A unit finally got in at two fifteen. Joe had arranged to meet Tua for a game of tennis up at the university courts at three. He hadn't thought he'd be cutting the time so fine. Where did it go? he wondered.

When the unit pulled into Wellington station, Joe had a mad rush to make it to the courts before Tua got tired of waiting and left. He jogged most of the way. This will teach me, he kept telling himself. Old slow-coach. The last minute dash kid, they call me. Always the same. Never learn. No wonder I drive Kath halfway round the bend. He knew he was running late but didn't know what the exact time was. When his watch broke down the last time he never bothered to get it repaired. Can't afford it, he had told himself. The bare necessities, like food and rent used up what money he had these days. It's odd though, he thought. It's not until you have so little money that you realise how so many things you take for granted are really only luxuries. The amazing thing was you somehow got along without them.

To his relief Tua was still there when he arrived at the courts. He was sitting in his car reading through some papers. Joe supposed they were to do with his insurance job or else his university studies.

It was good seeing Tua, for it didn't matter how badly he, or other people for that matter, thought of him at times, Tua was always good company. Joe had discovered a long time ago that no-one could lift him out of a depression more quickly than Tua.

Normally Tua greeted him with gusto; breaking into a short haka. And there were times when Joe, caught up in their spirit of the moment, would take up the challenge and join in. But this time Tua merely looked up and then glanced reproachfully at his watch.

'Sorry I'm late.'

'Half an hour. I was just getting ready to go.'

'I didn't know those bloody units from Lower Hutt were so few and far between.'

'Yes, they are,' Tua said. Then, with an action more typical of him, he shuffled the papers roughly together and in that positive way of his put them on the seat. 'Never mind, you're here now. Don't worry about it. Come on — let's grab a court.'

That's better, Joe thought. This's more the Tua I know. Tua got his tennis gear from the boot of his car and the two went around to the dressing sheds.

'You look hot,' Tua said.

'Ran most of the way from the station.' Joe was still a bit out of breath. 'It helped loosen me up though. I've been pretty screwed up lately. Better watch out in the game.'

'Not too good at home?' Tua asked.

'No, it's not that so much. Although things aren't too good there either. I had to go and see about my dole money.'

'Did you get it?'

'I'm not sure. The bastards leave you on tenterhooks. Make you sweat for it. But I think I got it all right. Won't really know till Thursday though.'

They talked about the dole for a while. Joe told Tua about his theory of how you had to approach these people when you were applying for it. How he reckoned you had to look all meek and mild.

Tua kept repeating while Joe spoke, 'That's the way. You've got the idea. Make the buggers feel great. They like to think they're playing God handing out that money. The buggers like that. That's the way.' Joe felt much better after that, for his conscience was never really easy.

They walked out on to the courts. Tua, as usual, was immaculately dressed for the occasion. Everything about him was spick and span. Joe's tennis gear consisted of an old short-sleeved sports shirt and baggy pair of black football shorts that he had picked up somewhere years ago. His sandshoes were filthy and coming apart at the seams. He wore no socks. He was never a conscientious dresser, so he supposed it was easy for him. But Tua always maintained that the right dress was half the battle with anything.

Joe lost the first set. Tua beat him easily, 6-2. Without a break they went straight into the second set. Tua beat him again but it was much closer this time. First Tua raced into a 4-0 lead and it looked as if he were going to win this set even more easily than the first. But Joe hung on tenaciously, steadied his game and slowed the pace right down. This had the effect he'd hoped for. For it threw his friend out of rhythm and Tua began making mistakes — over-hitting volleys and fluffing shots that should have been sitters. Doggedly Joe hung on, gaining more confidence, until he finally drew level at 4-4. Then he went ahead to a 5-4 lead. At this point Joe thought he had the game in the bag, but he hadn't counted on his friend's fighting spirit. Tua didn't like being beaten at anything. He raised his game and overhauled Joe on Joe's serve. Joe knew he was in trouble then. Tua aced him three times and took the game without Joe winning a single point. This made Joe feel that Tua had been just playing around with him through the rest of the set. He felt a bit depressed, but soon shook himself out of it. After all, he told himself, it's just a game. And he'd enjoyed it; especially the last set when he'd almost won. And it was good exercise. But he hadn't beaten Tua for a long time now. He wished Tua could see that he needed to win now and then. For a while he thought there might be some truth in what Tua said, about the right dress being half the battle. Perhaps it *did* give you some sort of psychological advantage. But he didn't really believe that.

In the dressing sheds afterwards, Tua cut Joe's hair. It was something they had arranged as a way of saving money. Tua carried the clippers and scissors around in the boot of his car. The hair-cutting was supposed to be reciprocal, but Joe noticed that his friend hadn't trusted his head to him yet. Afterwards, Joe wondered if it was really worth the trouble. Tua took far too much off for his liking. They didn't have a mirror, so Joe really couldn't tell what was going on. He could only guess by the amount of hair that lay on the floor. It turned out not too bad though. When she saw it later, Kath said she liked it. And anyway, Joe always thought that the only

131

difference between a good haircut and a bad one was about a fortnight. It was with his hair anyway. That was how long it took to grow again. The trouble this time was that Tua took too much of the top and exposed Joe's balding patch. Joe sensed his friend's shock when he saw how thin he really was on top. But good Lord, Joe told himself, I'm nearly forty now. What else can you expect?

Later, the two showered. Joe had forgotten to bring a towel. Normally Tua let him use his. Joe could see he was about to do so again, but Tua suddenly changed his mind and instead gave Joe a pair of old football shorts to dry himself with. Joe sensed something was wrong with his friend, but didn't know what. What with the rough haircut earlier and the desperate way in which Tua went about beating him at tennis, Joe felt his friend was somehow trying to humiliate him. But why? Still, beggars can't be choosers. And he was grateful that he didn't have to carry wet gear around in his bag, for he would have had to dry himself with his own clothing.

Later, out in the car, Tua showed him a watch he had bought for a younger brother's twenty-first birthday. It had all sorts of mod cons attached to it and had cost around fifty dollars. The expense appalled Joe. He couldn't help thinking what a bloody waste of money and how empty really. And a quick tally up in his head told him that he and his family could exist for a fortnight on the money. But he went through the motions of admiring it and passing the appropriate remarks.

They went up to the university cafeteria for a cup of coffee. Joe got Tua to show him how to fill in his income tax forms. But afterwards he was none the wiser.

Tua stayed on at the university to do some work; so Joe made his way down to the city on foot. Something was eating Tua all right. Any other time he would have offered to run Joe down in his car.

The five o'clock session of the movie he wanted to see had already started when Joe arrived at the theatre. He asked the girl in the ticket box what time the main feature started. She told him, not until after the interval. So Joe walked around the streets to fill in time. He thought of ringing Kath to tell her he'd be late coming home. But he was still smarting over the way she'd treated him that morning. So he decided against it. It would teach her to have a little more respect for him in future.

When he thought it was nearly time for the interval, he sat on the steps of the theatre opposite and watched. The people started coming out, in dribs and drabs, and the foyer slowly filled up. Still he waited, hoping there would be a larger crowd. It would make things a lot easier.

When he saw the foyer was as full as it was likely to be, he strolled across to a youth who was standing on the footpath smoking and watching the passing girls. Joe had seen him come out of the theatre earlier on.

'S'cuse me mate,' Joe said. 'Do they hand out pass-out tickets for half-time?' The young man looked quizzically at Joe, but shook his head. 'Thanks,' Joe said.

He slipped inside the theatre door and merged with the crowd. He pretended to study the posters on the wall so that his back was to the ticket box, in case the girl recognised him. He thought it very unlikely though. A movie crowd is a fairly anonymous one.

The buzzer went, warning that the picture was about to begin. The crowd started moving back into the theatre. When most of the people were inside and he saw the auditorium lights were out, Joe casually strolled past the two ushers on the door. Under cover of dark, he made his way up the aisle, peering along the rows for any seats that were still turned up. He'd found that it was a pretty safe bet that these seats would be unoccupied. As a rule, people didn't bother turning their seats up when they vacated them. By now his eyes had become accustomed to the dark and he spotted a couple of turned-up seats in a fairly good position. He sidled along to these and eased himself down, feeling a glow of joy. How much more you enjoy the old story of getting something for nothing again? That's a dollar saved anyway, plus sixty cents on a haircut — that's a dollar sixty. And the twenty-two dollars fifty-seven cents exactly from the Social Security — perhaps? All in all not a bad day's work. And with that half day's gardening at Watson's on Saturday, we might just be able to survive for another week or two yet. And don't forget the *Playboy* magazines. They cost about a dollar each — fancy people paying that much for the things. And the newspaper. They all add up. And you could never tell what might crop up in the meantime. You could survive all right, so long as you were prepared to pull your belt in now and then; do away with luxuries.

The film turned out a dud. But it didn't matter. One couldn't be too fussy when one got something for nothing.

After, he went across the street to the coffee bar. His stomach was beginning to rumble. He still had one banana left in his bag. He'd eaten the other one up at the tennis courts and the apple inside the theatre. He resisted a strong temptation to order a toasted sandwich, for he felt like something hot. Instead he took the banana from his bag — it was black and bruised by now — and ate that with his coffee. What a combination, he mused. The girl behind the counter looked across at him, but said nothing. There was a large notice above the counter saying that you weren't to eat food in there other than that bought on the premises. But if you're audacious enough, you can get away with anything, Joe thought. And anyway it was only a banana.

Joe tried to make up his mind whether to stay on in town or not; just wander around for a bit. Once I'm home, that's it, Joe thought. The same old suffocating, monotonous routine. Perhaps he could call into the 'Albatross' for a while and have a few drinks with the boys. Leo was sure to be there. He could get a loan from him to pay his way. But he felt a twinge of conscience; he hadn't even rung Kath yet to say he'd be late coming home. He made his way to the bus terminal and caught the nine fifteen.

He could tell Kath was still up, for the light was on in the lounge and he could see the flickering bluish light of the television set. Before going inside he slipped around the back and put the bag with the tennis gear inside the bach.

Kath was propped up on the couch, glued to the TV. He had expected to find her in the bad mood he had left her in that morning. And to start in on him as soon as he got inside the door; wanting to know where he'd been and why he was late. He had prepared himself for it. He had a cock and bull story ready, about how he'd been sent on a wild goose chase all round town looking for a job. Instead, she was surprisingly friendly. He shouldn't have been surprised though. Whenever he expected to find her in a bad mood she'd be in a good one; or vice-versa. He supposed this had something to do with his own frame of mind. On the way home he had steeled himself, ready to find her in a bad mood, because he was still feeling out of sorts with her over the morning's carryings-on. He could never guess what might have taken place in her mind in the meantime, for her mood to change as it had. It was a mystery to him. But he wasn't going to press the issue. It was just good to find her in an agreeable mood.

She never even bothered to ask him why he was late or where he had been. She just said, 'Your dinner's on the stove. Needs heating up.' After she'd greeted him with a friendly 'Hullo.'

Joe was on the point of telling her about the harrowing time he'd had looking all over the city for jobs, but decided that silence was golden. Leave well alone boy, he cautioned himself.

He brought his dinner into the lounge and ate it off his knee, watching television. There were a lot of people rushing about and shouting and sirens blaring and then some shooting. Joe felt a twinge of despair, recalling all the wasted hours he'd spent watching inanities like this. What had happened to Kath, he wondered? She has a good brain. And yet she'll watch this sort of thing night after night. It wasn't as if there was nothing else she could do. There were shelves full of unread books.

He couldn't make head or tail of what was going on, but the programme soon finished. Then the late news and weather came on. Kath got up and went into the bathroom.

Joe was slumped in a half-hypnotic trance by now, his eyes fixed on the attractive young continuity announcer who was telling viewers what was on screen tomorrow. He wasn't even aware of what she was saying.

Kath came out of the bathroom. Joe knew she would be heading off to bed. He wondered if she would stop to say good-night. This usually meant that she felt all right towards him. Or whether she'd carry on past and up the stairs. She opened the door and poked in her head. 'Well, good-night,' she said. Did he detect a query in her voice? He couldn't be sure.

'Good-night,' Joe replied, and added, 'I'm sorry about this morning. I'll leave my door open tonight.'

Kath slid the door closed and he saw her reflection through the opaque glass panel as she made her way slowly up the stairs. She was walking heavily. She seemed very tired.

Joe put the milk bottles and the cat out and went into the bathroom. While he was there he got an erection. Because Kath was in a good mood, thoughts of sex crossed his mind. But then the erection went slack. Kath had cooled him off a bit over the last weeks by insisting that he left her dissatisfied more often than not. It's all very well for her to say that, Joe told himself, when most of the time she just lies there. She doesn't seem to think she has to work for it also. Kath didn't usually become interested until quite late in the piece, so that Joe found himself doing all the work. Kath never bothered, or never liked to indulge in the preliminaries that he liked. She just liked their hands to go straight to where the action was. As if there weren't other parts of their bodies that needed touching as well. He wondered, with a start, if she might like it over with as quickly as possible, like he'd heard many women did. It was one great big bore to them. Christ, surely we haven't got to that stage? he thought. Or has it always been like that with her? This left Joe feeling very uneasy.

He checked to see if the children were tucked in. The sleeping children, looking so innocent and trusting, caused him to feel a sudden pang of guilt, about not being a good provider and for not being home with them that evening. He bent over and kissed them both tenderly.

He read for a while in bed, with the radio tuned softly in the background. It wasn't long before his concentration waned. He put the marker in the book, closed it and put it on the dresser. He had read only one page. What had happened to the nights when he'd lie in bed and read an entire book? he wondered.

He switched off the light and listened to the radio for a while. Then he switched that off too. He thought he would fall asleep in no time, for he was feeling very tired. But his mind kept wandering back to sex. And soon he had an erection again. He tried to ignore it, but it stayed with him. He began to find it pleasant and it got worse. It really ached. So he began to masturbate. Slowly at first, just to take some of the tension away, but then with gathering momentum. He knew he would have to finish it now. Halfway through his penis began oozing, he could feel it wet on his fingers. He thought that his balls would be full — bursting at the seams — because it was nearly a week since he'd had sex. It would be a waste just to let it go into the palm of his hand. He felt a powerful need to share it with Kath. He got up, as he had done countless times before it seemed, and made his way to Kath's door. He felt a sense of defeat. He supposed it was because he had wanted to punish Kath for telling him that he wasn't a good lover. She had really hurt him. He wanted to punish her by denying her sex altogether.

But now, drawn against his will, he eased open the door to Kath's room. Her odour enveloped him as he stood just inside the doorway. He knew there was no turning back now. A lump caught in his throat as he quietly approached the bed.

'Kath!' he said. 'Kath!' His voice had gone suddenly hoarse and he could hardly get the words out.

The Gathering (Extract)

21. SITTING ROOM. INTERIOR.
(Pan around faces, while 1st Pakeke continues speaking to Paul and Minister.)

MINISTER: He's just quoted another old Maori saying.

PAUL: What's that?

MINISTER: A saying about the severing of the umbilical cord.

PAUL: What's he referring to?

MINISTER: I think I know what he's getting at. Just hang on a minute. I'll explain to you later.

1ST PAKEKE: (Continuing his speech.)

MINISTER: (Leaning closer to Paul) He's just said that our symbols of pride and dignity are at home. The carved houses. The sacred mountains and rivers.

PAUL: (Just nods his head)

1ST PAKEKE: (Continuing speech. He concludes and sits down.)

PAUL: What did he say at the end?

MINISTER: He finished by quoting a Maori proverb.

PAUL: What was that?

MINISTER: He said something about Man being able to scale the
highest mountains and also being able to scale the
highest waves. But that he cannot trample on the
summit or the mana of Man. Because Man is sacred.

(There is a pause of some length before 2nd Pakeke rises to speak. During
this pause the crowd is expectant.)

PAUL: (To Minister) You're going to have to explain this. If
there's anything I should know.

MINISTER: Yes, well later...

(The 2nd Pakeke is on his feet and begins his tauparapara. Paul is looking
back at Minister wondering.)

PAUL: Why are you looking like that?

MINISTER: It's all right.

PAUL: Something's wrong.

MINISTER: Wait Paul...let's see what this Pakeke says.

(The song goes on. The camera pans around to find Auntie Nowa.)

21A.

KAREN: (Referring to the song) That's beautiful.

WIKI: If you say so. Who is that lady?

KAREN: The kuia?

WIKI: Yes! Stop showing on.

137

KAREN: She knew mum when she was a kid. I think she's our great aunt.

WIKI: She's beautiful.

(The song finishes and the Pakeke breaks into speech. Outside there is the sound of a car drawing up with no muffler and the squeal of brakes. It makes a great din. The Pakeke is thrown off guard and hesitates for a moment. Glances around distracted towards the source of the noise. The rest of the crowd in the room are also distracted.) Cut to:

PAUL: Oh God! What's going on out there?

MINISTER: That was not good. These people aren't used to the disrespect. They don't like it.

21B. Cut to:

WIKI: (She has quietly got up to peer out the window. She comes back and bends down to Karen) I'll bet I know who that is.

KAREN: Who?

(But Wiki has gone out the door.)

(2nd Pakeke continues his speech.)

PAUL: (To Minister) Is he saying anything important?

MINISTER: He's saying that in death a person is taken back to his or her loved land.

(Paul is by now getting the drift of what the elders are getting at. He starts to become a little edgy.)

WIKI: (In Paul's ear) Richard's here.

PAUL: Oh... What?... With some of his mates, is he?

WIKI: Yes. There's a carload of them.

PAUL: Have they been drinking?

138

WIKI: (Not very convincing) Why do you ask that?

(The Minister has not heard this.)

MINISTER: Paul! Listen now. He's saying that the symbols...

PAUL: (To Minister) Hepi,... 'scuse me a minute. (To Wiki)
What's he want?

WIKI: Just to come in.

PAUL: Bloody hell... we've got enough problems. (To
Minister) I've gotta go.

MINISTER: Eh?

PAUL: My brother's here...hold the fort.

(He leaves. The Pakeke stops in mid-sentence, distracted by the
movement. Then continues.)

22. HALLWAY. INTERIOR.
(Paul, Richard, Mob.)

(Richard standing at doorway with four mates. Richard has his back to
Paul, looking out. We read 'Mongrel Mob — Taranaki'.)

PAUL: You're not coming in here dressed like that man.
Jesus, what took you so long anyway?

(Richard turns to him. He looks as if he's going to cry.)

RICHARD: Wiki just told me Mum's dead! Why didn't you let
me know?

PAUL: You're never in the same place long enough. I tried
to.

RICHARD: I came because I heard she was sick.

PAUL: I tried to get hold of you long ago.

RICHARD: I might've got here in time if I'd known.

139

(Pause. Richard turns away for a second.)

> PAUL: (He is upset by the hinted accusation that he had not bothered to contact Richard, and the sight of the 'Patch' is too much for him.) Christ Almighty, man, did you have to come dressed in that outfit? What the hell do you think this is? There's a lot of old people inside.

> RICHARD: Look man. I've come. But I didn't come to see you. So just lay off, aye.

> PAUL: (Loud enough to be heard in sitting room) Mum's dead. Couldn't you've shown more respect than that?

23. SITTING ROOM. INTERIOR.
(As before — without Paul.)

(2nd Pakeke has stopped talking and everybody is listening.)

> 2ND PAKEKE: (In Maori) Listen to that e hine. Your children fighting. Fighting at your tangi. They don't love you like we back home love you. . . .

(Reaction on Karen.)

> 2ND PAKEKE: (In Maori) . . . so come home with us e hine.

(Karen doesn't know what to do. She starts to rise as if to go out — but the Minister signals her to stay. The argument continues out in the hall. Minister himself gets up and discreetly leaves.)

24. HALLWAY. INTERIOR.
(Paul, Richard, Mob, Lou has now joined them, visitors who are unable to fit into sitting room, Minister who now joins them.)

> RICHARD: I'm only here five minutes and you lean on me. And *you* talk about Mum being dead.

> PAUL: Well, couldn't you've got into something different. Just this once?

(Richard turns away for a second.)

MEMBER: (Mumbling to Richard) We're with you, Raho.

(Richard turns back to Paul.)

RICHARD: These are my clothes man. (He goes to enter house.
            Paul blocks the way.)

PAUL: You change your clothes first. You're not coming into
            this house like that. I told you there're old people in
            there.

LOU: (Appearing behind Paul) I'm with you, Paul.

RICHARD: If this wasn't Mum's funeral. I'd smash your bloody
            face.

PAUL: Look man. . . .

RICHARD: (Yells) Wiki! Come here!

WIKI: (Stepping from doorway to sitting room) I'm here
            Richie. What's the matter?

RICHARD: Have a word to big brother here, will you.

WIKI: Paul, you're being stupid. What about Mum?

PAUL: Look at him.

WIKI: (Topping him) That's Richard! (Quietly) Paul, lay off
            him just for once. For our sakes. For Mum's sake.
            These people in here might be more broadminded
            than you.

PAUL: No. . . .

WIKI: (To Richard) Come on, Richie. Come in.

RICHARD: (Angry now. Spits to one side) Ah, stuff him!

WIKI: Come on Richie, don't be stupid. (She pulls at him.)

141

PAUL: That's right, back your precious brother up. You're both alike anyway. Why don't you go out and stand in the bloody rain with him too.

(Wiki slaps Paul.)

PAUL: (Infuriated) You bloody bitch... (He goes to slap her back. Richard grabs him. Paul tries to swing at Richard. Misses. Richard grabs Paul. They wrestle around in crowded hallway. Richard's mates step up.)

(Lou comes galloping up through crowd. Scattering people. He tries to step between Paul and Mob.)

RICHARD: Don't you ever lay a hand... on Wiki again... Paul... or by Jesus, I'll...

PAUL: You might be big news with your mates, Richard.... But I can still take you.... any bloody time... I like.

(Lou stands in between Paul and Mob, threateningly.)

LOU: The first one steps up here'll cop it.

(Paul and Richard are struggling a little way in corridor. Wiki is trying to break Paul and Richard apart. The Minister arrives on scene.)

MINISTER: What are you fellows up to?

DAPHNEY: (She and Reta have come from kitchen on hearing commotion) For God's sake, Paul, I thought you had more sense than that. This is your mother's funeral.

RICHARD: (Over his shoulder to his mates) Cool it, you guys. This is my fight.... between big brother.... and me....

MINISTER: (To Paul) Take it easy Paul. Your brother has a right to be here. He's her son too.

DAPHNEY: (To Paul quietly) They can hear you in the sitting room.

142

PAUL: Look he.. . .

DAPHNEY: I don't care. What must they think. Go back inside and listen. I think it's important.

MINISTER: It is, Paul. You must know what has been said.

(Minister, Paul, go back into sitting room.)

WIKI: Come on Richie. You come through to the kitchen.

RICHARD: Where's Mum?

DAPHNEY: They've still got her at the hospital.

RICHARD: Ah! (He hesitates for a while, not sure what to do or say. Then he turns to his mates) Come on you guys.

(They all traipse through towards the kitchen. People make way for them, a little apprehensively.)

MOB MEMBER: (To Lou in passing) Some other time wanker.

LOU: Just name it, mate. You and me.

2ND MOB
MEMBER: (To Wiki) You got a beer out there?

RETA: We've got a cup of tea.

(There is a groan from Mob members. Lou tries to follow.)

RETA: We'll be all right Lou. Might be better if you stayed away.

LOU: You sure?

RETA: Yes.. . . Just keep an eye on Paul.

25. SITTING ROOM. INTERIOR.
(As before. . . without Wiki, Paul, Minister and Lou.)

(The Pakeke is speaking. Karen is looking lost on her own. Enter Paul,

Minister. Paul notices Karen and signals her that he's sorry. Karen moves quietly round room to stand with her hand reassuringly on his shoulder.)

MINISTER: (Picking up the threads of what the Pakeke was saying before the interruption) He was saying that the symbols of a person's status calls for his or her return to the mountains of their birth-place. He made reference to a chasm in the mountain.

ROWLEY HABIB: NGA PITIROIRANGI (1935; Ngati Tuwharetoa) was born at Oruanui and educated at Te Aute College and Ardmore Teachers' College (where be began to write). For two-and-a-half years he was a foreman for a scrub-cutting gang which consisted mainly of members from the Black Power and Mongrel Mob gangs. He lives in Wellington and has three children.

In 1975, with Hone Tuwhare, he took part in the Maori Land March from Te Reinga to Parliament. Since then he has become closely involved with Te Matakite o Aotearoa (the Maori Land Rights movement) and was one of the seventeen arrested on the Raglan golf course and jailed during a protest in 1978.

Rowley's stories, poems and articles have appeared in *Landfall, Mate, NZ Listener, Te Ao Hou, Arena, Cave, Te Maori, Te Awatea, The Sunday Times, Poet International, Ocarina (India), N.Z. Approach to English (U.K.),* and the *World Anthology of Contemporary Poets.* His stories have been published in *Contemporary Maori Writing, Short Stories by New Zealanders, One and Two, My New Zealand, Junior* and *Senior,* and *Ten Modern New Zealand Writers.* Together with Don Selwyn and Earl Spencer he wrote the script for the Tihe Mauriora television series in 1974.

He has been the recipient of two Literary Fund grants and in 1975 was the second person to receive the Maori Purposes Fund Board writer's award. In 1977, with Richard Turner, he made a film called *Ka Tutaki Nga Awa Rua (Two Rivers Meet)* on contemporary Maori poets. In the same year he founded, with Jim Moriarty, Te Ika a Maui Players (at that time the only Maori theatre group in the country). Since then the Players have performed his *Death of the Land* in most of the major centres of the North Island. A radio version of the play was twice broadcast on the National Programme in 1979 and later televised. A series of his short stories, *Tamariki,* has also been broadcast by Radio New Zealand, and he is currently working on a new play. Collections of his short stories and his poems are in preparation.

In 1979, *The Gathering,* Rowley's second television play (from which an extract has been taken for this anthology) was screened on New Zealand television.

Haare Williams

Go East Of Your Mountain

Go East of your mountain—

Go East of your dream
And let the light
Spin your yarn
And give form to shapes

Go East of the totara trees
Leave soft and silent shades
Like the drifting colours
Of a summer breeze

Go East of your mountain
Where fools and angels
Spend their odds
Motionless in time

Go East of the Penrods
And take a long drink
In the distilled springs
Of your voiceless ancestors

   'Ka rere nga kirehe
   O te rangi ki tona
   Wai unu ai
   E kore e mimiti'

Go East to the foot of the mountain
He founded himself a Home
Rest there — nothing said
Rest there — nothing said

Go East of the oily slickness
See a swelling richness syphoned
To Father a dying majority
And wait — to see the water, yet

145

Go East to your yesterday
My light sees your tomorrow
Today — I'm gone
My night sees your troubles

Go East to my fortress in the mountain
And there look through my mountain
Again you'll see the soldiers in the field
And this time the advance guards are real

Go East of your mountain—

E Noho Koutou

E noho koutou
Anei ta matau koha
Ko Tane Mahuta, ko te Ariki
O te Waonui-a-Tane
Kia tiria iho ki konei
Taku take
Taketake

'He kauri tonu' e ai ta tetahi
'He ngakau marohirohi tona
Tu te Ao, tu te Po
Ki a ia whakatupuranga'

'Kao' e ai ki ta te Kuia Whenua
'Ka pumau ia
Hei ona kura tonu
He pito i tiria
He aho tapu
He tohu mauri
He pihinga tetekura

Na aitua
Takoto kau te papako
He hokinga hinengaro ki te pito
O te oneone ki te oneone
Hinga atu ana he toa

146

Ara mai ra he toa
Roaka ana mai, na Papatuanuku
Hoki ana te mauri

Hoki ana ki te iti
Ki tona whaea ki a Papa
E takoto nei'

He kupu i rangona
Ka tiaho te marama
Ae ra
Kua tapu te whenua
Kua pumau te aroha e

Totara Tree

Before leaving
A totara was gifted
To the marae
To be planted
Symbolising our roots there

'A totara' said one
'Has heart
It'll be here for centuries'

'No' replied Whenua
'It'll be here forever
As part of the land
Like the burial of the pito
The sacred umbilical cord
It is part of the living soul
The planting is the emergence
Of a new life

At death
The body and soul are separated
The soul returns to the pito
And the body to the land
Life is born and reborn
In the land

Mauri — lifegiving principle
Abides in the womb of Papa
The land'

With these words
The meaning came
Land is sacred
Communal
Eternal
Whoever understood its sacredness
Could never wilfully violate it
Nor, forget it

To destroy it
Is to destroy a history
A people and a future

We planted
The totara tree
The ground freshly turned
Reminded us of a burial
Placing there a part of us
Our umbilical link
With people, land and
Ancestors.

E Ngata E

E ngata e
he poturi
to nuku atu
to kuare
hoki
kaore koe
e mohio

Engari
ko nga mea ngaro
me te kanapa
huarahi
ko koe anake

e taea
te inu

Koru

Behind the silent curve
Stands another man
Searching for beauty
Searching for truth

Searching for feelings
In the emptiness of Te Kore
Through the shadows of Te Po
'Til morning has broken

Koru designs
The corridors of the minds
And the rafters
Of the womb

Condensed and distilled
In tears and laughter
Welling deep within
The flowing springs

The seed uncurling
Sliding shoreward
On the sea's curve riding
The embryo of Aroha

   'Kei tua i te Koru
   He tangata
   He tangata
   He tangata'

Behind the silent curve
Stands another man
Neither brown nor white
But both .. .. ..

Tihei Mauri ora!

Kaponga

Titiro
ki te rito
o tenei
kaponga

E whakahihiko nei
i tona
Mauri
mai i te pokapu

He pikopiko
e raranga haere ana
i nga puawai
o tona pu-manawa

Ko ana
whakakikoranga
ko tona oranga
ka puawai
te ira tangata
ki te ao
ka kitea

Mokopuna

Silence
in the wharemoe
except for a small
boy

his kuia
humming
a lullaby from
yesterday

her story
in music and verse
echoes returning from the
shadows

Her work
and love
moves through her
song

and from her face
to her
expectant
mokopuna

like a river
moving down
to the sea, his
love

'Tell me another story'
'Aue, to hoha'
her thoughts sifting through
memories

She pushed back
her sleepiness
and the shadows
'Nanny . . . . .'

'Shhh . . . . .'
she continued
her mokopuna now long
asleep

Stride

My Maori side
Is intimately written
In stories of canoes,
Sailings, drifting,
Fishing, taniwha, whirlpools
Storms, and drownings
Privations, loneliness
Discoveries, barren places
And wilder places

The sea's unrelenting pull
In the blood of my ancestors

The sea
Scattering the seed of Hawaiki
Across Te Moana-nui-a-Kiwa
Across the unkind tides
Straddled by Kupe and Ngahue

My Maoriness
Taku taha Maori
Is rooted there — in the sea
My bones lie there
Not in the summits
Of the mountains

The swell is but a ripple
Which began in
Hawaiki nui
Hawaiki roa
Hawaiki pamamao
Its location in history
Yielding only to the sea's
Timelessness

Where is the song of Tangaroa
Once heard on a thousand beaches

Why then my people
This distaste
For the voyaging spirit

Have you become cultural seagulls
Lulled only to clean the coastline
Feeding on insubstantial flotsam
Fringing the sea's lure
Of intense meaning?

Why

HAARE WILLIAMS (1936; Te Aitanga-a-Mahaki, Rongowhakaata) was born at
Te Karaka, near Gisborne. He has been a lecturer at Auckland Teachers' College

and a Research Fellow at the University of Waikato. At present he is the manager of
Te Reo o Aotearoa for Radio New Zealand. As a writer, Haare is a product of the
Maori Artists' and Writers' Society which began in 1973. He was chairman of the
society for five years and edited its journal, *Koru*. His work has appeared in *Pacific
Quarterly Moana*, *Koru*, *Te Maori*, *Te Ao Hou* and *Marae*. Haare published a
collection of poems, *Karanga*, in 1981.

Bruce Stewart

Boy

I was five. My father waded the bush-edged river. Bent double. Carrying a
stag. Sweat, blood. Soaked his black singlet. Steamed in the frosty air.
  'Daddy, you got one. It's big Daddy. How many shots did it take?'
  'One.'
  'Can I carry your rifle?'
  'No, s'all right.'
  ''Cos I'm too little, eh Daddy.'
  'Yes.'
  'It was cold waiting for you, Daddy.'
  'Told you to stay home.'
  We drove home in silence. With me, he always seemed silent. Even sad.
I'd watch his muscles split a totara log into posts. Or stand behind a lonely
fence. While he broke a young horse. He never cuddled me like Mum.
Never called me 'Boy'.
  After my first day at school. I ran home crying.
  'Mummy, the kids keep pointing at me and calling me Maori. Maori.'
  She cuddled me all over.
  'I'm not a Maori, am I Mummy?'
  'Yes you are, boy, 'cause Mummy's a Maori.'
  She had crying eyes.
  I ran to my back bedroom. Sobbing. Father came home.
  'What's wrong with you?'
  'Nothing...'
  'Nothing. Crying for nothing.'
  'Leave him, Frank. The children were cruel.'
  'Cruel, eh. Be cruel back. Punch them between the eyes.'
  'Frank... Please...'
  'Frank...'
  'Sit up for y'r tea.'
  'I couldn't.' I sobbed. Quietly. I could hear them arguing louder and

louder. Mum broke crying. Father's anger came into my room. I was scared. Tried to get under the bed. Started hitting me. Hard. Mum, though little, pushed him aside. Covered me. Slept with me all night.

The next grey morning I'd made up my mind.

'C'mon boy. Get dressed, it's getting late.'

'I'm not going to school.'

'Yes you are.'

She dressed me. Washed my face with a rough flannel.

Her warm hand pulling my cold stubborn feet through puddles. Three steps to one.

'Mummy knows how you feel, boy.'

'You don't.'

'Please, boy, you are a Maori.'

'I'm not. Father's not.'

'Mummy will teach you things. You'll see.'

School had started. Mum pulled me right into the silent classroom. She whispered to the teacher. Teacher nodded. Whispered back. The kids stared. I stood behind Mum.

That day, a boy called me Maori pig. I hit him, with a milk bottle, between the eyes. Tried to pull his yellow hair out. The teacher strapped me, in front of the class. I didn't cry.

I was the only Maori in our little school. Failed in primer three.

John Jones became my friend. We walked home together.

'My sister's gone bad.'

'Did she steal something.'

'No. She's gone with a Maori shearing gang.'

His mother asked me inside. They had a deep freeze and a radiogram.

'Would you like a piece of cream sponge?'

'Yes, thank you, Mrs Jones.'

'Does your mother make your clothes?'

'Yes. She makes them all.'

'Lemon drink.'

'Yes, thank you. The sponge was nice.'

'Does your mother talk about her own people?'

'No, she doesn't.'

'She has no need, really, she's happy here.'

'Yes, she is.'

'Your father likes a clean house, doesn't he?'

'My mother's very clean, Mrs Jones.'

'You're a well-mannered boy.'

'Thank you.'

'It's hard to tell with you. You're almost like one of us.'

'Thank you, Mrs Jones.'

She was nice to me.

I had secrets. Used to wash my hands and face with a scrubbing brush. Sneaked some of Mum's white vanishing cream. Rub it hard on my hands and face. Never sat in the sun without a hat. I buried a baking powder tin in the garden. It was full of money, saving to buy my own farm. Couldn't help wetting my bed. Dad said I was lazy. Doctor told Mum I'd grow out of it... in time... When we stayed at relations Mum brought my rubber sheet.

My father's family are farmers. On sale days we'd go to town. I'd see them at the sale yards, talking to their friends. I'd run to them.

'Hullo, uncle. Hullo, auntie.'

'Er... hullo Bruce...'

They never seemed pleased. Always in a hurry. Often frowned a little.

All relations went to grandma's farm for Christmas. Their big cars slowly filled the car park. Uncle Joe was an All Black. He'd come in carrying his son, Jim, like a football.

'You've got a budding All Black there, Joe.'

'Yes, Frank. He's comin' up. Took him trainin' the other day. Went like a bomb.'

'He's a well-made boy, going to be tall.'

Aunt Hilda was quite posh. Everyone in their family had silver serviette rings, with their own initials engraved.

'I say, Frank, You're looking well!' (Her way of saying fat.)

'Feel good, Hilda. What'll it be? Whisky or beer.'

'Sherry, if there's any. Dry.'

'Bloody good price for wool, Frank.'

'I'll drink to that.'

'Me too. I'll drink to that.'

No-one talked to me, just a quick hullo. Smoke, laughter, and shyness. Drove me to a dark corner to sit with Mum.

We'd go for walks. Watch crawlies in the stream behind the cow bail. One day we followed the stream to a small valley. Shimmering green. Limestone cliffs encircled like a giant pipe organ.

'It's a fairy glade, boy.'

'Yes, Mummy.'

'This is our very own fairy glade.'

We watched the upside-down trees in the lazy river. Swam naked.

'Trees are people. Birds are fairies,' she'd say.

We'd watch fat pigeons sunning. Hug our magic rimu tree from opposite sides. Our fingers barely touched.

'Listen, the soil breathes.'

'What's the most important thing in the whole world, Mummy?'

'The soil, the sky.'

'Why, Mummy?'

'They are mother earth and father sky. Without them nothing could live.'

It started raining. We held hands. We sang. Our fairy glade sang too.

'You are my sunshine'. . . . .*my sunshine*
               my sunshine
                        my sunshine

We walked home. Catching the rain in our mouths. Still holding hands. Still singing.

'Remember these things I tell you, boy.'

'I will, Mummy. I will.'

Once at the beach. I saw Maoris eating sea eggs. Thought they were dirty. Didn't say. Kept everything to myself.

Mum helped me with my school work. Started doing well. At football, too, scored many of our team's tries. The parents and teachers cheered. I wanted to be an All Black, like Uncle Joe. I was bigger than the others. No-one called me names. Some of them shared their play lunch with me. Stopped wetting my bed. Worked hard at everything. In my dreams I planned. Had to win, especially against my cousins. Learnt to know people's tastes, by their dress, or speech. I made them like me. Even telling lies. Didn't have close friends though. Except Mum. She was sick most of the time now.

During a storm. On my own at the fairy glade. I found our magic rimu tree. Lying down. Dead. I ran home. Wailing with the trees.

'Why, Mummy. Why did the sky kill our tree.?'

'The sky didn't kill him. He was old. Go back. Look. Close to the ground. You'll see.'

I did. Baby rimu trees. Hundreds. The valley sang.

I started to learn with Mum's help. Slowly I began to see some truths about father sky, mother earth.

'You'll never know everything, boy.'

'Why, Mummy?'

'No-one does. You'll just learn enough to love them.'

'I hate Daddy.'

'One day, when you learn. You'll love him, too.'

'I never will.'

'Love makes love, boy.'

'Does it, Mummy.'

'Yes, boy, love. . . makes. . . love. . .'

I hated meal times. Father hung his razor strop over the chair.

'You make more noise than a pig.'

'Don't you ever bath?'

I wasn't allowed to speak at the table.

At seventeen I'd nearly finished college. There was to be a prize-giving ceremony. The students were to invite their parents. Mum knew I'd won three certificates.

'I'm proud of you, boy.'

'Thanks Mum.'

'University next.'

'Looks like it.'

'Better get ready. We'll be late.'

I went to my room. Hating myself. Swallowed mustard. Rushed to the bathroom. Sick.

'What's wrong, boy.'

'Sick, Mum.'

She saw the vomit. She knew. Didn't say, though.

'Better go to bed, boy.'

She tucked me in. Sat on the edge of my bed. Brown eyes brimming. Body tired. Couldn't drag me through the puddles now. Bottom lip started quivering. Cuddled me.

'I understand, boy.... I understand.'

She turned out the light. Closed the door. I lay in my vomit.

Mum went to hospital again. We visited her the day before the operation. As we left she held out her hand.

'Stay a minute, boy.'

'Can't Mum. Promised to meet John.'

'Please...boy...'

'Can't, Mum, I'll come back tomorrow. Promise.'

Her back hid her tears.

Phone ringing. Two a.m. Rush. Hospital. Ward sister met us.

'Are you boy?'

'Yes...'

'Before she went. She kept calling for you.'

Numb days. Followed numb days... Empty house without heart. Apron on its hook. People blurs. Coming and going. Offering soulless hands and distant voices slurred. Wishing me 'Hard luck. Sincere condolences. Deepest sympathy.'

Aunt Hilda. Tweed skirt and pearls.

'Be brave, time will heal. Life must go on.'

No tears in this loneliness. No-one to share.

Through the mocking whisky fumes. And prattle-chatter my Mum called from her bedroom.

157

'Boy.'

'Yes, Mum.'

The prattle stopped.

'Make me a cup of tea please.'

'OK. Won't be a minute.'

No-one stirred while I made tea. They stopped me before I opened the door. I fought them. Swore. Started throwing their bottles through the window. Finally, tackled from all sides. Broken. Like a young horse I once saw.

I went to our fairy glade. I sang.

'. . . my sunshine away'. . . . . *my sunshine away*

                      sunshine away

                                    sunshine away

                                          away. . .

I lay down beside our dead rimu tree. I stayed there all night. The valley wailed. I didn't cry.

In the morning I went home. They'd been looking for me. I heard someone say, 'Her relations are coming.'

'I didn't know she had any. She never said. . .'

'How did they know?'

'Maoris are like that. They just seem to know.'

'Where are they from.'

'Up north somewhere.'

Two black shiny cars stopped at the front gate.

'Christ. Look at the taxis. More money than sense.'

'Wouldn't think so by their clothes.'

The women were dressed in black. Men in working clothes. Worn, but clean. I was frightened. For a long minute no-one went to meet them. If Mum. . . If Mum was here she'd be rushing down the path. . . She always did. . .

I went slowly. They walked towards me too. The woman in front said: 'Tena koe. Boy.'

She cuddled me all over. . . . just like Mum. . . crying. . . kissing. . . she spoke in Maori. . . softly calling my mother's name. . . . rocking me too and fro. . . I started to cry too. Years of tears. . . mixing with hers. . . . all over our faces. . . . each of them did the same. The men pressed their noses to mine. Hugging me. I'd never met these people. Yet they were sharing my lonely grief. It was as if Mum had sent them. They asked if they could take Mum back to her family.

'No.'

'They asked if they could spend some time with her alone.

'No.'

They spoke of her as if she were still alive.

It was raining at the cemetery. Mum's people in sharp contrast to the dark suits. Umbrellas. Black ties. Heads bowed but erect. Stiff tearlessness.

Mum's sister, Hine, held both my hands. Uncle Heta spoke in Maori to Mum. He placed a greenstone tiki in the coffin. Aunt Hilda raised a haughty eyebrow to Uncle Joe. Mum's people sang in Maori. Dad's people shuffled uncomfortably. Uncle Heta put his arm over my shoulders. Felt strong, warm. Like *sunshine*.

I didn't hear the minister.

I saw Mum and I
swimming naked
through upside-down trees
hugging our friend
Rimu
talking to fat pigeon-fairies
holding hands, singing
while the rain
made our brown faces shiny . . . . *faces shiny*
                     faces shiny
                                       faces shiny

Papa

I stayed all night at the cemetery with Mum. Dad's people tried to get me to go home. Mum's people stood around, they didn't say anything, they fumbled with the fresh earth at times, I think they knew I wanted to be alone with Mum, they left before dark. It was warm lying next to Mum, the night was a blanket, some stars zoomed across the sky. There was so much to talk about, about school, about our fairy glade, about the gardens, about the chookies, cats, dogs, and our birds. Mostly I was worried about what I should do next.

I feel so young, Mum. I know I've done well at sport and I'm tall and all that, but really I'm younger than the other boys my age. Like, most of them have girlfriends, and they shave. Mr Matthews tells everyone I've got a lovely soprano voice. I hate it when he says that, Mum, because I'm sure the bass singers laugh at me. I haven't seen them laugh, but they duck behind the tenors so's I can't see them. The truth is though, Mum, I love singing the solo bits with the whole choir behind me. But I won't anymore. . . not singing soprano, I won't. And there's another thing too, Mum, I'm shy of girls, when they come close to me my face goes all red.

159

But it was warm on the earth next to Mum. Even when the sky started to flicker, and the change to the morning was warm. But as the blue paled, I felt a bit unhappy, it was like someone was taking off my blankets.

What now, Mum? I feel so rickety, what am I going to do? For a moment, just for a moment I looked up... there was a skylark... high above me.

She hung in a blue sky, singing tweedle songs. I listened, just as Mum taught me to listen at the fairy glade. It's true you know, what Mum told me, if you listen really hard, and if you want to, birds can tell you things. The skylark did, it was like Mum talking to me, telling me she'd always be with me. And to do what I thought was best.

When I got home I cut the back hedge; Mum had been at me for ages. I cut a big pile of kindling wood too. For the next week I did lots of jobs around home. I didn't feel like going back to school, but I did because I knew Mum would like that. My form teacher, Mr Bull, stopped me on the way in, he had a clipping from the funeral notices.

Simpson, on behalf of the school, please accept our sincere condolences for the recent and, I might say, untimely passing away of your mother er, ah... he quickly looked at my Mum's name on the clipping... er, Mrs Pare Simpson. Thank you Mr Bull, I said and sat down at my desk in the back corner of the class. We all knew Mr Bull's Second World War off by heart. He'd brought his photo album to school again. He was a tank commander.

Now here's a shot of myself with my tank. Here's another one with some of my company, you can see the tanks in the background. Now here's another one showing all the tanks on the move — you can just make out my head sticking above the gun turret. We were on our way to knock out Jerry. I might say, they were rugged days. We were chasing Jerry across the desert. It was cold, at nights we'd knock the top off a forty-gallon drum of petrol and set it on fire to keep us warm. By day it was hot, by God it was hot. We ran out of water once, but luckily we had the tankers full of beer. The Horis loved it. They wallowed in it, even washed in it.

Everyone in the class roared except me. It was like saying my Mum washes in beer. I knew my face was red, and I was kind of numb when I stood.

You are always going on about Maoris Mr Bull, I yelled.

Everyone stopped laughing. I could feel them staring at me. Some of them were whispering. Mr Bull's face went white and he took a while to answer. Sit down Simpson. I'm afraid you're over-reacting, though it's understandable in the circumstances. I'd like you to know Simpson that one of my aunties married a Maori. He was a well-known chief.

But I wouldn't sit down. It was like I was standing up for my Mum and

160

myself for the first time, and it felt good. My face was still red, I was still numb as I stomped down the aisle, stood in front of Mr Bull's desk.

It's not just this story Mr Bull, you're always picking on Maoris, why? Why do you?

Mr Bull jumped up and leaned across his desk, our faces were inches apart. You've gone too far this time Simpson. Leave the room and report to the headmaster. I'll be there in a minute. On my way out the class sniggered again. Mr Bull's face was smirky-looking. It was those faces that set me going, I was so mad I wanted to smash them all. Those smirky faces, I'd always seen them from my desk in the rear corner of the classroom. I threw a box full of chalk and some books at the class. I threw a duster, it bounced off Mr Bull's head, I felt so good. Mr Bull rushed me. I grabbed his blackboard pointer and swung it as hard as I could, it whacked him fair in the guts. He doubled up groaning but he couldn't have been hurt too bad, because by the time I was at the end of the corridor he was setting his boys out to catch me. I was flying because I was scared, and I felt good somehow. If I got caught the headmaster would make me feel a fool in front of the whole school. He wouldn't understand me, he never does. By the time I got home I'd run off all my angriness, I was trying to work out what to do next.

Some of Mum's photos and pieces of driftwood were gone. When Father came home I asked him what he had done with them.

I put the photographs in the top cupboard, I threw the driftwood out.

You got no right to throw out those things, you know Mum likes them. He stared at me as if I were simple or something.

It's about time you woke up young man, your mother's DEAD.

She's not, I know she's not. She'll always be with me. She said so herself. You're the one to wake up, not me.

I thought he was going to bowl me, but he didn't. He shook his head and went outside to his car, I followed him.

I'm leaving home.

You leaving home, that's a joke, you wouldn't last five minutes in the real world. You're a dreamer mate, and you're still a fat puppy. Mind you, I left home when I was thirteen. Any rate y'got compulsory military training coming up, it'll knock a bit of sense into you. Leavin' home, he chuckled. He drove off.

I found the driftwood and photos. I put them back the way Mum had them. Two cops and Mr Bull banged hard on the door. I slammed the door in their faces much faster than I opened it. I ran straight out the back way across the paddocks into the swamp and hid there until they were gone. I sneaked back, grabbed my bank book, went the back way to town. I felt good, I'd never been like that, I was always shy and quiet. Now I knew I had to leave home, seemed like my mind was being made up for me, it wasn't the same any more.

I bought a pack, sleeping bag, boots, woollen bush gear, and as much food as I could carry. I took off to the Tararua mountains.

For years I'd been looking at those mountains. It was as if there was something there, I don't know what it was, the snow, the bush, the bigness; it was that, and more.

I kept off the roads so as I wouldn't be seen. I kept thinking the cops and Mr Bull would be looking for me everywhere. My pack was heavy. A lot had happened in one day, I was tired and I lay down for a while in some shivery grass. I felt good though, like you must feel when you climb out of a wrecked car. As I lay there looking at the sky, the skylark came again.

Keep going, she said, keep going, and then she just seemed to fade out of sight.

I made it over the foothills by night. I camped beside a river, under some totara. I lit a big fire, because I was a bit scared, a bit lonely too. I sat on a log and swung my tea billy. I swung the billy lots of times, that night. Night time was the worst because I kept getting lonely as lonely. Sitting out there away from everybody. I was a bit frightened too. Frightened because I felt too young.

I thought about Mr Bull and the cops, about school. About our home, and father, and what it would be like if we were all together again. It was as though the whole world was against me and I was wishing the skylark would come back and say something; but skylarks don't come out at night. In the morning I pushed up through wet ferns. The bush was thick, it was hard to see where I was going, I knew if I kept going up I'd get somewhere.

At times the bush blanket thinned. I saw the mountains. They looked massive. Rearing out of the earth above me, like wild horses. There was one great high one. It was like a giant unbroken stallion. They were a morning blue colour. Then there was the quiet. It was a deep, far-away quiet. Everything was massive. All those peaks, somehow I knew I had to climb them — especially that wild unbroken one, the highest one.

I decided to call him 'Maori', because he reminded me of a horse my father couldn't break. In fact, Maori ran right over him, smashed some of his ribs. When he was better he stock-whipped Maori, nearly killed him. Never broke him though. He called him Maori.

It wasn't so lonely in the day time. There was so much to see, fantails flickering, red flowers, white flowers, and greenness, everywhere there was greenness. Now and again I'd stop and listen, the deep far-away quiet made me feel little. It was just about dark when I found an old hut. It had *The Whare* carved on a squeaky door. I cooked up some food. I sat on a silent log by the fire, listening to the river chatter. A mouse flicked across the corner of my eye. The more I thought about it, the more I smiled. Now if a mouse dawdled to the centre of the hut and lay down for a snooze, that'd really be something. I made up my mind to be friends with the mouse. Little things seemed so important, things I hadn't noticed before.

That night I dreamed about my posh Aunt Hilda, she was wearing Mum's greenstone tiki, everyone liked it. They were saying it was valuable. Someone offered her a lot of money and she sold it. That's my mother's greenstone, I shouted, but I couldn't stop them. They couldn't hear me. They kept on talking as if I wasn't there. I sulked and sat at my desk in the corner of the classroom.

I woke up, the hut was dark. For a long time I didn't know where I was. Then I heard the river chatter, the mouse flicked across the corners. I was too frightened to sleep, I got the fire going again.

The next day there was a lot to do and it was good; being busy was good, it kept my mind off the lonely things. I chopped firewood, and caught crawlies and eels, picked watercress. Nothing seemed more important than to climb some of those peaks, those wild horses. Above the hut, a rocky knob stuck out on its own. I wanted to climb it, even though it was late in the day, I took off.

It was a lot further up than I thought, I slipped and slid and went up the wrong way a few times, but I got there. It was nearly dark, but it didn't matter. Standing on top of that rocky knob I felt bigger. It wasn't a high knob at all, the Wild Horses peaks were a long way further up. But it was the highest peak I'd ever been on... and I'd climbed it, on my own. I did feel bigger. Everything was big, especially the silence. There was a close silence and a far-away silence. I stayed there till it got dark. Going up it felt good, going up and up and up. I got puffed and thought my legs wouldn't go on anymore, but I kept going.

Keep going, keep going, that's all I said to myself, trying to keep a rhythm as I plonked down each foot. Sometimes it was keeeeeeeep... gooooooooiiiing, and sometimes I was so puffed I couldn't say it — just thought it. I had to climb it. I wasn't strong like all those other Pakeha boys at school. They always seemed strong.

Standing on top of that 'wild pony' I felt stronger. Especially when I looked way down and saw the knob I'd climbed two days before.

I looked up, there was another higher peak. In the next few weeks, I had not time for anything else. I was breaking in those Wild Horses. 'Nelly' was easy. 'Mustang' was a rugged, steep, rock-faced one, he nearly broke me. 'Rocky' was a tricky one, I got a bit lost, I had to spend all night out and it took me two days to get over it. But I felt stronger and stronger. The higher I went the stronger I got.

The cops and Mr Bull and those posh Pakeha kids in my classroom, they were way down below me. Father went on about me being a dreamer and a fat puppy. I'd like to see him climb Maori. His head was going right into the clouds. But I knew what his head looked like by heart.

I slept well, I was away a long time before morning could see. Five deer chased down into a steep gorge. I didn't go fast. I kept to the main ridge and kept a steady 'Keep going, keep going, keep going, keep going'.

It was a clear day. A hot, hot day. Near the bush edge the trees were really stunted and I'd got a bit off the main ridge. I had to get down on my belly and wriggle through. The trees kept me down. They were trying to stop me from getting through. I hated it, got mad with them and I pushed and smashed branches off. I wasn't getting anywhere very much and I was covered in cuts and scratches. I was using up a lot of energy. I must have fought my way back to the main ridge because I landed on a track. I knew then I'd been struggling for nothing, there was a well-worn track. It had been made by the deer.

Through the stunted trees, I crashed out onto the tussock. Wild with myself because I'd used up so much energy. The track must've been only about five paces to my right all the time. It took me a long time to get my breath back. It wasn't just getting my breath back — it was getting my fire back. It was hard to overcome the hollow in my guts.

By the time I got cracking again, the sun was bouncing off the bare rock. It was hot. It was hard going. 'Keeeeep gooooiiiing, keeeeeep gooooiiiing.' Plod, plod, my singlet was wet through with sweat. I could hardly suck in enough air to keep my legs going. I was dry, all that sweat and nothing to drink and it was hot. Before I got to the top I could see the head above me. Tried to go faster but my legs wouldn't answer. I started getting ahead of my legs and that made me worse. As soon as I hit the top I stripped off my clothes, hung them over a rock. Stood naked and breathless all in one movement. It took me a long time to get my breath back. I wanted to collapse but I didn't. It was a complete victory I wanted... I didn't want the Maori to see me collapsing, on the finishing line. So I stood there, tottering. Slowly things started to get back into focus.

There was layer upon layer of ruggedness. Patches of wet rock glittering in the sun. Far below rivers winked their way to a green lake. Fuzziness hung low over the towns. From my high place I could see it all. I was above everything. All those wild horses. I'd conquered them. No wonder the skylark said I was doing right and told me to keep going. Of everything I could see, I was the highest. I looked down at my naked body. I wasn't a fat puppy anymore. I had a body like a man. I'd conquered Maori. Me, Boy, I'd done it. I raised both arms above my head, hands stretched right out and bellowed as loud as I could, I'm king, I'm king, I'm king, I'm king. It echoed back off all the rock faces. All those wild mountains shouted back at me, king, king, king, king, king, king, king.

164

I tried again in my new deep voice, but it didn't echo as much so I changed back to my high voice.

Look at me Mum.... Mum... Mum... Mum.

Look how high I am.... high... high... high.

I'm king, mum.... king... king... king.

Look at my new body.... new body... new body....

I stayed there raving, letting my hands slide right over my slimness to my toes and back again. Listening to the deep, far away quiet, and the close quiet. Night covered me. A warm blanket. I lay on the earth. I stayed all night on top of Maori.

Broken Arse

The first day Henry came into the Can, we could hear him cracking funnies and whistling all the way down the wing. Even while he was being stripped and even while they shore off his yellow hair, gave him a number, a well-pissed mattress, his boob blues — he still raved on. He lined up for scoff, tall; you could hear him even when his mouth was full of tucker.

'Hey man, she's a far-out pad. More like a hotel. It IS a hotel. When you think about it, it IS a hotel.'

And he laughed till the snot came out of his nose. He was a big man with a big laugh and made me feel good. I could see everybody's face spark up a bit. It was easy to see he was a country boy, trying to sound heavy, but you couldn't help liking him.

'She's sweet here, buddies, very sweet. Free keep, plus they pay me missus a wage. I'll tell yer she's a sweet one, buddies, a very sweet one.'

Tu and I were in the same slot. We'd come in together. He was the Kingpin. Everyone liked him. He always checked the new inmates out. After we'd finished our scoff we stopped by Henry's slot. He was hanging his boob gear on the nails behind the door. He was making his bed on the bottom bunk. He stopped for a bit when he saw his blankets were ripped and patched; his towel too was made up of four old towels. But he laughed again and poked his head through a ripped blanket.

'An' what's more, this patchwork stuff is big deal outside buddies, yeer big deal.'

He played a photo of his missus a bit like a trump card. She looked like one of those flimsy girls you see in the big cities, one of those girls with lots of smelly stuff on her sad-looking face. Didn't seem like Henry's sort of girl but he looked at the photo as if she was some kind of a star or something.

Tu couldn't take his randy eyes off the photo.

'You got a spunky missus Bud.'

'Oh. . .Tina-Marie you mean?' He tried to look surprised. 'She's not too bad — fuckin' good in the sack, yeer. Straight up and down she is, yeer, straight up and down.'

He went into a short trance, kept staring at the photo. 'She'll wait. . .yeer, she'll wait. . .'

Tu rolled a slow smoke and Henry kept on mumbling about her waiting and about seven years not being too long. . . but it was only for a moment 'cause he went outside his slot and shoved his card in its place above the door. The card said:

Athol Henry Bligh

Sentence:	7 years
Date of Sentence:	5.1.80
Date of Release:	5.1.87

He stood back hands on hips. 'Seven years, eh? Tha's a man's lag an I'll do it on me fuckin' head. With ease, buddies.' He punched the card and roared, 'With ease.'

His eyes were blue on white and bright. Brighter than any eyes I'd seen for a long time. Everyone started to look up to him cause he made you feel good. He looked so big. He was big. Tu looked at me with a knowing kind of nod. 'Too loud,' he whispered. 'A bit too loud.'

Henry got right into his lag. He played football, he played basketball. Most of his spare time was spent in the iron room. All sorts of stories went around the Can about Henry's muscles. Like lifting the back of the pig truck off the ground was hard to believe and so was the one about Henry tipping over the prison bull, Barney.

Tu and I went up to the iron room one Saturday to see Henry's muscles for ourselves. Tu could push more iron than anyone. We shoved our way through lots of little muscles, I say little muscles because they were standing around like apes. It was the same as being in church. The place smelt of iron and sweat and sort of stung my nose. There wasn't any sound except Henry's deep breathing, sweat dripped off his nose. He was shaping up to a great heap of iron.

'He's been building up to this for three hours,' someone whispered, so's we could be up on the action.

Henry moved into the heap of iron. It was more than Tu had lifted. He stood there for a long time breathing deeply and twitching his fingers. He bent down and gripped the bar like he was going to tear it apart; with a half shout, half scream hurled it up over his head.

'Chesses!'

'Fuckin' hell!' said all the little apes.

166

Henry ripped off his shirt in front of the mirror and struck a kind of Mr World pose and all the little apes oohed and aahed. His pumped up body bulged out all over the place. His veins stuck out and looked something like the roots of an old pohutukawa tree. Henry struck pose after pose. He twitched his muscles, he made them shiver. They were shiny with sweat. Everybody watched him. He was the new champion. He looked like a great white giant. I looked for Tu. He was standing with his back against the wall rolling a long slow smoke.

Henry developed a kind of a gorilla walk; guts pulled in and up to his chest, back muscles fully flexed so's his arms hung out from his body. Wherever he walked he managed to catch a glimpse of himself in the windows. The queens loved him, specially Sandra. Tu said she did a few free blow jobs on the side to get the top bunk in Henry's slot. One day Tu found them under the stage on the badminton nets. Tu was pretty sweet on Sandra. It seemed all the strong fellas got the best queens. Sandra was a Maori — somehow I knew Tu didn't like her being with Henry. Henry always showered in front of the mirror and even when he combed his hair he'd strike a pose.

Before the mail list was called Henry would be standing outside the Guardroom, waiting. I saw Piggy Screw one day censoring Henry's letter. He sniffed the scent and ripped it open. I could tell by the way his fat face lit up and by the way he was chuckling he was really caught up with the secret bits.

Henry looked like a hurt little puppy waiting for a bone. Piggy Screw kept reading. Henry waited.

'Oh, Bligh, didn't see you there. I just finished censoring your letter, here you are.'

'Th...thanks mister.'

'She's quite a girl, your Tina-Marie, eh Bligh?'

'Y...eah, yes mister.'

'Yes...quite a girl.'

And Henry would come swaggering up the wing offering all the boys a sniff of the scent his missus had splashed on the letter.

'Every day! Every day!'

Sandra didn't mind. The letters made Henry randy. It was Sandra who slept with Henry.

Henry went back to his slot and read and re-read the letter. He read in between the lines. By the time he had read it six times he was happy. He started doing his lag letter by letter, kept them all in a large cigar box with a yellow ribbon tied around. Tu found out where Tina-Marie lived. He was a Trustee and drove the Can's pig truck. He called in to see her every day. Everyone knew about Tu and Tina-Marie, everyone except Henry. Also Tu was working on something. I couldn't work out what it was, but he spent a fair bit of time in Piggy Screw's car. No one else knew he was talking to Piggy Screw. No one talks to screws much. But he had a way of saying things out the side of his mouth. Piggy Screw knew how to play the game too. He'd been with crims so long he was like one himself. His best mates were crims with lots of form. He was no match for Tu though. He was like most of the other screws, thick. Thick but cunning and dangerous. Well, that's what Tu told me.

Henry often talked about farming, about ploughing with horses. He'd been taught by his grandfather. He knew so much about the land. I liked his talk. When he talked about Tina-Marie though, he was sad, 'She taught me everything...I love her so much, I miss her so much...it hurts. Never had a girlfriend before.'

Henry got a whopping toothache, I was working with him cutting scrub in Piggy Screw's outside party. Henry was in such a bad way he could hardly speak. Plus he was too scared to see Piggy Screw 'cause Piggy Screw was starting to give him a hard time, making him do the dirty jobs. He called Henry 'Musclehead'. I said I'd go and see Piggy Screw for him.

Piggy Screw was lying down in the shade asleep. He always went to sleep in the shade while we worked in the sun. It's a wonder no one killed him while he slept. Enough fullas hated him. They always talked about it. But then he was so strong and fierce. Once he told us the best job he ever had was as a mercenary hunting niggers in South Africa. 'They had spears, we had automatic rifles.'

I got within ten yards of where he was sleeping. He jerked upright.

'Excuse me, mister. Henry Bligh has a really bad toothache, if I could get some kawakawa leaves from the bottom of this gully it would help him, mister.'

'A witchdoctor, eh,' he roared and his fat stomach shook. He got to his feet. 'Might just go down there and see Bligh, the Musclehead. I'm a bit of a witchdoctor myself, a WHITE witchdoctor.' Piggy Screw looked evil.

Or maybe he was lonely too, I didn't really know. He seemed to enjoy everyone hating him. He hated kid fuckers the most, that's what Tu said. By the time he got down to where Henry was he was puffing and sweating.

'Bit of a toothache, eh Bligh? Well, you just remember WHO you are and WHAT you're here for. Not a holiday camp, is it Bligh? No. WHO ARE YOU? Go on Bligh, YOU tell me, who you are?'

He kept prodding Henry in the chest with his forefinger. 'An whatcha here for, go on, whatcha here for.'

Piggy Screw kept pushing Henry down the hill. Henry mumbled back and Piggy Screw told him to speak clearly. We all knew Henry couldn't speak 'cause his gum was badly swollen up.

'Speak up like a man.'

I couldn't work out why he was so evil, so cruel. I couldn't stand it any longer. 'Please mister, Henry Bligh can't speak.'

'Well, what have we here. Witchdoctor speaks for the kid fucker. A bit of a kid fucker lover are y'? I thought there was sompin' queer about y'. Not as bad as a genuine kid fucker. Should cut their balls out I reckon.'

None of us believed it. Not Henry, a kid fucker! We all looked at each other and then back to Henry who was shaking his head.

'No!' he mumbled, 'No!'

Piggy Screw asked me to take Henry back to his slot.

'I'll send the nurse when I'm good and ready.'

All the way back I was trying to work out what happened...I knew Henry wasn't into little boys...he had Tina-Marie and Sandra...not little boys. What made Piggy Screw so awful? Maybe it was something to do with Tu...when he talked out of the side of his mouth to Piggy Screw.

There was a story about Piggy Screw finding a sack on the side of the road...it had a baby in it and it was still alive — he adopted it. The boy turned out to be a bit funny in the head, they said. Had to put him in a special home. He got a job as a screw for revenge, they said. He'd been at it 25 years. He was getting old for a screw but he could still swing a pick handle.

We waited in Henry's slot for the nurse. Everyone was in from the work parties, I could hear them in the showers. Henry was in a bad way. He tried lying down on his back but the hammering would make him jolt up again. He'd start pacing around his slot. I could see the pain was hammering him stupid. He was crying. He wiped away the tears and tried to make an excuse for crying in front of me, but I told him I cried too at times, and I didn't think there was anything wrong with it. He smiled a bit through his tears.

One hundred and thirty-six speakers told us it was scoff time. I left Henry in his slot; told him I'd be back after scoff.

In the dining room I could feel something was going on. Tu was the centre of it all. I could tell by the sly glances. A screw checked the muster. He whispered to one of the other screws. They both looked worried. Checked the muster again. Still one down. They checked for the third time.

'Lock the doors!'

'Who is it!'

No-one knew so they called the roll.

'It's Athol Henry Bligh.'

I could see Tu had it all going well. The boys were leading the screws on great guns.

'Bligh must've gone over the wall.'

'Yeah, he had a toothache. He probably jumped over the wall.'

'Bligh's a nutter.'

'He split, man.'

Piggy Screw came in, 'Shut up alla y'.' He asked the two screws where Bligh was. They said he'd gone over the wall.

The Super himself was called in.

'Bligh's escaped, Sir,' said Piggy Screw.

'Who is Bligh?'

'The muscle man, Sir,' said Piggy Screw trying to sound very polite, and he whispered something into the Super's ear.

'Oh God, no. Not him! Look, if the papers want to know what's going on, keep it quiet. Having someone escape is bad enough. Is that clear, mister?'

'Yes, Sir.'

It was good fun listening to it all. They seemed to have forgotten we were there. It was good too because we knew Henry was safe in his slot. Piggy had sent him there.

But I couldn't work out what Tu was up to. True, he was liked by everyone, they'd do anything he asked. We'd been through a lot together. He was doing ten years for trapping five cops up a blind alley and beating the shit outta them with a chain. He said they were white trash. Tu made out he was a bit silly, but he wasn't. He was always working something out...some way to get his own back. He'd always been the Kingpin, no one could match him. No screw was a match for Tu.

We were all ordered to our slots for an early lockup. Tu beat me to Henry's slot. I got there just in time to hear Tu telling Henry to keep out of sight.

'They think you've pissed off, man. Play along. They'll find you soon. And you'll get painkillers. Sweet?'

Henry nodded. He knew he had to be staunch. I could see he was in a bad way, his teeth must've been giving him one helluva hammering. Only wish I could have got those kawakawa leaves.

An hour after lock up Piggy Screw found him. We could all hear everything he said.

'B...Bligh, you kid-fucking bastard. Y' set me up, y'cunt.'

'You sent me to me slot to wait mister, f...for the nurse.'

'No I didn't, y' bastard, don't lay that on me or I'll cut y' balls out.'

He sounded pissed and evil. We could hear him kicking Henry in the ribs.

'That's (THUD) for saying I sent y' to your slot. Lies. That's (THUD) for pretending to escape, so by now the police are looking everywhere for you. (THUD) It's all over the radio, Bligh. (THUD) "Kid fucker at large". (THUD) "Everyone is requested to lock up their sons as Henry Bligh is loose." That's what they'll be saying.' (THUD)

We could hear a lot of scuffling, Piggy Screw was trying to shout, but it was coming out all muffled. Henry must've got him. It sounded as if Piggy Screw was being strangled. Henry could break his neck easily. Then we could hear Henry smashing Piggy Screw's head against the wall.

'Kill the bastard, Henry!' roared Tu so no-one could tell where his voice came from. Everyone started chanting. Banging the heating pipes with anything they could lay their hands on. Steel against steel. Ringing echoing ringing ringing. Stomping out the refrain. It was slow at first. Deliberate, heavy.

'Kill the bastard!'

'Kill the bastard!'

'Kill the bastard!'

It echoed and bounced from wall to wall. The whole place was going crazy and I was too, chanting along with the rest . It was good sticking up for Henry, he was a good guy... I mean, Tu reckoned all pakehas were trash and yet here we were stomping for Henry, a pakeha.

Suddenly I knew we were killing Henry. Because if he killed Piggy Screw he'd get life. We weren't helping Henry at all.

I looked at Tu. He was at the grill pushing everyone. Keeping it all going. He looked a bit porangi.

'Tu!' I had to yell. He swung around. I could see he was mad. He loved fights. He was in command of the whole prison.

'Tu!' I yelled again. 'Stop them, Tu, he'll get life.'

'You fuck up boy or I'll put y' down.'

'Y' can if y' like but you've got to stop all this.'

'Fuck up boy, I'll...'

He was going to drop me — we were close friends. Screws were running down the wing. The chanting stopped. We could hear three or four screws belting into Henry.

'They're kicking the shit outta Henry,' yelled Tu.

The screws were whispering so's we couldn't hear.

'Better get the nurse.'

'No, he'll live, serve him fuckin' right. He tried to kill me.'

They locked him up. They left. It was quiet again. Tu could see Henry's slot through the grill.

'There's blood all over the place,' he screamed. 'Henry's blood. Hey, you guys, Henry's nearly brown bread.'

The Can started winding up, you could feel it. You could hear it murmuring. Tu was still in command, leading everyone. 'They kicked the

171

shit outta him. The screw bastards. SCREWS FUCK SPIDERS!'

'Fuckin' screw bastards!'

'SCREWS FUCK SPIDERS! SCREWS FUCK SPIDERS!'

It was winding up again. Not only our wing but all the wings joined in. All chanting. All stomping.

'Get Bligh the nurse.'

'Get Bligh the nurse.'

'Get Bligh the nurse.'

It was building up. Nervous. Ugly. And I was right there caught in the fire of it all. Bashing steel against steel. Everybody stomping. Steel against steel ringing echoing ringing. Piggy Screw was running up and down the wing. Yelling through the peep holes.

'Cut out y' fuckin' racket. Cut it out or I'll come in and fuckin' do y'.'

But it stomped even louder.

'SCREWS FUCK SPIDERS.'

'SCREWS FUCK SPIDERS.'

'GET BLIGH THE NURSE.'

'GET BLIGH THE NURSE.'

Next thing we heard Piggy Screw on the loudspeaker. He was using his loudspeaker voice. 'Would inmates refrain from creating a disturbance. If not, we will be forced to take sterner measures. I repeat. Would inmates refrain...'

The more he tried to stop us the stronger we stomped. They poked a firehose into our slot. The force of the water slapped me against the back wall. The Can hissed back. Everyone, steel against steel, 368 of us all shouting and stomping. Tu and I stripped off naked. We danced in our madness. The prison shook. It all reached a high-pitched screaming sound.

The nurse came.

There was silence. The hate and the ugliness were still there, throbbing, but it was silent.

'Come on now, son, this will kill the pain.'

We could hear her making the screws run: she wanted hot water, clean sheets and blankets, she made them clean up the mess.

'How on earth did this happen?'

'One of the inmates got him. He'll live, won't he?' It was Piggy Screw talking in a hoarse whisper thinking we couldn't hear him.

'Liar!' Tu yelled so no-one could tell where his voice came from again.

'Bloody Liar!' came from a dozen slots. 'You got him bashed up. Y' liar.'

Piggy Screw left. We all knew he hated taking orders from a woman.

The Can never settled down that night. The stomping was still there; even when it was silent. It kept turning over. Every now and again the night shattered.

'Dirty, rotten, fuckin', screw bastards!' someone screamed in their half-awake fear.

I couldn't sleep — kept turning over and over and over.

By morning Tu had a new plan. He was always working on ways of destroying...though I wasn't sure who he was destroying...even in his sleep I could hear him mumbling things. I knew he didn't care about Henry now, 'cause Henry was a pakeha — of the 368 inmates 203 were Maori. Tu ruled the prison; he was the boss. The prison had a guard placed outside Henry's slot. As soon as we were unlocked Tu called a meeting in the showers.

'We've got to tell Henry to lay a complaint outside, to a magistrate. We'll tell the newspapers and the TV. Sweet?'

'Sweet.'

'We'll riot,' said Tu. But there was a long silence and he could see some of us weren't ready for the kind of riot he meant.

'You've got to. You all know how the bastards smashed up Henry. We can't let them get away with it. Let's tear this hell-hole apart. We'll wait till the screws are standing around at morning scoff and we'll grab them.'

Tu was talking fast and I could see most of his heavies were being swayed. I couldn't agree though, not about the riot I mean, we were no match for the screws.

'No riot, Tu,' I said.

Tu glared at me. 'Let's down the bastards,' he shouted.

'No. They'd get the army in,' I said. 'Better to have a peaceful sit-out.'

'No,' Tu shouted.

'Yes we can, Tu. We'll all go into the yard after breakfast and sit down. We'll do as you say, get a letter to Henry. Henry could lay a complaint. We'll let Henry know the whole boob is sitting it out.'

Everyone agreed. Everyone except Tu.

After morning scoff Tu chased Sludge, one of the pakeha Kingpins. Chased him past the guard outside Henry's slot, to the shitter at the end of the wing.

'You fuckin, thievin', white, trash bastard, I'll bean ya!' yelled Tu.

'Issat so, black? You'll be brown bread when I've finished with y'. All you Maori cunts are gutless. Y're only good in numbers!'

He shouldn't have said that, because it was only meant to be a decoy. Tu dropped him and stood kicking the shit outa him.

The screw took the bait and rushed down to the shitter. 'C'mon you two; break it up or you'll both be charged.'

I slipped a note under the door to Henry.

'Henry,' I whispered, 'chin up. Read this. We're all with you.'

After breakfast 136 speakers ordered us to parade for work. The screws could see something was wrong, they looked a bit scared. Piggy Screw was back on duty. He must've been expecting trouble because it was his three days off. He had an unhappy face but he knew we loved trouble. We could see him reaching for the microphone.

'Would all inmates get on parade.' He waited for a while. All the young screws were standing beside him. They were nervous-looking.

No-one moved. No-one said a word. We all sat there, 368 of us all waiting. None of the screws would come out into the yard. They were too scared. They stayed close to their microphone, close to Piggy Screw. I could see him reaching for the microphone again.

'Would inmates elect a spokesman. The spokesman should come forward and inform us of your grievance.'

Tu whispered, 'You go boy, Henry's more your friend than any of us.'

It wasn't easy for me walking up to the guardhouse and telling them we were going to stay there until we knew Henry Bligh had got a magistrate.

'What's he want a magistrate for?'

I could see he was going to play games with me so I left the guard room and walked across the yard.

We were strong, all being together. Nothing they could do to us. It was a kind of safe feeling. 368 of us lying there in the sun. No-one talking. With my eyes closed I thought of my old koroua, Tane. Must be he's thinking of me too. Wish I was with him in the bush. The birds were singing in the bush outside the prison.

Sun.

Bush.

Birds.

Tane.

So gentle.

I was drifting. Dreaming. Floating. In my dream I could see myself...lying down there with the 368...heaps of walruses...sunning ...I looked happy with my eyes closed. The tui in the kowhai were busy. It's hard to remember all the things of aroha Tane taught me. He said it would take a lifetime to learn its meaning. The sun heals. Tane says aroha always wins. Takes a long time. But it always does. He said it is the only way.

I woke up suddenly. For a while I didn't know where I was. Kind of lost. It was Henry. I saw him limping out of the guardroom. The Super, Piggy Screw and the four other screws were crowded into the guardroom. Smirking behind bullet-proof glass. Henry was all cleaned up, bandaged, and in some new recreation gear. He limped slowly. Something was wrong.

174

Later on Henry told me what happened. He said he'd got our letter and he'd only just swallowed it when the screws came for him. He was marched before the Super himself. He was offered a roundie and a cup of coffee. Piggy Screw was there, he was being really nice.

'Sit down, Bligh.'

The Super showed Henry to a comfortable chair. 'You know, Bligh, you're in serious trouble attempting to escape.'

'But I was sent to my slot...'

'It's no good going over that again, Bligh. We know what you were trying to do.'

Henry tried to say something.

'Listen Bligh, you're in big trouble so shut up and listen. Just remember WHO you are and WHERE you are!'

Henry hung his head. 'Yes, Sir.'

'Another cigarette? More coffee?' Henry nodded. No inmate was allowed cigarettes or coffee.

'Well, it's like this, Bligh. You're doing seven as it is... and you've got a girl waiting for you outside, eh Bligh?'

'Yes, Sir.'

'And she's quite a girl judging from her letters. Well, we're taking this into consideration and we are not laying charges and I know you will not take it any further, will you Bligh?'

'No...no, Sir.'

'No what?'

'No, I won't take it any further, Sir.'

'That's talking sense, Bligh. Now you can have this packet of cigarettes. The nurse will see you and you can sit in the sun. There's no need for you to work for the next couple of weeks. I'll fix it with the nurse.'

There were 368 of us all watching Henry limping. He looked really sore. Behind the glass the screws smirked. Something was wrong. Henry stopped. He was smoking roundies!

'What...he's smoking roundies!'

'He's fuckin' scabbed.'

'Wassa score?'

'He's cracked up.'

The Can started winding up again. This time it was against Henry. He just stood there on one spot. In the middle of the courtyard shaking his head.

'I couldn't...sorry, but I couldn't.'

'Scab.'

'White trash.'

'Broken arse.'

'BROKEN ARSE!'

175

'BROKEN ARSE!'
'BROKEN ARSE!'

The stomping started again. Henry knew he'd blown it. He looked back to the guardhouse to the Super and the screws. It was almost as if he'd wanted to take back the things he'd said. But the guardhouse was empty, the screws were gone. Henry hung his head. The stomping started building up.

'BROKEN ARSE!'
'BROKEN ARSE!'
'BROKEN ARSE!'

The more they chanted 'broken arse' the more Henry sunk to his knees. It was like a giant hand was crushing him into the ground. He wept right out there in front of everybody. He couldn't control himself. Snot and tears running down his face. And all the time the stomping beat out the refrain, 'broken arse, broken arse, broken arse'.

'Crying,' said someone.

'Crying like a mad woman,' said another.

'Shit, now I've seen it all, a man crying in front of everyone.'

'Fuckin' hell, makes you want to throw up.'

Some of the 368 took off, ran to their slots. Squirming.

'Never seen anything like it before.'

I went out to see Henry. I'm not into being a hero, in fact I was really scared. But it was as if Tane was pushing me out. Helped him to his feet. Put my arm over his shoulder and helped him back to his slot. It was awful...the brokenness was awful.

That night they demolished Henry. They stomped for two hours. The screws pretended they never heard it.

Henry spent a week lying on his bed. He couldn't eat. I managed to get him a few scraps. He was too frightened to leave his slot. Everywhere he went they called him Broken Arse.

Two weeks later when Henry went up to the iron room, they hissed at him.

'White trash.'

He pretended not to hear, but it was written all over his face. He piled a great heap of iron on the bar. It was heavier than he'd lifted before. He was going to try it cold.

He walked around the bar. This hissing stopped. He stood in front, deep breathing, fingers twitching. It was his last chance to come back. He grabbed. Lifted, pushed and pushed but it wouldn't go right up. It was lopsided, started toppling over. He fell. Screamed. He'd ruptured something in his groin. He tried to get up.

'He's fucked himself.'

'Must've dropped a piston.'

'He's got a broken bum bum, hehe.'

'The original broken arse.'

When he got back to his slot someone had done a shit in his bed. They had thrown shit all over the walls. The had rubbed it over the photo.

Henry went into hospital. He came back on crutches ten days later. Wherever he limped he was called Broken Arse. He lived for his missus's letters, but they weren't coming every day. Sometimes it was three days before he got one, even then it was often a scribbled page. We all knew Tu was rooting his Tina-Marie.

Henry wasn't seen much now. He slid along the walls, feeling his way. His left shoulder drooped. He was always seeing the Chaplain or the nurse. He didn't work. The nurse said he was too sick. He slept most of the time, didn't even read, just slept.

I used to go to his slot as much as I could. He liked to see me, I liked to see him too. He always sparked up a bit when we talked about our grandfathers, about the bush, the mountains.

He couldn't keep his slot clean. He never had a shower. His great body was withering away. On film nights Henry used to sneak in after lights out so's he'd miss the hissing. But the 368 knew. One night the film clacked on about a woman becoming tired of her man. When she finally climbs into the best friend's bed, the 368 spat out...

'An' that is Broken Arse's missus.'

In the dark Henry picked up a chair and smashed it down on Tu's head. He downed two screws. He cut a furrow through the 368, leaving a bleeding heap. And all the time making half-dog, half-man, noises. He rushed back to his slot and swallowed razor blades. Henry went into hospital again. When he was well enough he was committed to the nutter. Henry's head was electrocuted. Months later he was brought back.

'Broken Arse is back.'

'He's a fuckin' robot.'

I saw him starting across the yard from the guardhouse. He was swinging his legs like they were dead logs. His head was screwed to one side...it looked crooked. The further he walked out into the yard the slower he went. He looked back at the guardhouse — Piggy Screw and his mates were just staring. The closer he got to the spot where he went down on his knees, crying, the place where they chanted 'broken arse', the more he started to twitch. He couldn't go past it. He just stared at it like he was staring right into hell itself. His eyes were rolling. His head twisted...evil...his arms twitched. His fingers were bent...different ways. He froze. He looked like a statue...like a statue of what Whiro must look like. It was not Henry at all. I went out to him, so did the others, even the screws, even Piggy Screw. My guts was burning, it was all mixed up

177

with love and hate and anger, all at the same time. Only the whites of his eyes were showing. He was breathing all right, but it was as if he were dead. His face was twisted and frozen with a look of deep hurt...deep pain. Tears were streaming out of his white eyes. The tears were the only warm part I knew about him. It ripped at my guts. I was full of tears too. So were many of the others. Piggy Screw looked different, his bottom lip was quivering.

'Poor bastard,' someone whispered.

'Makes you feel stink all right,' said Piggy Screw. 'I gotta boy in the nutter...be about the same age...he's got yella hair too...makes you feel fuckin' stink all right.'

Piggy Screw was hugging Henry, the tears were streaming down his face too. 'Found him stuffed in a sack you know... no-one wanted him... no-one loved him, no-one at all...'

It was sad seeing Piggy Screw crying out there in front of the others. He looked shattered, even broken, right out there where Henry went down on his knees. It seemed the same giant hand that crushed Henry was crushing Piggy Screw.

Tu was standing in the shadows, up against the back wall. So were all his Maori heavies. There were about 80 of them, they seemed to enjoy the brokenness. Henry and Piggy Screw...hugging.

We could all feel the stomping. It was a slow, deliberate stomp, though there wasn't a sound. They were stomping their feet, swaying their bodies from side to side like a haka. They stomped. Broken arse, broken arse. You couldn't hear a sound. They looked so black, so ugly, so strong.

Henry and Piggy Screw looked so pale, so weak, so broken.

Tu rolled a large, slow smoke.

BRUCE STEWART (1936; Ngati Raukawa, Te Arawa) was born in Hamilton and grew up in the Wairarapa where he was educated at Wairarapa College. He is the founder of Tapu Te Ranga marae in Island Bay, Wellington, and is currently the president of the Maori Artists' and Writers' Society. He started writing in 1974 while attending a writers' workshop with Michael King when he was on parole from Wi Tako. He has since been involved in writers' workshops with Christine Cole Catley and Fiona Kidman. In 1979 he read 'Broken Arse' at the New Zealand Writers' Conference and in 1980 both Bruce and Alistair Campbell were given grants by the Queen Elizabeth II Arts Council and the Ministry of Foreign Affairs to represent New Zealand at the 5th triennial ACLALS Conference in Fiji at the University of the South Pacific. Later in the same year he attended a Pacific Writers' Conference in the Cook Islands, also organized by the University of the South Pacific. He was instrumental in setting up the Art of the Maori festival at Pipitea Pa in 1981. His stories have appeared in *Alumni, Te Kaea, Shirley Temple is a Wife and Mother* and on Radio New Zealand. A book on Tapu Te Ranga is in preparation as is a collection of stories.

Vernice Wineera Pere

Song From Kapiti

Some people there are
who survive
on the promise of summer.
Such are the inhabitants
of the Paekakariki coast,
in dwellings nestled against
cliff-face and ragged clay
in the full winter fury
of the open ocean.
I watch a lone sea-bird
who sits woodenly
on a wind-ravaged crag,
his feathers ruffled
by the cold southerly
straight from the Antarctic.
The sparse toe-toe
lean with the wind,
and trail feathered fronds
over the wild, grey beach.
They reach chill fingers
into my heart.
I am that bird
frozen by the southern wind,
my wings wooden
in the cold salt air.
I am the child of the Ngati-Toa,
seeking my place
in a mainland society.
I am she learning to sing
the sad-sweet songs of a people's soul.
I am the lone bird
alive in a limbo of longing,
enduring the winter world,
surviving
on the slim promise
of a future summer.

The Boy Named Pita

The boy named Pita
hangs in the blackened corner
where the streetlight's blue glare
cannot reach.
Around him, the chewed-up road
is tiled with flattened soda cans,
round coins of bubblegum
and pop-top tabs, glinting
silver exclamation marks
upon a dark page.

On Iosepa Street, an old woman
watches TV, the grey screen
flickers blue shadows through
the small room.
Her bare, brown feet
folded against lauhala matting
soft on skin,
she only half-perceives the fantastic parade
of police shows, soap commercials,
and the good life's din.

In the soft black night,
surrounded by sophisticates
he knows vaguely from school,
the boy named Pita
is snared in a conversation
that slithers across the sidewalk,
sinks fangs into his throat,
until salt stings his cheeks
wringing understanding from him.

Hearing rapid English
she cannot comprehend,
mouthed words she cannot catch,
the old lady's ears are tuned
to the tattered screen door's latch
she hopes will rattle and slam
soon, very soon,
announcing her grandson's
coming home.

At Porirua

Knee-deep in water
we clawed the sand,
and laughing,
dug fat pipis from their bed.
Now grown,
I finally understand
your hollow call
that froze us then
with dread.
An accident —
football —
a tram —
snatches from an adult
air of shock.
The urgent toll calls
and telegrams,
your slow, old hands
winding up the clock.
And how, the long, grey journey
into town
we did not count
the sleepy station shops,
but stared upon
your white and furrowed frown
afraid of what awaited
when we'd stop.

How strange,
that children's sea-side laughter rings
with ashen echoes of such long-gone things.

Bitter-Sweet

I searched in vain
for an old house
in a street of old houses.
I couldn't even find the street.
I wanted at least
to swing again the rusted gate,
and walk the path

of broken bricks
to the yard
behind the house.
I wanted to find
the big old mulberry tree
and the furry-leaved loquat,
— the hiding places
where I pretended freedom
high above the ties
of childhood far below.
And so,
I hoped I might find
some good things
rummaging in the litter
of remembered years.
But I searched in vain
for the old house
in the street of old houses.
Thinking about that now,
it's probably just as well,
for to be honest with myself,
I know,
way down inside,
I don't really want to find
that house again.

Wellington, Circa 1950

The winds were always there.
The southerly, up from Antarctica,
baring teeth that tore your clothes,
hair, skin, even flesh from off your ribs
then licked your bones
with that infinitely cold tongue.
And sometimes the northerly,
no less cruel, snarling down the gorges
north of the pa, clawing branches
off the eucalyptus trees, roofs
from wooden houses, frail, every nail
creaking in the onslaught.
Then we'd hate to go outside

for more wood, the few lumps
of coal you bought with shillings
kept safe within your coin purse.
Someone had to though,
and I avoided the guilt of seeing you
trussed in that thin overcoat
in the brute wind, the flimsy scarf
whipping about your grey hair,
the axe ever-poised in the air
as you fought to let it drop
against the wet logs
on the chopping block.
So I'd go, stepping beyond
the slamming of the time-lock door
into the animal day,
the whole world writhing,
snakes in the trees,
dogs howling down the sky,
the picket fence rocking, possessed
of something terrible, unseen.
Then the empty rooms of that house,
damp with their view of the grey sea,
the bleak sky, became
the only womb of warmth left
for a fifteen-year-old adrift
in a storm, a grandmother's fading year
the sole companion.

VERNICE WINEERA PERE (1938; Ngati-Toa, Ngati-Raukawa) was born in
Wellington and grew up in Porirua Pa. She lives in La'ie, Hawaii, with her
husband and seven children, where she graduated Magna Cum Laude from the
Brigham Young University — Hawaii Campus. Vernice has taught English and
creative writing at that University and she is currently an editorial assistant at its
Institute for Polynesian Studies.

A former editor of *Kula Manu*, a Hawaiian literary journal, her poetry has
appeared in *Te Ao Hou, Eve, Kula Manu* and *Ensign* (USA). In 1978 The Institute
for Polynesian Studies published her first book of poems *Mahanga: Pacific Poems*.
In 1979 the Polynesian Cultural Centre brought out *Ka Po'e o La'ie*, an anthology
of the poetry of La'ie edited by Vernice. She has two further books in preparation.
Mahanga: Pacific Poems was the first collection of poems by a Maori woman writer
to be published.

Pere's work looks towards both New Zealand and Hawaii and in so doing
reminds us that contemporary New Zealand writing is more and more coming to be
seen as a part of Pacific writing generally.

Bub Bridger

Girl In The River

She stood knee-deep in grey mud. Water lapped to her waist. She wore an old woollen pullover and brief colourless shorts. Her face and arms were streaked with mud and bits of shining green river weed clung to her hair. She had long strong hands with fingernails painted bright coral. On the bank behind her purple violets and irises blossomed in little clumps and against a huge old plum tree rested a big garden fork and wheelbarrow.

She pulled the weed from the water, reaching into it up to her elbows, dragging the heavy mass against her. She held it there, squeezing out the water and then she braced her legs in the mud and swivelled to heave it up on to the bank behind her. The stench was sickening. She kept rubbing her nose and forehead into her shoulder then throwing back her head gulping the clear cold air above her.

Across the river, hidden by dense lupins, a man watched her. He had been watching her for weeks. He had seen her scything the rank grass that reached the first branches of the plum tree. Clumsily at first, wielding the heavy wooden handle with chopping strokes and then gradually getting the rhythm of it and swinging the curved blade. He saw her mow the stubble so that from the plum tree at the edge of the river there was a stretch of smooth unbroken green up to the cottage. She planted orange and lemon trees, and silver birches and wattles and nectarines and apples. She grew flaxes and toi tois down by the river and in the little dips and hollows of the bank she put the violets and irises. He saw her long arms and legs turn gold in the sun and her hair burn.

At first the man discussed her with his wife. He spoke of the 'brazen bitch across the river going about half-naked'. His wife went down to the river to see for herself and was shocked and angry. She wondered if there were some way they could complain about the way the girl flaunted herself. She talked it over with friends and neighbours and took a group of them down through the garden to the river.

The girl saw them standing on the far bank in a forbidding line and for a moment she was startled, then she stood up and waved to them. They saw her long legs in the faded shorts and the shape of her breasts under the tight shirt that stopped some inches above her waist, showing the bare golden flesh. They stared at her and then they turned and filed through the lupins back to the house. She watched them, leaning against the plum tree, frowning at their retreating backs.

The women decided to sign a petition and send it to the Mayor. They

184

strongly requested that he inform the police of the girl's shameless exposure of herself in an area where they had all lived quietly and decently for years. They mentioned her two small children. That they should be taken from her and given a chance to grow up as good citizens in a Christian atmosphere. But the Mayor didn't answer the petition and they wondered whether he had ever actually received it.

After that the women never went near the river and when they heard the girl laughing and shouting with the children they would go indoors and close the windows.

The river was small and slow moving so that logs and branches and discarded plastic containers got caught in the strong weed and stayed there lining the banks. The summer had been long and the water dropped several feet. The branches and weeds trapped the water at the river's edge and turned stagnant and sour. The winter was cold but it brought little rain and the girl hated the still, stinking mess below the bank. She would stand under the plum tree watching the growing tangle encroaching a little further into the stream and one spring day she brought the wheelbarrow and the fork down to the bank.

The man watched her step down into the water. Her summer skin had paled but the long legs and high breasts were still as arrogant as ever. He saw her cringe as her feet sank in the soft mud.

Downstream a dozen or so mallard ducks observed her. She and the children had been feeding them for months and now they swam closer, quack-chattering hopefully for stale bread. She smiled at them and the man in the lupins heard her talking and swearing happily at them as she plunged bright painted nails into the river weed. The cold water didn't worry her. After a long time he could see the sweat gleaming on her forehead and the pile of weed on the bank grew so high she had to start another.

The children played behind her on the long sloping lawn. Now and then they came to watch and they poked the pile of weed with enquiring fingers.

'Don't touch it,' she warned. 'It stinks.'

Around midday she climbed out of the water and went up to the cottage with the children.

The man rose from the lupins and groaned with pain. The knees of his trousers were wet and his face and hands were blue with cold.

His wife had prepared lunch and when he came inside she stared at him.

'Good God, are you ill?' she asked.

He shook his head without looking at her.

'I've been weeding.'

'Well, don't do any more — you look dreadful.' She served him hot soup and watched him with concern. The soup warmed him and his hands stopped trembling. After lunch, his wife said, 'I'm going over to Doreen's. I wish you'd come with me — you haven't seen the kiddies for ages.'

'No', he said, 'you go on over. I'll see them at the weekend.'

'Well then,' she hesitated — 'Don't go back to the garden. Stay here in the warm and watch telly.'

When he heard the car start he went through the house and watched from the window for the girl. She came out of the cottage with the children. They were playing with a big yellow ball and halfway down the lawn she drop-kicked it high in the air. They screamed and raced to catch it.

'Don't kick it down here', she called, 'you'll lose it in the river.'

She had cleared several yards and she stood on the bank with her hands on her hips, smiling and humming her satisfaction.

At the window, the man stood with clenched hands, whispering softly and rapidly. When the girl was back in the river, he slipped out of the house and ran crouching and crab-like to the damp hollow in the lupins.

She moved carefully out into deeper water, lifting each leg with difficulty from the mud. When she reached the mesh of logs and branches, the water covered her breasts. She was suddenly frightened of the oozing slime gripping her legs and in panic she lunged, kicking powerfully to release them. She fell face down into sharp twigs that ripped her face and arms. For a moment she lay there. The branches sank beneath her and the weed gripped her hands and legs. She pushed her head and shoulders back out of the water and then slammed forward in a frenzy, out into the middle of the river. The water ran smoothly about her and she floated with it, gasping and whimpering her relief. The man in the lupins rose and started forward.

She drifted limply down the stream for several yards and then she turned and swam back with long easy strokes. The children still played with the ball. She felt a great surge of joy to see them safe and laughing and unaware. She called to them and they came running, squealing their surprise and delight to see her swimming.

'Can we come in? Please? Can we come in too?' They danced about on the bank waving their arms, yelling at her.

'No! No it's too cold — stay up there.' She blew kisses to them.

She tackled the branches and weed from midstream, completely at ease now. She pulled logs free and pushed them into the current. A tangle of weed broke away. She worked steadily, treading water, tearing the branches apart and guiding them into the stream. She loosened big clumps of weed, dragging them into the flow, swimming back again and again for more. And finally she was aware that the smell had gone. The water ran clear and clean past her bank. She swam up and down, searching the

186

riverbed for snags that might give anchor to floating ribbons of weed from upstream and tossing them up on the bank.

At the moment when the girl made up her mind to brave the mud and get out of the river, the woman found her husband in the lupins. He heard her gasp and he cowered at her feet, unable to look at her. Then his head sank to the damp ground and he began to cry.

The girl pulled herself up on to the bank and lay there, exhausted. Her face was bleeding and her arms and legs were criss-crossed with scratches. Her coral nails were broken and filthy. She rolled over with an effort and saw the fork and the wheelbarrow.

'Tomorrow I'll cart that weed away,' she said.

The Circus

One early spring night, a night of soft drifting rain and unseasonable warm, three people were involved in an odd encounter. A middle-aged man and woman who knew each other well, or perhaps didn't know each other at all, and a stranger whom neither of them had ever seen before and never saw again.

The man's name was Jeremy Schaffer. He was fifty but could have been ten years younger. He was short and broad-shouldered, with dark bushy hair and pale blue eyes in a clever attractive face. There was an ex-wife somewhere and a couple of adult children. His present bachelor existence suited him, but it also worried him. He couldn't help the feeling that it wasn't quite proper to be unmarried at fifty. He had several woman friends. One of them was Nora Shannon. She was a big glowing woman in her forties, red-haired and dark-eyed. She was in love with Jeremy Schaffer, desperately, painfully in love, as a young girl loves.

When they met, he was attracted by things about her which later appalled him. In the beginning, he had her safely pigeonholed in his mind as a happy being, full of life, uncomplicated but exciting. He found he enjoyed her company without having to try very hard. He was more relaxed with her than with any other woman he knew. And then he began to notice things about her which startled him and revealed that the simple genial woman he had imagined her to be, did not exist.

The truth was that when she met him, she lost her balance. She fell in love straight away. She was joyous and honest and unwary. And when it was too late, she couldn't help herself. Then on that warm spring night, something happened to her. Nothing really changed, but things were never quite the same again.

He called for her at nine and, as usual, he was exactly on time. She often wished he might be a little late or even early, but he never was. She was ready, which wasn't usual, tall and stunning and in those first few moments, excited and flushed as a girl at the sight of him. He never liked that in her, he felt she always did everything to excess, and his disapproval replaced the genuine feeling of pleasure at the thought of seeing her again. She saw it at once, in the tight smile, in his perfunctory greeting of her.

'Oh Christ!' And then she leaned forward as she always did, and kissed him. He felt the swift response and he pulled away a little and smiled at her. She didn't see the relaxing, the gentleness. Her eyes were glazed with tears and she turned from him. But as they drove she panicked at the silence and began to talk quickly with a prattling gaiety that horrified him.

'Guess what? I got a chain-letter today and if I don't answer it within twenty-four hours terrible things will happen to me. Mrs Someone in Timbuctu broke the chain and dropped dead and the President of Somewhere did too and now he's no longer president. But a lowly farmhand in the Scottish Highlands did the right thing and he's made millions!'

'Are you serious?'

'What do you mean?' she asked sharply.

'Well — it all sounds like so much bullshit!'

'Of course it's bullshit! Chain-letters are bullshit! I told you about it because I thought it would amuse you.'

'Did you really get a chain-letter?'

She thought of the silly little note on her desk threatening dire misfortune if she failed to send it on. 'I'll send you a copy,' she said coldly, 'and if you don't answer it — you drop dead!'

They drove the rest of the way in silence.

The party was still in the awkward early stage. People sipped their first drinks and waited for the ice to crack. It always did when Nora arrived and despite the misery of the car ride she sailed into the big room with Jeremy in her wake, stopping to hug people, waving and calling to others, noticing happily the sudden ripple of pleasure at her arrival. Somebody brought them drinks and she moved easily about the room talking and laughing and already flirting with the men she knew, while their wives smiled their acceptance. They were never offended. They said Nora was too honest, too open. But she wasn't — it was simply that she didn't covet their men. Her flirting was harmless. She would have been happiest standing with Jeremy, talking with him to others, but she knew he disliked that. He circulated as she did, but from choice. Yet he was quieter than she and he sought out men he knew, chatting almost instantly about sport, although his blue eyes took in everything and in seconds he was aware of the most attractive women in the room. Two or three of them he knew intimately and he acknowledged them with quick secret half-smiles while he talked to their husbands about which side was likely to win the cricket. His interest was genuine. He liked few things better than to watch or discuss cricket or rugby with men. He could never have discussed them with women.

A couple of hours later, Nora was in full swing. Inwardly she was aware of Jeremy's every move but nobody could have guessed, Jeremy least of all. Occasionally his eyes sought hers and he felt a glow of pleasure seeing her at the centre of an attentive and admiring group. Sometimes he would go to her and for a time they would be close, but she never relaxed for long. She watched and waited for his mood to change. He felt the tension and it puzzled and annoyed him. He would make some excuse and move away from her.

After four or five gins Nora became restless. The music was a quiet background for the conversation which was easy now and relaxed. But she had no desire for conversation, because about then her brain and her tongue fell out of step. She became a little befuddled. Nobody noticed because she took pains to hide it. Her dark eyes widened and her voice softened to a husky drawl. Actually, at that stage, her eyes tended to narrow and her tongue to thicken. The mental and physical effort to prevent such a betrayal was difficult to summon, but years of practice prevailed. She stopped circulating and sought out a comfortable chair to curl up in, feeling sleepy and ready to go home. From across the room, Jeremy watched her and thought how relaxed and lovely she looked. He wanted to take her home and make love to her.

The chair was very comfortable and in a few minutes Nora knew she had made a mistake. If she stayed there she would fall asleep. She stood up with an effort and crossed the room carefully through the laughter and chatter to the door. In the hall the air was cool and she breathed deeply, standing with her eyes closed, grateful for the empty darkness. When she opened them she saw a couple in each other's arms right at her feet. Had she taken another step she would have trodden on them. She smothered a tipsy laugh and swerved away to the open front door. Outside the rain fell softly and the street lights shone yellow and beckoning. She went eagerly down the steps, wide awake now, walking out into the middle of the street lifting her face to the rain.

Jeremy's car was parked before a big shabby house with long windows wide open to the street. Loud music beat from the windows. In the shadows of a huge leafy gum before them, a tall skinny boy was listening. He leaned against the trunk with closed eyes, one bare sandalled foot tapping. Inside the house a crowd of young people were dancing and she stopped to watch them, open-mouthed with surprise and pleasure. Jeremy found her there and watched her for a moment. Then he unlocked the car and threw her shawl and bag on to the seat.

'Nora,' he called, 'let's go home. Your things are in the car.'

She turned, smiling at him. 'Isn't it beautiful? Just listen!' She held out both hands to him. 'Dance with me Jeremy!'

'Here? In the street?' He smiled his amusement. He felt all his inhibitions about her melt. Rain gleamed in her hair and glistened on her face. He leaned forward and touched her cheek. 'Let's go home.'

'Yes! But dance with me first.'

'No, come on — don't be silly.' He reached for her hand and kissed the palm gently. 'We're going home.'

She pulled her hand away. 'No we're not — I want you to dance with me.'

'When we get home,' he said, moving away from her and slipping in behind the wheel of the car.

'You bastard,' she said softly, 'you narrow conservative bastard!' She turned her back on him and stared up at the windows. Music from the bright room poured all around her and she ignored him.

'Nora! For Christ' sake! You're not twenty-one — get in the car!'

She spun to face him, incensed, shouting.... 'Ahhhh! You'd dance with me then! You'd stand on your bloody head if I were twenty-one!'

Jeremy folded his arms across the wheel and lay his head on them. She had shattered everything as she always did with her crazy impulses and her mad refusal to act her age.

Then the boy stepped from the shadows of the gum tree and leapt the fence with a long bound.

'Lady! I'm twenty-one and I'd love to dance with you!' He bowed. A deep exaggerated swoop with one skinny arm flung wide, long brown wet ringlets hiding his face.

Nora stared at him. He tossed back the long hair and she gazed at the crooked smiling boy's face.

'We're wasting the music.'

She laughed.

Jeremy heard her and lifted his head. She was looking up at the boy, rocking, bubbling with laughter. He opened the door to get out, then stopped. He saw her, arms outstretched, her head thrown back like some big flamboyant bird, dancing in the rain. The boy led her. They swayed and stamped and circled, their feet shuffling, their heads dipping and shaking, leaning to each other then bending away in the amber light of the street lamp. A goose-woman and a heron-boy in a queer erotic ritual. It seemed endless. Jeremy watched them with shock and revulsion. He saw Nora's face and he hated her then. Her smile was intense and sly. The boy knew it and he wheeled around her, laughing and triumphant.

Then suddenly, it was all over. The music stopped and he saw them fall into each other's arms. Nora reached up and kissed the boy full on the mouth. He held her for a long time and then she pulled away and came to the car, sliding in beside Jeremy without looking at him or speaking.

'You bitch,' he said, 'you common bitch.'

She stared at him coldly and shrugged. He wanted to hit her hard across the mouth. Then he knew he didn't want to hit her at all. With an effort he started the car and as they moved away, Nora turned and waved to the boy. He waved back with both skinny arms crossing and uncrossing like floppy scissors above his head until the car turned at the corner.

After a time Jeremy spoke.

'Do you want to go home?'

'Yes I do.'

'Very well.' His voice hardened, but more than ever before he wanted to make love to her.

When they reached her flat he said, 'Goodnight Nora.' For a moment she hesitated, then she caught up her shawl and bag and got out of the car. She looked remote and calm and secretive. He was suddenly uneasy. 'Nora?'

She smiled at him and moved away.

'I'll give you a ring,' he called.

'Oh — yes. . . .'

She knew he would. Tomorrow, or the next day, or the next week, he would call and she knew she would be waiting as eagerly as ever for the sound of his voice.

But for the moment, she didn't care if he did or he didn't or if she never ever saw him again — and relief flowed through her like a cool stream.

The Stallion

When we moved to the house in the valley my mother said, 'Don't ever come home through the shortcut, come up over the hill road.'

'Why?' I asked.

'Because of the stables. You're not to go near the stables.'

'Why?' I asked again.

'Because I said so. They're not very nice people.'

'Who aren't?'

'Stable people. They're rough and if I ever catch you coming home that way. . .'

So I rode to school on the bar of my brother's bicycle and walked the long way home in the summer heat through the dust and burnt brown grass.

191

At the new school the teacher sat me next to Elsie O'Leary. Elsie's father owned the stables.

For the first few days I was wary of her and then I forgot about it because she was nice. We walked home together as far as the turn-off and she skipped along the short-cut while I trudged up the hill.

When she found out I lived a couple of hundred yards past her house, Elsie said, 'Why don't you come home through the short-cut?'

'Because I'm not allowed to,' I said uncomfortably.

'Why not? Your brother does.'

I shrugged. 'I'm just not allowed to.' And I turned up the long road.

'You're mad!' Elsie called after me.

I hunched my shoulders and made myself small in my embarrassment and shame. The metal handle of my school case grew wet and I kept changing hands and wiping the sweat down my skirt. Hating Elsie O'Leary.

My brother came home full of tales about the O'Leary boys. They could ride racehorses bareback and were all going to be jockeys when they grew up.

'Their big brother's a jockey already,' my brother said, 'and their father owns "The Shah".'

'What's "The Shah"?'

'He's the biggest, blackest horse you've ever seen and he's just like a wild beast.'

I shivered, and that night the biggest blackest horse was running through my dreams and away over the valley hills like a storm.

All the next day at school I questioned Elsie O'Leary about the horse, my misery of the day before forgotten. In the end she grew impatient.

'He's just our stallion.'

'What's a stallion?'

'We breed from him.'

'What's breed?'

She scowled. 'It's putting him to the mares to get foals.'

'Foals,' I murmured. 'Baby horses.'

'Yes. You have to have a stallion to get the mares in foal.'

'Oh.' And while I was thinking about that and getting ready for another question she grinned at me, her pretty brown-elf face suddenly sly.

'Do you want to see him?'

'The horse?' I whispered.

'Mmmm.'

'Where could I see him?'

'Along the short-cut.'

'He's *there!*'

'Yes. He's fenced in by the short-cut.'

192

'Oh Elsie,' I breathed.

'Do you want to see him then?' Her brown eyes slanted at me — laughing and devious and foxy.

'Oh yes! Oh I do, Elsie!'

'But you're not allowed to take the short-cut,' she said softly.

I shuddered with excitement. 'I don't care — I'm coming.'

Walking past the turn-off I felt no guilt. I looked at Elsie O'Leary and smiled. Elsie smiled back.

My mother is wrong, I thought. She *thinks* she knows, but she doesn't.

Elsie held out a small hand and together we ran down the short-cut to the huge wooden fence.

He was standing on the far side of the enclosure, whinnying to the mares. Bigger, blacker than in my dreams. Wilder and lovelier and more fearsome than anything I had ever seen.

I stared and stared.

'Elsie,' I breathed, 'have you ever touched him.'

'Touched him!' she blinked at me. ' 'Course I haven't! Nobody can touch him except Dad and my big brother!'

'Elsie, are you very frightened of him?'

'I'm scared stiff!' she muttered.

'I'm not,' I said softly.

'I'll bet you are! Everybody is — even Dad sometimes. Only my big brother isn't.'

'If I got in the paddock would he kill me?'

'He'd smash you to bits!'

'With his hooves?'

'Yes!' she was staring at me.

'I'm still not frightened of him.'

She caught my arm tightly. 'You're not going in there though, are you?'

'No!' I shook her hand away, 'but I'm going to stick my neck through.'

'No! Don't put your neck through!' She grabbed at me. 'Oh God! I'll get murdered for this,' she whimpered. But I was kneeling in the lush grass and I pushed my head under the big wooden bar at the bottom..

'Please,' Elsie moaned, 'please take your head out.'

'I won't.'

I pushed my head in further until my shoulders and chest were through. Elsie, wailing and cursing, was trying to pull me away. I kicked at her, 'Get away Elsie O'Leary!'

The stallion still called to the mares.

'You mad fool!' Elsie sobbed. 'That black devil will get you and I'll get the blame!'

I wriggled a little further under the fence.

'Hey! Black devil! Come and get me!'

The great head turned on its satin neck and the huge body was suddenly still. Then screaming and rearing and plunging he came for me. Hooves and thunder and rage.

I stayed there, half under the fence, until the noise of him, the screaming and the pounding and the terrible ragged breathing was almost above me. Then I rolled sideways and over and over away from the fence.

Elsie had gone.

I crouched in the grass and watched him. Still screaming, he flung back his giant head and lifting the glistening shoulders and forelegs he hung there for a moment and then slammed the slashing hooves down the heavy fence. I could see the huge eyes rolling and mad in his fury. Again and again he raked the fence, striking the broad timbers with hooves like knives.

'I love you, big black horse.' I whispered. 'I love you, I love you.'

And then somebody grabbed me by the hair and pulled me to my feet.

'What the hell are you doing? You mad little bitch!'

He hit me across the cheek and I went spinning against the fence on the other side of the short-cut.

When I turned he was talking to the stallion. Standing right against the fence, reaching through, and saying over and over, 'Easy boy — easy boy — easy now — easy...' and slipping through the fence smooth as a cat, stroking the taut muscled neck with sure soothing hands until the rage was stilled and the marvellous head relaxed.

He came sliding back through the fence. 'You'd better go home.'

'Yes,' I said.

'You're a little Montgomery aren't you?'

'Yes.'

'You look like your brother.'

'Yes. And you're Elsie O'Leary's big brother.'

'How do you know that?'

'Because,' I said, 'because with the horse.'

His eyes slanted and he smiled at me.

'Go home now.'

'Yes.'

And I went running along the short-cut and began to cry. The great black horse and Elsie O'Leary's big brother and the long green grass and the clear summer sky were spinning, spinning, spinning.

When I was nearly home I fell into the cool sweet grass and cried and cried for a very long time and never knew why.

BUB BRIDGER (1924; Ngati Kahungunu) was born at Napier and has lived in Wellington most of her life. She began writing in 1974 while attending a writers' workshop with Michael King. (Bruce Stewart was another member of the same workshop) and participated in a subsequent workshop with Christine Cole Catley. Her stories have appeared in *The NZ Listener* and *Shirley Temple is a Wife and Mother*. In 1979 she read 'A Wedding' at the 2nd New Zealand Writers' Conference in Wellington. Bub is currently completing a collection of short stories for Cape Catley.

Henare Dewes

Tihei Mauriora!

Strange thing happened today
applied for a flat in Remuera
got knocked back
cause I'm a maori,
funny that!
Hell! I can't even speak the lingo
don't even know my maoritanga
whatever that is.
Once I spoke Maori
but the teacher strapped me
and made me learn pakeha so hard
and respect pakeha so hard
and be like a pakeha so hard,
I'm real good at it now
got papers to prove it too
yet I still couldn't get this flat
cause I'm a maori
funny that!
I should've bowled that landlord
but I'd have gone to Paremoremo
bugger that!
that's where lots've maoris go.
Funny that!
I'd go back to my marae
If I knew where it was
and prove, I'm not
an Uncle Tom.
Aue!
I wish those pakehas

would make their minds up
about who I belong to
that's the worse of being half 'n' half,
the pakeha half is always
getting the maori half in trouble
funny that!
In my next reincarnation
I'm coming back
as a full blooded maori,
that'll scare the tutai
out of all those
pakeha staticians.
I'm going to Ponsonby tommorrow
gonna get another flat,
this time,
I'm gonna be a Samoan
Tihei Mauriora!
whatever that means.

Whakarongo

Who will gaff the tuna stream
and tickle nga taraute
and collect the kina
kutai and pipi
pick the puha and bitter cress
set the hinaki
make the bread to buy the kai
for te huatahi,

eh! . . . . . . who!

Who will lie
to flapping ears
and teach te reo Maori
patere and mihi
point the tapu place of rest
of 'tipuna me' mythology
and scratch the rib
that crease the skin
the nose to dry
and the eyes not look for me

eh!......who?
Aue!
as usual nobody listens to me
in this stinking prison.

Te Ao Hou

My people cry out
but the baskets of food are empty
and the promises that filled them,
nurture the thistles
of abandoned courtyards.
Behind glass panes
the tekoteko stares helplessly
while the manaia
bows his head in shame,
and the shopkeeper keeps on smiling.

I see confusion
in eyes that avoid mine
and sense anger
in the clenched fists upon their backs.

E tu ra!
hold tight your maoritanga
lest your calabash overflow
with the greed of today,
and the death of yesterday
is a meaningless wave of tomorrow.

HENARE DEWES (1942; Ngati Porou) was born at Waipiro Bay on the East Coast. He was one of a small number of poets who published in *Rongo* (initiated by Te Huinga Rangatahi o Aotearoa). At times writing from prison his work has also appeared in *Te Maori*, *Te Ao Hou* and the *NZ Women's Weekly*. At present he is completing a book to be called *Te Karanga* based upon a Maori family caught up in the urban migration.

Mana Cracknell

The Last Fish

Fish, the offspring of
Tangaroa. Who will eat the
last one?

A Bearing At Sea

A piece of wood drifts
North to South.

Heaviness

Turn an attentive ear
to the clicking of flax.
A death sign of my sadness.

MANA CRACKNELL (1948) was born on the Maahia peninsula. He began writing in 1964 when at Hato Paora College in Fielding and did two readings at Te Kaha. A past-president of the University Maori Club when he was at the University of Auckland he was also the Maori representative at the first World Youth Conference sponsored by the United Nations, in New York.

His work is influenced by the whakatauaki and pepeha forms, and the Japanese haiku.

Patricia Grace

A Way Of Talking

Rose came back yesterday; we went down to the bus to meet her. She's just the same as ever Rose. Talks all the time flat out and makes us laugh with her way of talking. On the way home we kept saying, 'E Rohe, you're just the same as ever.' It's good having my sister back and knowing she hasn't changed. Rose is the hard-case one in the family, the kamakama one, and the one with the brains.

Last night we stayed up talking till all hours, even Dad and Nanny who usually go to bed after tea. Rose made us laugh telling about the people she knows, and taking off professor this and professor that from varsity. Nanny, Mum, and I had tears running down from laughing; e ta Rose we laughed all night.

At last Nanny got out of her chair and said, 'Time for sleeping. The mouths steal the time of the eyes.' That's the lovely way she has of talking, Nanny, when she speaks in English. So we went to bed and Rose and I kept our mouths going for another hour or so before falling asleep.

This morning I said to Rose that we'd better go and get her measured for the dress up at Mrs Frazer's. Rose wanted to wait a day or two but I reminded her the wedding was only two weeks away and that Mrs Frazer had three frocks to finish.

'Who's Mrs Frazer anyway,' she asked. Then I remembered Rose hadn't met these neighbours though they'd been in the district a few years. Rose had been away at school.

'She's a dressmaker,' I looked for words. 'She's nice.'

'What sort of nice?' asked Rose.

'Rose, don't you say anything funny when we go up there,' I said. I know Rose, she's smart. 'Don't you get smart.' I'm older than Rose but she's the one that speaks out when something doesn't please her. Mum used to say, Rohe you've got the brains but you look to your sister for the sense. I started to feel funny about taking Rose up to Jane Frazer's because Jane often says the wrong thing without knowing.

We got our work done, had a bath and changed, and when Dad came back from the shed we took the station-wagon to drive over to Jane's. Before we left we called out to Mum, 'Don't forget to make us a Maori bread for when we get back.'

'What's wrong with your own hands,' Mum said, but she was only joking. Always when one of us comes home one of the first things she does is make a big Maori bread.

Rose made a good impression with her kamakama ways, and Jane's two nuisance kids took a liking to her straight away. They kept jumping up and down on the sofa to get Rose's attention and I kept thinking what a waste of a good sofa it was, what a waste of a good house for those two nuisance things. I hope when I have kids they won't be so hoha.

I was pleased about Jane and Rose. Jane was asking Rose all sorts of questions about her life in Auckland. About varsity and did Rose join in the marches and demonstrations. Then they went on to talking about fashions and social life in the city, and Jane seemed deeply interested. Almost as though she was jealous of Rose and the way she lived, as though she felt Rose had something better than a lovely house and clothes and everything she needed to make life good for her. I was pleased to see that Jane liked my sister so much, and proud of my sister and her entertaining and friendly ways.

Jane made a cup of coffee when she'd finished measuring Rose for the frock, then packed the two kids outside with a piece of chocolate cake each. We were sitting having coffee when we heard a truck turn in at the bottom of Frazers' drive.

Jane said, 'That's Alan. He's been down the road getting the Maoris for scrub cutting.'

I felt my face get hot. I was angry. At the same time I was hoping Rose would let the remark pass. I tried hard to think of something to say to cover Jane's words though I'd hardly said a thing all morning. But my tongue seemed to thicken and all I could think of was Rohe don't.

Rose was calm. Not all red and flustered like me. She took a big pull on the cigarette she had lit, squinted her eyes up and blew the smoke out gently. I knew something was coming.

'Don't they have names?'

'What. Who?' Jane was surprised and her face was getting pink.

'The people from down the road whom your husband is employing to cut scrub.' Rose the stink thing, she was talking all Pakehafied.

'I don't know any of their names.'

I was glaring at Rose because I wanted her to stop but she was avoiding my looks and pretending to concentrate on her cigarette.

'Do they know yours ?'

'Mine?'

'Your name.'

'Well...Yes.'

'Yet you have never bothered to find out their names or to wonder whether or not they have any.'

The silence seemed to bang around in my head for ages and ages. Then I think Jane muttered something about difficulty, but that touchy sister of mine stood up and said, 'Come on Hera.' And I with my red face and shut mouth followed her out to the station wagon without a goodbye or anything.

I was so wild with Rose. I was wild. I was determined to blow her up about what she had done, I was determined. But now that we were alone together I couldn't think what to say. Instead I felt an awful big sulk coming on. It has always been my trouble, sulking. Whenever I don't feel sure about something I go into a big fat sulk. We had a teacher at school who used to say to some of us girls, 'Speak, don't sulk.' She'd say, 'You only sulk because you haven't learned how and when to say your minds.'

At last I said, 'Rose, you're a stink thing.' Tears were on the way. 'Gee Rohe, you made me embarrassed.' Then Rose said, 'Don't worry Honey she's got a thick hide.'

These words of Rose's took me by surprise and I realised something about Rose then. What she said made all my anger go away and I felt very sad because it's not our way of talking to each other. Usually we'd say, 'Never mind Sis,' if we wanted something to be forgotten. But when Rose said, 'Don't worry Honey she's got a thick hide,' it made her seem a lot older than me, and tougher, and as though she knew much more than me about the world. It made me realise too that underneath her jolly and forthright ways Rose was very hurt. I remembered back to when we were both little and Rose used to play up at school if she didn't like the teacher. She'd get smart and I used to be ashamed and tell Mum on her when we got home, because although she had the brains I was always the well behaved one.

Rose was speaking to me in a new way now. It made me feel sorry for her and for myself. All my life I had been sitting back and letting her do the objecting. Not only me, but Mum and Dad and the rest of the family too. All of us too scared to make known when we had been hurt or slighted. And how can the likes of Jane know when we go round pretending all is well. How can Jane know us?

But then I tried to put another thought into words. I said to Rose, 'We do it too. We say, "the Pakeha doctor," or "the Pakeha at the post office", and sometimes we mean it in a bad way.'

'Except that we talk like this to each other only. It's not so much what is said, but when and where and in whose presence. Besides, you and I don't speak in this way now, not since we were little. It's the older ones: Mum, Dad, Nanny who have this habit.'

Then Rose said something else. 'Jane Frazer will still want to be your friend and mine in spite of my embarrassing her today; we're in the fashion.'

'What do you mean?'

'It's fashionable for a Pakeha to have a Maori for a friend.' Suddenly Rose grinned. Then I heard Jane's voice coming out of that Rohe's mouth and felt a grin of my own coming. 'I have friends who are Maoris. They're lovely people. The eldest girl was married recently and I did the frocks. The other girl is at varsity. They're all so *friendly* and so *natural* and their house is absolutely *spotless*.'

I stopped the wagon in the drive and when we'd got out Rose started strutting up the path. I saw Jane's way of walking and felt a giggle coming on. Rose walked up Mum's scrubbed steps, 'Absolutely spotless.' She left her shoes in the porch and bounced into the kitchen. 'What did I tell you? Absolutely spotless. And a friendly natural woman taking new bread from the oven. '

Mum looked at Rose then at me. 'What have you two been up to? Rohe I hope you behaved yourself at that Pakeha place?' But Rose was setting the table. At the sight of Mum's bread she'd forgotten all about Jane and the events of the morning.

When Dad, Heke, and Matiu came in for lunch, Rose, Mum, Nanny and I were already into the bread and the big bowl of hot corn.

'E ta,' Dad said. 'Let your hardworking father and your two hardworking brothers starve. Eat up.'

'The bread's terrible. You men better go down to the shop and get you a shop bread,' said Rose.

'Be the day,' said Heke.

'Come on my fat Rohe. Move over and make room for your Daddy. Come on my baby shift over.'

Dad squeezed himself round behind the table next to Rose. He picked up the bread Rose had buttered for herself and started eating. 'The bread's terrible all right,' he said. Then Mat and Heke started going on about how awful the corn was and who cooked it and who grew it, who watered it all summer and who pulled out the weeds.

So I joined in the carryings on and forgot about Rose and Jane for the meantime. But I'm not leaving it at that. I'll find some way of letting Rose know I understand and I know it will be difficult for me because I'm not clever the way she is. I can't say things the same and I've never learnt to stick up for myself.

But my sister won't have to be alone again. I'll let her know that.

Parade

Yesterday I went with Hoani, Lena, and the little ones up along the creek where the bush begins, to cut fern and flax. Back there at the quiet edge of the bush with the hills rolling skyward and the sound of the sea behind me I was glad I had come home in response to Auntie's letter. It was easy there, to put aside the heaviness of spirit which had come upon me during the week of carnival. It was soothing to follow with my eyes the spreading circles of fern patterning the hills' sides, and good to feel the coolness of flax and to realise again the quiet strength of each speared leaf. It was good to look into the open throated flax blooms with their lit-coal colours, and to put a hand over the swollen black splitting pods with the seed heavy in them.

And I thought of how each pod would soon cast aside its heaviness and become a mere shell, warped and empty, while that which had been its own heaviness would become new life. New growth and strength.

As we carried the bundles of fern and flax that we had collected and put them into the creek to keep fresh for the morning I was able to feel that tomorrow, the final day of the carnival, would be different from the ones recently passed when realisation had come to me, resting in me like stone.

'Please come for the carnival,' Auntie's letter had said. And the letter from my little cousin Ruby: 'Please come Matewai. We haven't seen you for two years.' I had felt excitement in me at the thought of returning, being back with them. And I came for the carnival as they had asked.

It was easy this morning to feel a lightness of spirit, waking to a morning so warm and fullscented, with odours rising to the nostrils as though every morning comes from inside the earth. Rich damp smells drenched every grass blade, every seeded stalk, and every cluster of ragwort thistle and blackberry. Steaming up through the warming rosettes of cow dung. Stealing up the stems of lupin and along the lupin arms, out on to the little spread hands of lupin leaves.

And a sweet wood smell coming from the strewn chips and wood stack by the shed. A tangle of damp stinks from the fowl yard and orchard, and from the cold rustiness of the cow-holed swamp. Some of the earth morning smells had become trapped under the hot bodies of cows, and were being dispensed, along with the cows' own milk and saliva smells, from the swinging bellies and milk-filled udders as the animals made their way poke-legged to the milking sheds. That was what it was like this morning.

And there was a breath of sea. Somewhere — barely discernible since evening had been long forgotten and the night had been shrugged aside — somewhere the sea was casting its breath at the land. It was as though it were calling to the land, and to us as we woke and walked into the day, 'I'm here, I'm here. Don't forget about me.'

The sun fingered the ridges of hills as we pulled the flax and fern from the creek and began to decorate the truck for the parade. We worked quickly, tying and nailing the fronds and leaves into place. And when we had finished, Uncle Hirini drove the truck in under some trees where the sun could not reach it, while we went inside to change into our costumes.

Auntie had sent all the children to wash in the creek, and as I watched them from the window it was like seeing myself as I had been not very long ago. As if it were my own innocence that they cast on to the willow branches with their clothes. Light had filtered through the willow branches on to the creek's surface, spreading in small pools to the creek banks and on to the patches of watercress and shafts of reed.

The sun had put a finger on almost everything by now. It had touched our houses and the paddocks and tree tops, and stroked its silver over the sea. The beach stones were warming from the sun's touching, and black weed, thrown up by the sea, lay in heaps on the shore drying and helpless in the sun's relentless stroking.

I watched the bodies falling into water warmed from the sun's touching, and fingers, not his, squeezing at large bars of yellow soap. Fingers spreading blistery trails of suds up and over legs and arms. Bodies, heads, ears. 'Wash your taringas.' Auntie from the creek bank. Backsides, frontsides, fingers, toes. Then splashing, diving, puffing, and blowing in this pool of light. Out on to the banks, rubbing with towels, wrapping the towels around, scrambling back through the willows, across the yard where the sun caught them for a moment before they ran inside to dress. It was like seeing myself as I had been such a short time ago.

Auntie stood back on the heels of her bare feet, puffing at a cigarette, and looking at me through half shut eyes. Her round head was nodding at me , and her long hair which she had brushed out of the two thick plaits which usually circled her head fell about her shoulders, and two more hanks of hair glistened under her armpits. The skin on her shoulders and back was pale in its unaccustomed bareness, cream coloured and cool looking. And there was Granny Rita stretching lips over bare gums to smile at me.

'Very pretty dia. Very pretty dia,' she kept saying, stroking the cloak that they had put on me, her old hands aged and grey like burnt paper. The little ones admiring, staring.

Setting me apart.

And I stood before them in the precious cloak, trying to smile.

'I knew our girl would come,' Auntie was saying again. 'I knew our girl would come if we sent for her.'

We could hear the truck wheezing out in the yard, and Grandpa Hohepa who is bent and crabby was hurrying everyone along, banging his stick on the floor. 'Kia tere,' he kept on saying. 'Kia tere.'

The men helped Granny Rita and Grandpa Hohepa on to the truck and sat them where they could see, then I stepped on to the platform which had been erected for me and sat down for the journey into town. The others formed their lines along each side of the tray and sat down too.

In town, in the heat of late morning, we moved slowly with the other parade floats along the streets lined with people. Past the railway station and shops, and over bridges and crossings, singing one action song after another. Hakas and pois.

And as I watched I noted again, as I had on the other carnival days of concerts and socials, the crowd reaction. I tried not to think. Tried not to let my early morning feelings leave me. Tried not to know that there was something different and strange in the people's reaction to us. And yet I knew this was not something new and strange, but only that during my time away from here my vision and understanding had expanded. I was able now to see myself and other members of my race as others see us. And this new understanding left me as abandoned and dry as an emptied pod of flax that rattles and rattles into the wind.

Everyone was clapping and cheering for Uncle Hirini and my cousin Hoani who kept jumping from the truck to the road, patterning with their taiaha, springing on their toes and doing the pukana, making high piping noises with their voices. Their tongues lolled and their eyes popped.

But it was as though my uncle and Hoani were a pair of clowns. As though they wore frilled collars and had paint on their noses, and kept dropping baggy pants to display spotted underwear and sock suspenders. As though they turned cartwheels and hit each other on the head, while someone else banged on a tin to show everyone that clowns have tin heads.

And the people's reaction to the rest of us? The singing, the pois? I could see enjoyment on the upturned faces and yet it occurred to me again and again that many people enjoyed zoos. That's how I felt. Animals in cages to be stared at. This one with stripes, this one with spots — or a trunk, or bad breath, the remains of a third eye. Talking, swinging by the tail, walking in circles, laughing, crying, having babies.

Or museums. Stuffed birds, rows of shells under glass, the wing span of an albatross, preserved bodies, shrunken heads. Empty gourds, and meeting houses where no one met any more.

I kept thinking and trying not to think, 'Is that what we are to them?' Museum pieces, curios, antiques, shells under glass. A travelling circus, a floating zoo. People clapping and cheering to show that they know about such things.

The sun was hot. Auntie at the end of the row was beaming, shining, as though she were the sun. A happy sun, smiling and singing to fill the whole world with song. And with her were all the little sunlets singing too, and stamping. Arms out, fingers to the heart, fists clenched, hands open, head to one side, face the front. Piupius swinging, making their own music, pois bobbing. And voices calling the names of canoes —Tainui, Takitimu, Kurahaupo, Te Arawa...the little ones in the front bursting with the fullness of their own high voices and their dancing hands and stamping feet, unaware that the crowd had put us under glass and that our uncle and cousin with their rolling eyes and prancing feet wore frilled collars and size nineteen shoes and had had pointed hats clapped down upon their heads.

Suddenly I felt a need to reach out to my auntie and uncle, to Hoani and the little ones, to old Rita and Hohepa.

We entered the sports ground, and when the truck stopped the little ones scrambled down and ran off to look for their mates from school. Auntie and Hoani helped Granny Rita and Grandpa Hohepa down. I felt older than any of them.

And it was hot. The sun threw down his spinnings of heat and weavings of light on to the cracked summer earth as we walked towards the pavilion.

'Do you ever feel as though you're in a circus?' I said to Hoani who is the same age as I am. He flipped onto his hands and walked the rest of the way upside down. I had a feeling Hoani knew what I was talking about.

Tea. Tea and curling sandwiches. Slabs of crumbling fruit cake, bottles of blood warm fizz, and someone saying, 'What're you doing in that outfit?' Boys from cousin Lena's school.

'Didn't you see us on the truck?' Lena was saying.

'Yeh, we saw.' One of the boys had Lena's poi and was swinging it round and round and making aeroplane noises.

Mr Goodwin, town councillor, town butcher, touching Uncle Hirini's shoulder and saying, 'Great, Great,' to show what a great person he himself was, being one of the carnival organisers and having lived in the township all his life amongst dangling sausages, crescents of black pudding, leg roasts, rib roasts, flannelled tripe, silverside, rolled beef, cutlets, dripping. 'Great.' He was Great. You could tell by the prime steak hand on Uncle's shoulder.

Uncle Hirini believed the hand. Everyone who saw the hand believed it too, or so it seemed to me. They were all believers on days such as these.

And the woman president of the C.W.I. shouting at Granny Rita as though Granny were deaf or simple. Granny Rita nodding her head, waiting for the woman to go away so she could eat her cake.

It was stuffy and hot in the hall with the stale beer and smoke smell clinging to its walls and floor, and to the old chipped forms and sagging trestle tables. Bird dirt, spider webs, mice droppings. The little ones had had enough to eat and were running up and down with their mates from school, their piupius swinging and clacking about their legs. Auntie rounding them all up and whispering to go outside. Auntie on her best behaviour wishing those kids would get out and stop shaming her. Wanting to yell, 'Get out you kids. Get outside and play. You spoil those piupius and I'll whack your bums.' Auntie sipping tea and nibbling at a sandwich.

We began to collect the dishes. Squashed raisins, tea dregs. The men were stacking the trestles and shifting forms. Mrs President put her hands into the soapy water and smiled at the ceiling, smiled to show what sort of day it was. 'Many hands make light work,' she sang out. We reached for towels, we reached for wet plates to prove how right she was.

Outside, people were buying and selling, guessing weights and stepping chains, but I went to where Granny Rita and Grandpa Hohepa were sitting in the shade of a tree, guarding the cloak between them.

More entertainment. The lines were forming again but I sat down by old Rita and Hohepa out of the sun's heat.

'Go,' Granny Rita was saying to me. 'Take your place.'

'I think I'll watch this time, Nanny.'

'You're very sad today, dia. Very sad.'

Granny Rita's eyes pricking at my skin. Old Hohepa's too.

'It's hot Nanny.'

A crowd had gathered to watch the group and the singing had begun, but those two put their eyes on me, waiting for me to speak.

'They think that's all we're good for,' I said. 'A laugh and that's all. Amusement. In any other week of the year we don't exist. Once a year we're taken out and put on show, like relics.'

And silence.

Silence with people laughing and talking.

Silence with the singing lifting skyward, and children playing.

Silence. Waiting for them to say something to me. Wondering what they would say.

'You grow older, you understand more,' Granny Rita said to me.

Silence and waiting.

'No one can take your eyes from you,' she said. Which is true.

Then old Hohepa, who is bent and sometimes crabby said, 'It is your job, this. To show others who we are.'

And I sat there with them for a long time. Quiet. Realising what had been put upon me. Then I went towards the group and took my place, and began to stamp my feet on to the cracked earth, and to lift my voice to the sun who holds the earth's strength within himself. And gradually the sun withdrew his touch and the grounds began to empty, leaving a flutter of paper, trampled heads of dandelion and clover, and insects finding a way into the sticky sweet necks of empty bottles.

The truck had been in the sun all afternoon. The withered curling fern and drooping flax gave it the appearance of a scaly monster, asleep and forgotten, left in a corner to die. I helped Granny Rita into the cab beside Grandpa Hohepa.

'This old bum gets too sore on those hard boards. This old bum wants a soft chair for going home. Ah lovely dia. Move your fat bum ova Hepa.' The old parched hand on my cheek. 'Not to worry dia, not to worry.'

And on the back of the truck we all moved close together against the small chill that evening had brought in. Through the town's centre then along the blackening roads. On into the night until the road ended. Opening gates, closing them. Crossing the dark paddocks with the hills dense on one hand, the black patch of sea on the other. And the only visible thing, the narrow rind of foam curling shoreward under a sky emptied of light. Listening, I could hear the shuffle of water on stone, and rising above this were the groans and sighs of a derelict monster with his scales withered and dropping, making his short sighted way through prickles and fern, over cow pats and stinging nettle, along fence lines, past the lupin bushes, their fingers crimped against the withdrawal of the day.

I took in a big breath, filling my lungs with sea and air and land and people. And with past and present and future, and felt a new strength course through me. I lifted my voice to sing and heard and felt the others join with me. Singing loudly into the darkest of nights. Calling on the strength of the people. Calling them to paddle the canoes and to paddle on and on. To haul the canoes down and paddle. On and on —

'Hoea ra nga waka
E te iwi e,
Hoea hoea ra,
Aotea, Tainui, Kurahaupo,
Hoea hoea ra.

Toia mai nga waka
E te iwi e,
Hoea hoea ra,
Mataatua, Te Arawa,
Takitimu, Tokomaru,
Hoea hoea ra.'

Mutuwhenua (Extract)

I was nine years old when we found the stone. Grandpa Toki was alive then and my parents and I had gone to his place because a man from the council was to be there to discuss with my grandparents and the rest of the family a road that the council wanted to put through our settlement to open up more land in the area. My grandparents' place is a mile or so from our place, on a small rise, with the hills stacking up behind. And from somewhere in the hills comes a creek which in times of heavy rain can swell and flood the flat land of the gully.

The man from the council had his son with him, and while the adults were talking the boy and my cousins and I went down to the creek to play.

Spring was unfolding from the end of a sodden winter, pushing up new shoots of grass along the edge of the creek which was now returning to its normal flow. The wet had flogged the gully. Banks had pulled away and slid into sticky mounds along the ferny edges of the bush. Shingle, heaped by the awry spilling of the creek, had filtered mud and rotting debris into reeking piles.

I don't know who noticed the stone first. Its shape made it different from the other stones and pieces of stick lying at the bottom of the creek. Lying in the water it had no colour at all. The boy and my cousin Toki lifted it out on to the bank between them. It was about a foot in length, tongue-shaped at one end and tapered towards the other. We dried it on our clothes and sat on the bank talking about it in the way that we always used to talk about the special stones or shells we found. Or about our coloured bits of glass. Now and again we stroked our hands along it or held it to know its shape and its heaviness or to feel it warming to our touch.

Then we began to wonder how it had got there in the creek. And, suddenly, the boy, who was older than any of us, said, 'It came in the floods from the hills and it took years and years to get here. It's hundreds of years old.' He picked it up and walked towards the house and we followed with our eyes popping. Not because of what the stone was, but because of the hundreds of years and because of how it came, taking ages and ages.

'Look what I found,' he said, and there was sudden silence in the kitchen, with all eyes on him and what he held.

'Well,' his father said. He took it from the boy and weighed it in his hands, looking about at all the adults. But they too had become stone in the leaping silence of the room.

'Well,' he said. 'Must be worth a coin or two.' But they didn't move or speak.

'In the creek,' the boy said into the long moment. 'Just lying there.'

Then my grandfather said, 'It goes back. Back to the hills.' And we all waited.

'Come off it,' the man said. 'Can't you see?'

They didn't answer him.

'Well, look, think of it this way. What use is it to anyone back there in the hills. Who can see it there?'

He told the boy to go and put the stone in the car and kept talking about how they could all share. 'It was my boy who found it,' he kept saying. 'But it's your land. There's something in it for everyone.'

While he was speaking I saw my father beckon my cousin Toki to him and whisper; then Toki slipped away.

The man was angry later when he went to the car and found the stone had gone. He accused my grandparents of many things but they were quiet and said nothing.

After the man and his son left, my cousin took the stone from under the house where he'd hidden it and gave it to our grandfather. The older ones spoke together. Then Grandpa Toki and my father went, taking the stone, far back into the hills, and returned without it. They told us how they had stood at the top of a rise and thrown the stone piece into a deep gully. And the next day they went back again with a tractor and graded the top of the hill down into the gully where the stone was, covering it with fall after fall of rock and earth.

I often think of that piece of stone lying at the bottom of the gully buried under a ton of rock and earth. And when I think of it I can feel its weight in my hands and the coldness of it, and I can see its dull green light. And it always seems that I can feel it and see it better now than I could when it was just like another shell or piece of coloured glass. As though part of myself is buried in that gully.

Whenever my cousins and I talk about that time I know they feel the same way too. And I have often wondered what the Pakeha boy's feelings would have been had he known what our older ones did with the stone. I saw him stroking his hands along the tapered handle and watched him curl his fingers about it and I wondered if it warmed in his grasp. I watched him look way into the hills with quietness shining from his face, so it is difficult to know. Perhaps the stone is part of that boy too, though I think not.

But what I'd wanted to tell Graeme during those days before our wedding was not so much the story of the stone, because that would have been easy enough. I'd wanted to tell him about the significance to me of what had happened; wanted him to know there was part of me that could never be given and that would not change. Because of my belief in the rightness of what had been done with the stone, my clear knowledge at nine years of age of the rightness (to me), I can never move away from who I am. Not completely, even though I have wanted to, often.

There is part of me that will not change, and it is buried under a ton of earth in a deep gully. The ngaio tree will age and die. Or perhaps it will not age. Perhaps the wind will have it in spite of its protectors, or perhaps it will be in the way and will go under the axe one day. But the stone with both life and death upon it has been returned to the hands of the earth, and is safe there, in the place where it truly belongs.

PATRICIA GRACE (1937; Ngati Toa, Ngati Raukawa, Te Ati Awa) was born in Wellington. She was educated at St Mary's College and Wellington Teachers' College. At present she is teaching English (specialising in English as a second language) at Porirua College.

Her collection *Waiariki* (1975), was the first book of short stories by a Maori woman writer. This was followed by the first novel by a Maori woman writer, *Mutuwhenua — The Moon Sleeps* (1978). *The Dream Sleepers and other stories* (1980) and *The Kuia and the Spider* (a book for children) followed. Her stories have been reprinted in *Contemporary Maori Writing* (1970), *Short Stories by New Zealanders One* (1972), *Short Stories by New Zealanders Two* (1974), *My New Zealand* (1974), *New Zealand Short Stories — Third Series* (1975), *Ten Modern New Zealand Story Writers* (1976) and *NZ Listener Short Stories* (1977). With Hone Tuwhare she appeared at the first Writers' Conference at the University of Papua New Guinea in 1976 and was invited in 1977 to the SPACLALS Conference at the University of Queensland where she read with Witi Ihimaera. She has also been involved in the New Zealand Book Council's Writers in Schools scheme and the Maori Artists' and Writers' huis and she read her work at the Second New Zealand Writers' Conference in 1979.

Patricia was awarded the first Maori Purposes Fund Board grant for Maori writers in 1974 and this was followed by a grant from the New Zealand Literary Fund. She is a recipient of the Hubert Church Prose Award (1976). Her stories have been broadcast in English by Radio New Zealand, and South Pacific Television produced her story 'The Dream' in Maori for *Pacific Viewpoint* (1979). Her work has also been translated into Russian and Swedish.

Hirini Melbourne

He Whakaaro Huri Roto

Ehara au nā tēnei ao,
Engari nā te aroha i wae aku mātua.
Ko aku kahu, ko te mauri me te wehi o oku tīpuna.
Ko aku kupu whakaaro, ā rātau tikanga.
E kare, ko aku waiata me aku tangi rā ō rātau roimata
A hā hā!
Ka puta he Māori.

Ko au tō tamaiti hei waha i ō kōrero.
Kia pai tō whakaako i a au.
Ko aku taonga tīpuna ki roto i taku ngākau.
Ko ā te Pākehā ki aku pūkoro.

I whānau noa, kore noa au
Kuaretia koe me hau hoki e

E ngā whaea o te ao hou
  Huri whakaroto
Hoatu he waiora Māori hei note mā tō tamaiti!

HIRINI MELBOURNE (1949; Tuhoe) was born at Whakatane. Currently he lectures in Maori at Waikato University. A former editor of Maori publications for the School Publications Branch of the Department of Education (1975-78) he edited *Te Wharekura* and *Te Tautoko* and he initiated the forthcoming series *He Purapura*.

Hirini's work has been published in *Te Kaea, The NZ Listener, Education, Nexus, Salient, Koru* and the *School Journal*. Also a composer, he scored the guitar track for *Two Rivers Meet*, Richard Turner and Rowley Habib's film about contemporary Maori poets. His record *Children of Tane* records his New Zealand bird songs and with another group of songs to be released under the title *Friends of Maui* they were heard on Radio New Zealand during Maori language week (1979).

Taunoa Kohere

Selections From A Diary

A long absence from those of my kind, fiction of some future age,

I narrate, elegant ingenu,
An eagle lost at sea, a shadow cast in bronze.

Bands of elders control the palace-gates
And mines are worked by foreign hands —
A scribbler in this new currency, I seek
The salute of the man crying in his solitude.

Pigs run from the hills, with rain on their backs,
To marvel at the dying of a poet. A final audience,
And his fine rhetoric thrills to the bone; already
They think toward statues in the park.

It shall be like this when the figurehead goes
From the crest of a rising vessel; how it was
When godly men walked among the people,
Or Christ, regally attired, was seen by peasant eyes.

(A ship lies beached upon the rocks, a drunken captain
Dreams of gold beyond his reach. A child intent upon its furious noise,
Summer confesses neither its sterility nor its images of gold.)

Yes, I too am a yeoman of sorts, as such fellows go,
And my truth shall not do for this age. Nothing less than
The thunder and dialect of the mute in speech.

TAUNOA H. KOHERE (1948; Ngati Porou, Rongowhakaata, Kati Tahu) died in 1969 while a student in English at Victoria University. As a student at Hastings Boys' High School he had published in the *Herald Tribune* and later appeared in university student publications. James Bertram described him as one of his most gifted students, someone likely to have become a writer of distinction. His grandfather, Reweti Kohere, was a notable writer and edited several Maori newspapers which ceased publication with the Depression.

Atihana Moana Johns

He Pakete Kanara

She used to live along the beach a bit from Hemi's place, and every time Hemi went past to the store on his horse she would poke her head out the window and yell out for a packet of candles or tobacco or something from the store. Hemi didn't mind at all but just for fun he tried to sneak past now and again, but he seldom got past. The window would creak open and she would yell, 'E Hemi! Tikina he pakete kanara.'

   She was getting old — too old to go fishing, and she didn't go out much except to the road when anyone came past. But her voice was still strong — a bit hoarse but strong, and on a clear still evening you could hear it from the other end of the valley calling for her house cow or from out in the bay cussing her dog. It was a reassuring part of the valley running back in a long narrow funnel from the sea like the sound of the breakers out on the reef, night after night without fail. You had to pass her place to get out of the valley and you couldn't do it without her yelling out or passing the time of day with you in that strong voice of hers.

   Her children had grown up and left. They came back now and again but mostly she was alone, with her dog and her house cow and passers-by.

213

Anyway her and Hemi settled into a regular arrangement once her youngest son left for town. He got her things twice a week from the store and delivered them to her door. About once a week he stayed to read her the news — quite by accident to begin with, or so it seemed at the time. One of her mokopuna had his School C. results in the paper. She peered at them but said she couldn't read without her glasses. A long time afterwards Hemi realised she couldn't read at all and she didn't have any glasses, but he played along.

She wanted to know about everything, even the football and how Cherrington and J.B. got on for Auckland last Saturday. Especially she was keen on the Korean war because she had a mokopuna over there. She'd squint into the distance and wonder how he was getting on in the winter snows of Korea. To her there was no summer in Korea.

When Hemi got bored with reading her the news he'd make some excuse to go, like he hadn't chopped the wood yet or he had to go and bait the set line. Or else he would make up the news like: 'At halftime the score was nil all. But after halftime things began to hum for North Auckland. First a scissors between Peter and brother J.B. found J.B. between the Auckland posts. Five nil. Then it was Cherrington between the posts after a fifty-yard run. Ten nil. Then, while Auckland was still recovering, a dummy, two sidesteps, and a burst past the scrum carried old Mihi Rapata between the posts. Fifteen nil.'

And old Mihi Rapata, realising that she'd been taken in but enjoying it all the same, would yell, 'Taureka!' and hit Hemi with the tea towel as he went out the door.

And so the days passed. Hemi felt a certain responsibility towards old Mihi living alone like that. When the valley was still full of people it was different. There was always someone around, but then only the Hetas, Pirinoas, Hemi's family, and old Mihi were still there. She wouldn't move to the city with her children like some of the old people did.

With nearly everyone gone the valley was quiet. Hemi often said that he would rather talk to Mihi than the cows. When someone died however it was different. Back would come everyone living in town to the old meeting house and Mihi would stand by the door and welcome them with her long sad karanga. That was her job as long as Hemi and most of them could remember. And at night she led the waiata and by the grave she led the hymn singing. It was strange really. It took a tangi to wake up the valley. There was old Bill Pirinoa, the chief orator, up and down the marae and big Tom Heta at the back of the dining room in charge of the cooking and Hemi's Dad circulating amongst the Ngati Kotiti as he called the town Maori, joking along as he went.

But then the buses and cars would disappear out of the valley and back to

214

town again. A few would linger on in their old houses looking out of place in their new clothes. Then they would leave and the valley would settle down until the next tangi. It took a few days for Mihi to get back to normal but she never forgot her packet of candles. Nothing made her forget that.

Soon it was Hemi's turn to leave for boarding school and perhaps for good. Mihi seemed to accept it, much better anyway than Hemi's mother. She was always suspicious of Pakeha education even though Hemi was going to a Maori school. Certainly Hemi could never remember his mother going out of her way to be nice to a Pakeha and she seldom spoke English. Anyway she cried when the taxi stopped outside Mihi's where the road ended, and Hemi had doubts for the first time about going away. Before that he couldn't wait, but — but he got on the taxi like so many before him since the last war and he was away. Once the taxi was out of the valley and through the gumfields past the store to catch the bus in the main road, only the future wound before him on the road to Auckland and beyond.

Mum had cried on his shoulder as if the Pakeha were taking her son away to gaol. Dad had put on his best show — or tried to — joking about how the cows can milk themselves now, or maybe he ought to get a milkmaid like the ones he saw in England during the war. He had a quaver in his throat but his handshake was firm and reassuring. And Mihi's strong voice frightened the taxi driver a bit but she was her usual self. 'Come back and take J.B.'s place, e hoa. And don't worry about me. Your father can get my packet of candles now.'

Hemi couldn't quite forget the old valley and the bay. On some nights he thought he heard the waves breaking out on the reef and for a while he worried about his mother. He spoke Maori as often as he could just for her sake. Once a fortnight he had to write home and he was happy to do so, knowing that he would be lucky to hear from them. He could imagine his father reading his letters to his mother who couldn't read English or didn't want to, so Hemi always wrote half of it in Maori. It would be just like his father to add a bit here and there like Hemi did for old Mihi. Hemi hoped that Dad would read Mihi his letters too and he never forgot to ask Dad to give her his aroha and to tell her he was playing centre just like J.B. and he always finished with: P.S. Send me some money.

By June, Hemi had not got any letters from home. He had never seen an autumn like that in Hawkes Bay — brilliant red and yellow English trees and bare silver in winter. The frosts went clean through his jersey on his way to breakfast. The football season was half gone and Hemi played in one of the lower teams, although he never said that in his letters. But one Sunday in an interhouse match everything clicked, as he used to say to old Mihi. He scored after selling a dummy. Five nil. Near the end he intercepted and scored again. Ten nil, the end of the game, and the shield for his house. Just like J.B. That night he wrote all about it in his letter for Dad, and Mihi too of course, and late that night he heard the breakers drumming out on the reef.

The next day he was still feeling pleased with himself. Some of his housemates gave him an extra square of butter that morning at breakfast. And, at last, at lunch time he got his first letter from home. He saved it for after lunch and went under a tree near the chapel to read it — only two pages long and written in Dad's neat standard-six writing. It said:

Dear Son,

Sorry we couldn't write sooner but you know how it is with me writing letters. Me and your mother are very well and we hope you are too. Looking forward to having you back for the holidays — to milk the cows. Don't go to Auckland with those useless relations of yours. Come back here. Your mother is as fit as a fiddle and kicking the cows out the bail no trouble at all. Grumbling as always.

Son I have some bad news. Your old tupuna Mihi passed away last week. The tangi is over now and everyone is gone. I wasn't sure if the school would let you come so I didn't send you a telegram. No money to pay your fare anyway.

When I went to get her things at the store she was all right. But when I came back she was on her bed. Ka mate ke. Too late to get a doctor. You know, we got her suitcase out to put her clothes in to bury them with her and we found about four dozen packets of candles in it.

Old Mihi was fond of you but don't feel bad about it. We all have to go some time. And . . .

Hemi blinked the tears from his eyes. He did not want to believe that anyone could be so lonely but, knowing what it was like in that valley, he knew in his bones that it was so. Mihi would have been pleased to know how well he played that Sunday, and on the way back to the classroom to get his books he wondered who was going to do the karanga outside the old meeting house for the next tangi.

Hemi The Pokokohua

All his relations said he was a kind and good boy. He was quiet, they said, so most of the time no one took all that much notice of him and he wasn't there as far as they were concerned. Only their image of him — quiet, kind, good, clever, obedient and obliging.

Most of the time, Hemi didn't mind this a bit. It was very useful at school. The teachers didn't worry too much about him. Someone else always got the blame for anything that went wrong — not him. He was too good.

But just now and again this image used to annoy him. He wasn't real — only an image derived from his tribe — good, kind, clever, obedient. Why couldn't he be real like his relations? And sometimes the isolation set him off on long walks along the beach and into the cave at the end to talk to himself. He often used to think that maybe he was tapu.

Very rarely did he break this image. Once he burst out swearing on the playground. The teacher growled instead at poor little Tuti. And little Tuti accepted it gracefully — almost as if he too wanted to preserve Hemi's tapu image. Another time Hemi set the gorse alight near the school and almost burnt down the outside toilets. The teacher growled at the person who provided the matches. 'You shouldn't have been there', was all Hemi got.

And so it went on. He was a reputation, not a real person. Maybe he was different. Not like the others. He was somebody that the rest of the community had made tapu and set apart. When he tried to wipe out the image they looked the other way. They weren't going to have Hemi spoilt. They knew that he was a good boy and that was that. It was no use him trying to prove them wrong.

So Hemi would give up trying and play along — even improving his image by being the brightest at school, the cleanest, no kutus in his hair, always a clean hankie, and clean nails. No, Hemi couldn't do nothing wrong they all believed. Not their Hemi.

But Hemi grew older — old enough to drink, smoke and play around with the girls like the others. At twelve years he tried drinking and could remember that when he finally grabbed the bottle underneath the tree that night down by the beach, while everyone sat around singing and Tare sat on the crate, no-one took the least bit of notice. He was so anonymous he drank more than anyone.

Boy, did he get drunk. He lurched around but all those red fire- and beer-lit faces didn't respond. They sang on and the guitar strummed along without missing a beat. He might just as well have been his own shadow up there on the tree, dancing and flickering with the flames.

Hemi was too drunk to care about his image or anything else any more. His head reeled and the ground bumped and dipped under him. Something deep inside him was let loose like a raging taniwha out of the deep cave and before his party mates on the beach realised it, Hemi had pushed Tare off the crate and was on top of him punching wildly. Tare was bigger and stronger than Hemi. To this day he does not know why he picked on Tare. Could it have been that Tare was so popular?

217

Anyway Tare threw Hemi off him and rolled over to get up. Then, bash! Hemi had grabbed a bottle and bashed him on the head with it. Poor Tare was out.

The taniwha in Hemi stopped, and backed away from what it had done. All those red faces stared at them in awe. In the silence only the waves scraped the sand along the beach. Hemi, scared, backed out of the firelight. By then the others had rushed over to revive Tare. Someone spilled beer over his drooling face and rubbed the bash on his head. After a while Tare, holding his head and groaning, sat up.

He didn't wait for any more. He stumbled off along the beach towards home and the beer warmth returned to slur his way along the sand. Halfway along he heard Tare call out in the clear night, 'Hey you bastard! Come back here! I'll fix you boy if I catch you! You Pokokohua!'

Hemi didn't go back but he dragged to a halt. It had occurred to him even through all that struggling in his head that no-one had insulted him like that before. No-one. Not good Hemi. Oh no. Not good, kind Hemi who was so good at school and all that. A pokokohua might be a rotten bastard but at least a pokokohua was real — was somebody real that you could touch and insult. Hemi didn't think exactly like this of course but the words sang in his head and swirled around with the beer — Pokokohua, Bastard, Pokokohua, Bastard. Hemi made a drunk tune out of them and slurred them into a rhythm as he said them out loud — Pokokohua, Bastard, Pokokohua, Bastard. The more he said them the lighter he felt. The image had fallen to the ground with the beer bottle. Hell! Man was he happy! He had to flop down on the sand and laugh like anything. Back at the party the singing had started up again, so nothing too much was wrong with Tare.

Hemi was still saying those words when he got to bed that night. He was very happy and tired. The taniwha in him curled up and went to sleep with a contented smile on its face. Hemi at last was noa.

By next morning of course everyone knew about it and his Mum and Dad didn't take long to find out either. Just a quick phone call from Auntie Wahanui who didn't like Hemi's Mum for some reason. Mum couldn't believe it. Full of Christian morality, she turned on Hemi and ripped into him. She just couldn't blame anyone else. She had to face it. Her boy who was going to be the first parson, teacher or doctor from Rangiawhia was a drunk who nearly killed someone. Waste the schooling, the scholarship, the confirmation at Church, everything. He was just a koretake like the rest. When her taniwha ran out of rage, she turned back to the stove and carried on with the breakfast crying quietly to herself.

Dad tried to be angry too but his taniwha was never any good at it. He felt an odd sense of pride in his son. The fact was, that he was never very happy about him and his good behaviour and everything. While other men's sons were out with the gang fishing and stealing watermelon his was usually in his room reading a book. But now, he looked at his boy in a different way. Fancy that, he kept saying to himself, fancy that. Then he remembered that he should be angry about it instead of pleased and he sent Hemi off to milk the cows. Hemi could feel the warmth of the new strange wondering look in his father's eyes as he went to the shed. For a change he didn't mind milking the cows one bit.

Things were different for Hemi after that — not suddenly of course but gradually. Everyone at Rangiawhia had to accommodate the new image he had drunkenly created for himself down on the beach that night. They began to accept him and not set him apart like his mother did for divine or educational purposes. He became the leader of their gang and Tare became his second in command. Well, after all, strong as Tare was, Hemi was still the cleverest. His mother no longer had the burden of grooming him for greater things in the Pakeha world and all his relations began to accept him as just another pokokohua like themselves. Even at school in his last year he got the strap and he notched them on his belt like the other pokokohua.

That was a while ago now. Hemi and the rest of Rangiawhia have all moved to the big city. Hemi is still the top man in his gang, secure in his identity and social position down at the public bar of the Station Hotel. He never did get to use that scholarship he won at Rangiawhia and he missed out on all that boarding school education. He was quite happy being a pokokohua in town.

ATIHANA MOANA JOHNS (1937; Ngatikahu, Te Rarawa, Te Aupouri) was born in Kaitaia and grew up at Whatuwhiwhi in Northland. He lectures in Maori Studies at Hamilton Teachers' College. He was educated at Te Aute College and Victoria University. His stories have appeared in *Te Maori*, *Te Ao Hou*, and *Short Stories by New Zealanders One*. A collection of his short stories is in preparation.

Te Aniwa Bosch

The Two Sisters

The family had been travelling for two days and nights and arrived at their new home in the city just before lunch on the third day. They sat in the truck, Mum, Dad, Hine the eldest, Ngahere, the boys Tame, Johnny and Wiri, and baby Moana, looking with dismay at their new home. Mum's brother had got them the house and it looked terrible. The front section was overgrown with weeds, the windows were just managing to hold on with broken hinges and the front gate was lying on the ground.

Hine thought of their other house back at the pa. Many memories of it raced through her mind as she sat there. She closed her eyes and then opened them.

'Well,' Mum sighed. 'Here we are.'

The street was deserted except for a dog and a couple of kids. The family began to unload the truck. Then Tame walked down the street looking for a fish and chip shop, taking his two younger brothers Johnny and Wiri with him. Hine and her father started to tidy up the inside of the house. As usual, Ngahere, the lady of the family, did as little as possible until Mum told her to put Moana to bed. Ngahere came out of the room as Hine went in.

'You all right, baby?' Hine whispered.

Moana looked absolutely beautiful lying across the bed with her tear-stained face half smiling in sleep.

'Don't you be afraid,' Hine said. 'We'll be all right.'

She came out and joined Mum and Dad and Ngahere in the kitchen. Mum had boiled the kettle for a cup of tea.

'E hoa,' Mum said to Dad. 'I wonder what they're doing now back home?'

'The same as always,' Dad answered. 'We've only been away a coupla days.'

He knew Mum was feeling homesick and Hine knew it too. Mum hadn't wanted to leave the pa, but she had to because there was no work at home for Dad and Tame.

'We have to make the best of it now,' Ngahere declared, smiling in that grown-up way of hers.

'Yes, dear,' Mum answered.

Just then the door opened and in came Johnny and Wiri, loaded down with groceries and chattering excitedly. Close behind them was Tame with a big parcel of fish and chips.

Mum looked at them silently. She looked at the fish and chips.

'Yes, we have to make the best of it,' she said.

The next day, Ngahere suggested that she and Hine should take Johnny and Wiri to be enrolled at the primary school not far from the house.

'E Ngahere,' Mum smiled. 'You always seem to know the right thing to do. You know a lot about the pakeha ways. Yes, you and Hine take your brothers to school.'

Hine felt a little put out that Ngahere had made the suggestion. After all she was the eldest, not Ngahere.

'You might know the right things to do, miss,' she said to Ngahere as they walked with Johnny and Wiri to the school, 'but when we get there I will do the talking.'

Ngahere shrugged her shoulders and nodded her head.

They arrived just before morning playtime. Hine and Ngahere went into the school office and a teacher took the two boys off to look at the playground. Hine filled in the boys' enrolment forms and the headmaster asked her to post the boys' birth certificates in to him, giving her the addressed envelope for them.

Afterwards, the headmaster took the two girls to the classroom where their brothers were playing. He called Johnny and Wiri over and after telling them who he was, asked if they would like to stay on at the school for the rest of the day.

'Yeah,' the boys replied. Then, before waiting for an answer they ran off to play.

It was then that Ngahere raised that sweet voice of hers.

'Please, Sir,' she asked. 'Could you help me? I was told of a girls' college quite near here. I wonder if you would write the address down for me as I would like to go over there now.'

It was obvious to Hine that the headmaster was taken with that Ngahere's charm.

'Yes,' he replied. 'I know the college you refer to.'

He wrote the college's address down and passed it to Ngahere.

'Oh thank you,' Ngahere smiled.

In the corridor she turned to Hine.

'Come on. We haven't got all day.'

They managed to find the college, not knowing how they did it, and Hine was so wild with Ngahere that she said Ngahere could just enrol herself. Not that Ngahere minded. She liked being the lady and doing things herself and, after getting to the college she knocked calmly on the door of the headmistress's office.

'I'm so sorry to bother you,' Ngahere apologised. 'But I do want to start school as soon as possible so I took the liberty of coming here today and hope I can start school next Monday. If that's all right, Madam.'

Like the headmaster in the boys' school, the headmistress seemed to take to Ngahere straight away. She talked with Ngahere in a way which appeared quite foreign to Hine. Snatches of the conversation came through to her like the headmistress asking about 'previous reports' and Ngahere replying, as always, with 'Of course, Miss Smith,' but Hine couldn't really understand what was happening.

Ngahere filled her own forms in. Her black hair, tied back in two tidy ponytails, hung down in front of her as she wrote. When she had finished she sat up and with a flick of her head her ponytails settled back behind her

221

shoulders once more. As they stood up, the headmistress said; 'Yes Naeere, I think we'll get on just fine. Come along with me and I will introduce you to your new teachers and classmates.'

Hine trailed behind them. She could hear Ngahere chattering gaily. Then just before they entered the classroom, Ngahere smiled brilliantly at the headmistress and said; 'Excuse me, Miss Smith. My name is Ngahere. Not Naeere. I hope you don't mind my correcting you.'

'Of course not,' the headmistress replied. 'And I'm so sorry Ngahere that my pronunciation was incorrect. Thank you.'

With that, the headmistress took Ngahere into the classroom. Hine waited outside, getting angrier and angrier.

After completing enrolment at the girls' college it was rather late so Hine decided that they should get a bus back home. She asked a passer-by which bus they should take and where to catch it from. The two sisters waited at the bus stop, Hine watching Ngahere angrily, until she couldn't stand it any longer.

'Boy you were posh all right,' she said to Ngahere. 'I hope I'm not disturbing you, ha! Where'd you learn to talk like that? Kotiro whakahihi!'

Ngahere knew she'd hurt her sister.

'I'm sorry, Hine,' she apologised.

'Ha!' Hine spat.

At that moment, the bus arrived. Hine hopped on first and by the time Ngahere had got her ticket Hine was already seated beside another woman. Feeling sorry for herself, Ngahere found herself another seat. She knew that Hine had a right to be angry but good heavens, you had to talk nicely to the headmistress of such a big college. After all, the first appearance was always the most important and Ngahere didn't want the headmistress to think she was just another 'Maori'.

Flustered, Ngahere sat there, watching Hine who refused to look at her. Then Hine pulled the cord because they were nearing home. As she got up from her seat she knocked over another person's shopping. Ngahere went to help pick up the parcels and because Hine didn't look like she was going to apologise, Ngahere said, 'I hope you don't mind, sir.'

'Oh no, Miss,' the man said. 'Thank you very much.'

The girls got off. Hine was more upset. She walked as fast as she could, keeping way ahead of Ngahere. But Ngahere ran to catch her.

'Look, Hine,' Ngahere began. 'I'm sorry. Let's forget about it for now, ay? We have to make the best of things.'

Hine looked at her sister and began to soften. Ngahere was so pretty. She spent a lot of time washing and brushing her hair, and cleaning her face and this annoyed everybody because she spent such a long time in the bathroom with the door locked. Hine admired her and was proud of her really.

'All right,' Hine nodded.

They walked on home together. As usual, Ngahere shot straight through the kitchen (on her way to the bathroom no doubt) but Hine went to help Mum.

'Where's baby Moana?' she asked Mum.

Mum was wild.

'Huh!' she answered. 'You remember the baby now, ay? Where you been all day! Leaving me here in this new place all alone. Dad and Tame out looking for work. You and your sister taking the boys to school. Where you been?'

'You know where I've been, Mum,' Hine said.

'Well it doesn't take this long to enrol two kids at school.'

Hine didn't know what to say. She looked at the clock and saw that it was very late indeed. As usual, she was getting the blame for Ngahere's actions. She felt tears come to her eyes at the unfairness of it all.

Just then Ngahere herself came in, her face pink from her wash, her hair pulled up onto the top of her head. She kissed Mum's cheek and smiled.

'Am I famished,' she said. 'What's to eat, Mum? What's to eat, Hine?'

Hine looked at her.

'Get it yourself, Ngahere,' she yelled. 'We're not your slaves.'

She ran out of the house and into the backyard. She sat on an upturned bucket and cried hot tears. She wished the family had never come to this awful place. She wished that they were back home at the pa. She leaned against the wall and looked at the sky and wondered if she would ever be happy here.

'Hine?'

It was Ngahere.

'What do you want, miss.'

'I brought you a sandwich. Here.'

'I don't want it.'

'Hine. Please. I'm sorry. I didn't mean to show off at the college. I can't help it. I wanted to show that headmistress I wasn't a dumb hori from the backblocks.'

Soon, Ngahere herself was crying too. And the two sisters hugged each other.

'Oh look at this damn place,' Hine said after a while, gesturing to the house and overgrown backyard.

'We have to make the best of it,' Ngahere said. 'And of ourselves too. I think we're all a bit homesick today.'

'Mum sure is,' Hine answered.

Ngahere nodded.

'But we'll make out,' she replied.

They heard Mum calling to them. Ngahere hastily wiped at her tears and smoothed down her dress. Hand in hand, she and Hine went into the house.

Broken Silence

Ripeka looked around her with a sense of hopelessness. The house was a mess, but at least she was all right. She drew her hand across her face and her fingers caught in the dishevelled mess of her hair. She tore her hand free and limped into the bathroom. She ran some cold water into the basin and immersed her stinging face into the water. Blood from her broken lips stained the basin.

Oh God. Eighteen years old and yet she looked like an old woman. Both her eyes were swollen and already the skin was blackening around the left eye where her husband had hit her. It hurt to cry. Her body ached with that familiar dull throb of pain. How much more could she take? How much more?

She sat on the lavatory seat. She had run away from home at fifteen leaving behind her parents and thirteen brothers and sisters, run away with her pakeha because he had promised her a good time. Good time all right. Two kids and regular hidings, insults and shit, and being thrown out of so many flats and houses that she couldn't remember one from another. Good time.

In the bedroom the baby began to cry. With a sigh, Ripeka went to attend to him. He lay there on his back with his fists clenched, his mouth wide open, crying. Crying. Crying.

Ripeka stared at him. Crying. Crying.

'Shut up,' she screamed. 'Shut up. Shut up.'

Unaware of what she was doing, she picked up a pillow and placed it over that horrible red face with its hole of a mouth.

The child pushed at the pillow. For a moment, its fists clenched tightly together. The noise of its breathing became soft and snuffled. Then everything became quiet.

Only the beating of Ripeka's heart filled the small prison of the room. It echoed against the four walls.

And Ripeka sank to the floor and buried her head in her hands. She rocked herself like she used to do as a child. Then she stood and went into the kitchen where her other son, Tommy, was playing with pots and pans. Banging them together loudly. Smiling at her.

She looked at him. She pulled the old pushchair out of a cupboard in the corridor. She picked Tommy up and put him into the pushchair, and wheeled him out into the street.

It was so calm outside. The street lights weren't on yet but the whole world seemed to be settling down for the night. The breeze was just enough to sooth her aching face. Without hesitation, Ripeka wheeled the pushchair down the street and into the driveway of a lighted house seven doors down. Trying not to make too much noise she wheeled Tommy close to the back door. Without looking at him, she knocked on the door and then moved swiftly back toward the street. She did not look back.

In the distance she saw a telephone box. She walked towards it, entered, and dialled '111'. She gave her address to the impersonal voice on the other end and then hung up. She walked back to the outside of the house and hid herself in a clump of trees opposite. The pain of her body once again throbbed its way into her head as she waited. She closed her eyes and moaned, trying to contain the pain within herself. She felt her body convulse and, all of a sudden, thick gouts of blood vomited from her lips. Oh God. Oh God.

Dimly she heard the siren of an approaching police car. She watched, like an onlooker detached from the drama that began to happen. Her vision blurred and became a flashing red light revolving on top of the police car. She saw two men go into her house.

Blood spurted again from her mouth. Nobody heard her painful sigh nor saw her collapse in the shadows of the trees. The two policemen went about their business not knowing that she was dying a few feet away from them.

Taki Tamihana went to the door. He felt afraid because he had had a dream, a premonition. He had been up since daybreak because of the dream. It had frightened him.

Even the baby had been fitful all night. And the dog too had been howling constantly at the moon. He had gone out to let it off its chain and it had disappeared into the reserve near his house.

Taki opened the door. Two men stood there. Cops. They asked to come in and Taki took them to the kitchen. They sat down while he made them a cup of tea. He set three cups on the table. *Why three when there were only two cops?* The action worried him.

One of the policemen forced a hearty smile.

'Fine day, ain't it?' he said.

The other policeman shifted his feet.

Taki sat down opposite them. Clumsily, he asked, 'Bad news?'

In the bedroom, his wife, Rere, sat up with a start. She heard the sound of talking in the kitchen. She got out of bed, wrapped her top blanket around her body and padded toward the kitchen to see what was happening. At the door, she heard the news: their daughter, Ripeka, was dead. So was one of the children.

'Aue,' she cried.

The room revolved as she fell to the floor. Quickly, Taki picked her up and carried her into the bedroom. They wept together before Taki returned to the two policemen.

'You better tell me how it happened,' he said.

The words rolled over him. Manslaughter. Sordid business. Assault. And as he listened he remembered his dream. He had seen Ripeka as a young child, crying, running toward him, her pigtails banging up and down on her back, calling for him.

And he thought of his young daughter and her vitality. And he felt anger and sadness about her death.

Finally, the two policemen left. He went to Rere. They sat together on the bed, grieving, and Rere's keening echoed from the four walls of the room.

The tangi was held up north and Taki and Rere took the bodies of their daughter and grandson by car to the funeral. It was a big tangi and all the relations of the family were there to mourn the death of one of their daughters and her son. Taki drifted through the funeral in a dazed mood. It wasn't until he heard the dull thud of soil on the coffin that he began to feel the real hurt of his loss.

With a cry which opened up the heavens he called to his daughter. In the pouring rain he screamed her name. As the thunder reverberated in the sky he cursed the world, the people, the circumstances, which had caused his daughter's death.

'Why?' he called. 'Why? Why? Why?'

And he clenched his fists and knelt at the fresh-turned earth and the rain fell upon him.

TE ANIWA BOSCH (1938; Te Aupouri, Ngapuhi) was born at Wainui in North Auckland. She is now a secondary school teacher in Palmerston North. In 1976 she was awarded the Maori Purposes Fund Board grant for writing in Maori and in 1977 she was given a Literary Fund grant to continue her work. Her stories have appeared in *Te Ao Hou*, *Te Maori*, *Wharekura* and *Ocarina* (India). She is currently at work on two novels, one of which is an historical novel concerning the Ngapuhi.

Rangi Faith

The Wait

Te Rauparaha
and his soulless fleet
like a tidal wave
smear
and
gut
the land;
Onawe
is said
to be their death-place.
Aue! It is
like a toy
to them;
the pilot fish
of the monster Onawe
they will
slaughter tomorrow.
Tonight they
will feast loud
for them
who are
listening silently
in the sea-dark.

The Last Battle

I

Tonight they will
feast loud
for us listening
silent in the sea-dark;
retiring within walls
like the crab we
pump ourselves full
of final pride, fill

the corners of our shell,
waving our masked fear;
we sing the last songs
without warmth —
there is death
between our teeth
& in our eyes;
the final kiss
of lovers' lips
fall on cold stone
as meres clenched,
we face the last stars.

II

There were some, the old ones,
I was told, who couldn't lift
their heads for the shame,
and many tried to run.
You and I played
on the flax flats
where they died.

Prelude To The Baptism Of Murderers Bay

So the long night fell
on the unknown South Land:
musketoons, sabres, pikes
laid out,
& the cannons quilled.
Morning found the Heemskerk
and the Zeehaen
riding at taut anchor,
the cockboats swinging,
and the canoes plunging
into the wide-eyed bay.

Te Pa Nui O Hau

As silently
as possible
they moved in the half-light;

heads and weapons
we could see
bobbing through the bush
to the water's edge,
and to the narrow neck of rock
separating the peninsula
from the mainland;
here, at Tara-o-Kura,
they prayed
to the spirit of the red rocks
to keep their stronghold safe
(which was not proved to be the case)
until their return.
Each warrior dipped
his hand into
the cold waters of the bay,
and softly daubed the boiling rock
so that it would remember its part,
and stay awake,
and light their way back.
But when they returned,
panic-stricken,
from their mission,
they fled past
the place of redness and knew,
because of the Darkness,
that it had forgotten them.

Corrosion Of Values

Two sticks of dynamite
make short shrift
of the hanging rock;
the charcoal drawings
peel away,
burst open,
and collapse outwards
& downwards:
> eagles, men,
> taniwha, dogs
> falling through
> the air.

The dust rises,
and keeps on
        rising;
the caves
cease their
        bellowing.
The trucks move in.
In a valley below
the quarry,
there is a hole,
an emptiness
in the cliff
        (the spearthrust
        in the side)
sphagnum masks
the chisel's mark,
but it is there & well.
In Frenchman's Gully,
the birdman is
        crucified
behind cyclone
netting, a Yale lock,
and iron stakes;
he offers himself,
but all appeals are lost;

the man who executes lines
executes himself. . .

The Dolphin

I am fishing
for blue cod and herring and
watching periodic terns dropping
like bricks turned to paper
on the struggling sea,
when he appears
as if clocks,
important events,
people
waited patiently for him —

early morning
offshore cruiser,
old man dolphin —
the sun pouring off
Ethiopic skin,
the certain dorsal fin
splicing the silence,
the sea;
time's unwavering journey
to beginnings,
to endings.

Spring Star

My dog howls
at the sea booming
over the
windthrown pines;
he is not alone.
Pukekos scream
in the spring
darkness;
it is the time
of the star
across the moon,
it is time
for the sighting
of new mountains.

RANGI FAITH (1949; Kati Tahu) was born in Timaru but grew up in Temuka.
He was educated at the University of Canterbury and is currently teaching primary
school. He lives with his wife, son and daughter at Woodend Beach.

Rangi's poems have appeared in *Islands*, *Te Ao Hou*, *NZ Bookworld* and *Pacific Quarterly Moana*. He is currently preparing a collection of poems tentatively titled *The Third Eye*.

Witi Ihimaera

The Child

— Haere mai, mokopuna, she would say.

And always I would go with her, for I was both her keeper and her companion. I was a small boy; she was a child too, in an old woman's body.

— Where we going today, Nanny? I would ask. But I always knew.

— We go down to the sea, mokopuna, to the sea...

Some people called my Nanny crazy, porangi. Whenever I heard that word, my heart would flutter as if a small bird was trapped in there and wanted to get out. My Nanny wasn't porangi, not to me.

But always, somebody would laugh at her and play with her feeble mind as if it was a kaitaka, a top which you whipped with flax to keep spinning. They would mimic her too, the sudden spasms that shook her body or the way she used to rock her head when her mind was wandering far away.

Dad, he told me that those people didn't understand or that they were only joking. But I'd see the sharp flints gleaming in their eyes and the cruel ways they lashed out at her. I would yell Stop! Don't you make fun of my Nanny. I used to hate them all.

I loved my Nanny. I would pat her on the head and hug her close to me. And she would whimper and put her arms around me too.

— Where my rahu, she would ask me. Where my rahu?

And I would help her look for it. I knew always that the basket would be under her bed, but Nanny, she liked playing pretend, so I'd play along with her.

— I don't know, Nanny, I'd tell her as we searched in all the dark corners of her room. Is it in the drawer? No, not there. In the wardrobe? No... might be in the corner, ay? No. Where you put it, Nanny? Where?

And all the time, she would answer me in a vague voice, just like a little girl.

— I don' know, mokopuna. I don' know where I put my rahu. It's somewhere. Somewhere here, somewhere....

We'd play the game a little longer. Then I'd laugh.

— Here it is, Nanny! Here's your bag!

Her eyes would light up.

— You found it, mokopuna? You found my rahu? Ae, that's it, that my rahu.

I would put it in her hands.

— You ready to go now, Nanny? I'd ask. We go down to the sea now?

— I put my scarf on first, ay, she would answer. Might be cold, might be makariri. . . .

Those other people, they never saw my Nanny the way I did. And some of the kids at school they used to be funny to her. Willie Anderson, he would make faces and act all crazy. He would follow Nanny and imitate the way she walked. His father caught him once, and gave him a good hiding. But Willie didn't feel sorry; he only hated Nanny more. And he told lies about her. We had a fight after school one day. He was tougher than me and he won. But I didn't care, not even when he told some other kids I was porangi too.

I had my Nanny; I didn't need anybody else.

— You fullas just leave my Nanny alone, I told them. Don't you touch her even.

Willie, he just laughed and threw dust at me.

But he was only jealous, because he'd thought that when Nanny was staring in the sky, she was looking at nothing.

— No! I've seen what she looks at, Willie Anderson, I've seen her world. She's taken me there.

Willie didn't like that. He never like being left out of things. That's why he was jealous.

— Come to me, Nanny, I would say.

And she would come and lift her head so that I could put her scarf on her. She would sit very still and very silent, and her lips would move without saying anything. The words were soundless.

— Yes, Nanny, I would answer. We're going down to the sea soon. Just wait your hurry. No don't say bad words to me. Nanny! I heard what you said that time! You're a bad girl!

My Nanny, she knew when I was angry with her. Her eyes would dim and she would fold her hands carefully in her lap. Sometimes, a small drop of spittle would trickle from her mouth.

— I'm sorry, mokopuna, she would whisper slowly.

I'd wipe her lips.

— Don't cry, Nanny. I was only playing. Don't be a crybaby, don't be a tangiweto!

And her eyes would light up, and deep down in them I'd see a little girl beginning to smile.

— You're cunning all right, Nanny! I would say. Those are only pretending tears! I know you, Nanny! So no more cry, ay? Come on, we go to the sea now. Haere mai.

And she'd put her hand in mine.

My Nanny, she used to be all right once. She never used to be porangi all the time. But when Nanny Pita died, something happened to her; I don't know what it was. Something. Perhaps it was because she found herself all alone and she was scared. Something.

I know she never used to be funny because Dad showed me some photos of her when she was young. She was pretty!

She used to be very slim and she had a shy way of smiling. Looking at her photos, you had the feeling that she wanted to tell you something, even after all these years. You waited for her lips to open, knowing that if they did, her words would be soft and beautiful.

But Nanny never spoke to me from her photos; she just kept smiling, and her lips curled around my heart and made it smile too.

— Where you going, Heta? Mum would ask.

And I would tell her, sometimes afraid that she might say, No, you and Nanny stay home.

— Me and Nanny, I would answer, we're going down to the beach for a little walk. Won't be long, Mum.

— Okay, but you look after Nanny, ay. If it gets cold, you put your jersey around her. If it starts to rain, you bring her home straight away. And don't get up to any mischief down there.

— All right, Mum.

And I would turn to my Nanny.

— Come on, Nanny. It's all right. Mum said we could go. Come on, come to me, Nanny. Give me your hand. Don't be afraid.

And together, we'd walk out of the house.

Sometimes, my Nanny she'd be just like she was before Nanny Pita died, as if she was waking up from a long moe. She'd laugh and talk and her body wouldn't shiver all the time. But after a while, her mind would go to sleep again.

When she was asleep like that, I'd have to help her do things. Nanny couldn't even feed herself when her mind went away!

— Come to me, Nanny, I would say. And she'd sit down, and I'd put a tea towel around her neck to stop the kai from getting on her dress. Open your mouth, Nanny. Wider yet. That's it. There we are! Wasn't that good? This kai's good ay! And she'd nod her head and make her moaning noises which meant she wanted some more. So I'd fill her spoon again, and she would smile to show she was happy.

— What that thing? Nanny would ask as we walked along the road.

And she would point to a house, a tree, a car or an animal grazing in a paddock. She liked pretending she didn't know what things were.

— That's a horse, that's a fowl, that's where Mrs Katene lives, that's a kowhai. . . I would tell her.

And she would repeat my words in a slow, sing-song voice.
— A tree, a manuka, a fence, a horse.... No, that not a horse, that a hoiho, mokopuna.
— That's right, Nanny! I would say. You're cleverer than me, ay! You know all the Maori names; I don't, Nanny. Your mokopuna, he's dumb!
And she would giggle and do a little dance. Sometimes, she'd even sing me a song.

> *Tahi nei taru kino*
> *Mahi whaiaipo,*
> *Kei te wehenga*
> *Aroha kau ana...*

And her quavering voice would lift its wings and circle softly in the air.
Nanny liked to sing. Sometimes, she'd be waiting at the door for me when I got home from school, and she'd have the guitar in her hands. Kepa, my brother, he gave me that guitar and learned me a few chords. But I didn't know how to play it proper. Nanny didn't mind, though. As long as I strummed it, she was happy. We'd sit on the verandah, she'd press my fingers to the strings, and as I played she would sing, one song after the other.
And sometimes, Dad would come and join us. 'What a racket!' he would say. 'Here, give that guitar to me.' And he would tune it and say to Nanny, 'Come on, Mum, we sing your song, ay? Ready, steady, go!' My Dad, he could play that guitar! And him and Nanny, they could sing as good as anything.

> *He putiputi koe i katohia....*
> You're just a flower from an old bouquet,
> I've waited patiently for you, each day...

That was Nanny's song. Her Pakeha name was Violet, and everybody called her that name because her Maori name was too long. And my Nanny, she was just like a violet; shy and small and hiding her face in her petals if the sun blazed too strong.

— We're almost there now, ay, mokopuna, Nanny would say.
And I would nod my head.
— Ae, Nanny. Almost there. Almost at the sea.
Nanny always said that same thing every time we reached the short cut to the beach. She'd hurry along the road to the gate. Beyond it, a path led through a paddock and down the cliff to where the sea was. Nanny, she would run a little ahead of me, then look back just to make sure I was following. She didn't like being alone.
— Haere mai, mokopuna! she would yell. Hurry up! The sea!

And she would cock her head to the wind and hear the waves murmuring. Then she'd run along a little further and flutter her hands at me to hurry.

I used to pretend not to hear her, and just dawdle along.

— Ay, Nanny? What you say? I would call.

And always, she would flutter her hands and lean her head into the wind.

My Nanny, she loved the sea. She and Nanny Pita used to live in a house right on the beach. But when Nanny Pita died, she came to live at our place because Dad was the eldest of her children. Dad, he told me that Nanny wasn't really porangi; just old and lonely. He didn't know how long she'd stay with us because she was as old as Nanny Pita.

— You look after her and you love her, he said to me. Nanny, she might go away at any time. So while you have her, you love her, ay? I told him I would make Nanny so happy that she would never want to leave. But Dad, he didn't understand that I knew my Nanny wouldn't go away. He just smiled sadly and put his hands around my shoulders. Some day, he said. Some day. . . .

Sometimes, late at night, I'd hear Nanny crying because she was lonely. I'd creep softly down the corridor to her room and brush her tears away with my hands.

— You're too old to cry, I'd growl her. But she'd keep weeping, so I'd hug her for a while. Turi turi, Nanny, I'd whisper. I'm here. Don't be afraid.

And sometimes, I'd stay with her until she went to sleep again.

— Here's one, mokopuna! she would yell. I got one!

And she would hold up a sea shell she had found.

My Nanny, she thought I liked shells; I don't know why. Maybe it was because when she first came to stay with us, she saw a paua shell in my room. Whatever it was, every time we went down to the sea, she'd wander along the beach, looking for shells to give to me.

— You want this one? she'd ask. And she'd cock her head to one side and look into my eyes. Sometimes, she looked so hardcase that I'd laugh.

— Okay, Nanny! We take it home.

Then she'd look very happy and drop the shell into her rahu.

— We taking you home, she would tell the shell. We taking you home for my mokopuna.

And every now and then, as we walked along the beach, she would let go of my hand to get another shell glittering on the sand.

— I already got enough, Nanny! I would yell.

But always, she would show it to me and cock her head as if she was asking a question.

236

— All right, Nanny, I would sigh. We take this one home too.

It used to be good just wandering along the beach with Nanny. If it was sunny and the sea wasn't rough, she'd let go of my hand more often, and wander off alone. I didn't mind, because I knew Nanny wasn't really alone; she was wandering with Nanny Pita on some remembered day.

But sometimes, a seagull would scream or cast its shadow over her head. Then she would stop and begin to tremble.

— It's all right, Nanny, I'd say. I'm here.

And she would reach out for my hand.

— You won't leave me will you, mokopuna? she would say.

— No, Nanny, I would answer. Turi turi now.

And we would walk together again. Nanny, she never left me when the sea was stormy. She used to be very scared and hold me very tight. Seaweed, it frightened her. She'd look at the waves and see the seaweed rising with them and whimper, afraid that she'd be caught by the long, black fingers.

And sometimes, she would make me scared too.

— We go back home now, ay? I would ask her.

— Ae, we go home, mokopuna. Home...

And she'd clutch her bag closely to her, and the shells would clink and scrape against each other.

One day, my Nanny, she wasn't home when I got back from school. I looked in her room, I looked everywhere, but I couldn't find her. Mum got worried and went to get Dad. But I knew where she'd be.

I ran down the road.

— Nanny! Nanny!

I don't know why I was crying. Perhaps it was because she had gone without waiting for me.

— Nanny! Nanny!

I heard the sea murmuring as I ran along the path, toward the cliff. I looked down to the beach.

My Nanny, she was lying there...

— *Nanny!*

I rushed down the cliff toward her. I hugged her to me.

In her hand was a sea shell.

— Yes, Nanny, I said. That's a good one, that's the best one you've ever found for me. We put it in your bag, ay? We take it home. We go home now, we go home...

But she didn't answer.

Her mind had wandered far away, and my Nanny, she had wandered after it.

— Haere mai, mokopuna, she would say.

And always I would go with her.

— Where we going, Nanny?

— We go down to the sea, mokopuna. To the sea. . .

Tangi (Extract)

The mountains are coming closer. Clouds are lowering upon them swirling down with drifting grace, shedding eternal tears. The earth is a desolate sea, howling in darkness.

A train moves slowly into Palmerston North. For a quarter of an hour it stands at the station. Then it leaves Palmerston North. Away from the brightly lit city it thunders, toward the towering mountains. Far, far on the other side of them, lies Wellington.

Into the darkness. Into the night.

This is a silent world. People are weeping but I do not hear them. Women are wailing, but I do not hear them. All around me are the sights of people grieving, of despair and of distraught mourners. But no sound. No sound.

The church service, held for father on this marae, held in front of him, has ended.

And my grandfather, who led the service, has been the first to kiss my father before the casket is closed. The family has followed him, the old people, the young children, and father's children too. Each in turn has taken off his shoes and crawled onto the porch, to lie beside him and whisper his farewell.

I too, have stroked his hair. I too, have let my tears fall upon him. And I too, have kissed him.

Now, the whispered farewells are ended.

Uncle Pita speaks to me but I do not hear him. He motions me to follow him. He also motions to Uncle Wiremu and Uncle Arapera, two of my father's brothers, and Kani Heta and Hoki Kahurangi, two of my father's friends, to join us. Together we walk through the grieving crowd toward Rongopai.

The mourners open a way for us. The women are gaunt, the men are grave. The children look at us, afraid. The crowd opens and there in front of me, Dad waits. *Tama you'll have to come home. Dad's dead.* The sun shines on the closed casket. It gleams on the silver inset upon which are inscribed the words: Rongo Mahana Born 1916 Died 1972. Part of the casket is covered with a feather cloak, rippling across the porch with the bronze fire of a moth's wings. At his feet, the flower wreaths are a blaze of dazzling colours. The photographs of Dad, displayed on the porch, flash in the falling sunlight.

Uncle Pita steps onto the porch. He bends over my mother where she kneels, her arms spread across the polished wood. *Mum was just lying there as if she was waiting for Dad to wake up.* He speaks to Mum. She shakes her head and clutches more tightly at father. Uncle Pita speaks to her again and holds her shoulders. My sisters too, they come to prise her away.

Her fingers claw at the casket as she breaks her clasp. Her head arches back, her hands reach up to tear at the sun.

And there is a storm among the mourners. Women gather round my mother, weeping with her. *Come home, son.* Marama and Hone are afraid. Mum looks at them, dazed, and then gathers them into her arms. The children seem to calm her. She reaches for her black scarf and puts it over her hair. Wiki and Mere help her to stand. She sways, almost falls. *Come home, Tama.* But her face is calm now. She stands. She waits.

My shadow falls across the marae and each step I take is into that shadow. The dust swirls at my feet. Upon the porch, father is waiting.

Uncle Pita beckons me forward. I step among the flower wreaths toward him. I kneel on the other side of the casket. Together, Uncle and I lift the feather cloak from the casket.

The other men come onto the porch. We are the pall bearers. We wait while the hearse reverses slowly through the crowd toward father. The hearse stops, the door swings open. And carefully we lift father from the porch. *I must go home, Mr Ralston.* He is so heavy, so heavy. And although it is only a few steps to the hearse, it seems a long journey. The doors close behind him.

And people gather at the glistening windows, and palms press silently on the glass.

Another car draws up near the porch. The photographs of father, the flower wreaths and the feather cloak, are placed inside it. My mother steps into a funeral car. My sisters and brother step in after her. Mourners begin to move to the road. Already, some of them stream toward the hill where the graveyard is. Others are stepping into their cars. Headlights are being switched on, like a coronet of moons around an eclipsing sun.

I join my mother and my family. Mum sits in the back seat. Ripeka and Wiki are with her. Hone and Marama encircle her with their arms. Mere has gone to her own car.

The car begins to move. It follows the hearse as it slowly moves through the mourners to the gate. The mourners make way. Behind us, the other funeral cars begin to follow.

And glimpsed for a moment is the grief-stricken face of my sister, Mere.

The car bumps through the gate. It turns onto the road, following the hearse. *No, Mr Ralston, he was not an old man.* Far ahead, the road streams with people walking, slowly walking, crying out to the hill, announcing that my father comes. People are clustering round the hearse. Auntie Ruihi is among them. Her lips are moving. She speaks to father.

I look away. Away from the road, away from the hill. I see the homestead and it seems to me as if I am there, watching from a window. I see people walking along the road which winds through the village. They raise swirls of dust. A long line of cars shines among them, more swinging into view. The cars come from Rongopai. They are heading for the hill. People are clustering there. People are streaming up the hill toward the graveyard.

The road unfolds through the green fields. This is my home, this is my whanau. This is Waituhi. *Where are you going, coz? I'm flying home, Kopua.* I look upon my village and suddenly the light begins to fade. A shadow advances across the landscape. It ripples across the houses. The wind and clouds are gathering at the hill. It always rains when a Maori dies.

The coldness strikes with a sudden blast of wind. The sky begins to darken, a shadow across the sun. The sky comes to embrace the earth. No sound. No sound.

I look back. The cortege extends along the road behind us as far as I can see. Rongopai is for a small space of time, deserted. I look forward. Before me, the hill is rising higher. People are stumbling toward the graveyard. At the foot of the hill, a large throng of people wait. They wait for father to come.

The car begins to slow down. The crowd thickens at the windows. In front, the hearse comes to a silent halt. The doors swing open.

E pa...

For a moment, the world is a blur of rushing shadows. Black veiled faces mourn with soundless agony. Then, there is Uncle Pita with the other pall bearers, beginning to take father from the hearse.

I step from the car and open the door for my mother. We embrace. Then she breaks our clasp and gathers the children to her. Mere joins us. *Don't weep my sister. I am here now.* Together we walk through the bustling crowd to where father is waiting.

Uncle Pita motions to me. Before I go to him, I turn to my mother.

— E ma, be strong e ma.

But she does not hear. I take my place beside the casket. Father is so heavy. I can feel his body moving inside the casket as we carry him through the crowd.

My heart is breaking. My tears are falling. And a storm is gathering across the hill. *Dad waits for you at Rongopai, Tama.* The sky is thick with lowering clouds, surging and lowering. The day is darkening, becoming ashen. The air is shifting, swelling and subsiding. The mourners must struggle against the currents as they climb the hill. The wind and clouds are coming to farewell father.

Beyond the hill, the sun is shafting sunlight upon another world.

Uncle Pita signals a rest. We lower the casket to the ground. Each of us is lost in our own thoughts. My mother comes to rest her head against the casket. Behind, more mourners are streaming up the hill. *Dad waits, Tama.* Above, mourners are waiting at the graveyard. Waiting where headstones and crosses prick at the ashen sky. *Tama, he waits.*

Rain begins to fall. It splashes on my mother's face. It splashes upon my father's casket. Then Uncle Pita motions us to take him up again. He is so heavy my father. But one step. Then another. *And one step further now.*

Through the rain, carrying father. Through the press of mourners. The rain streams from their faces. The path is becoming muddy and trickles with rivulets of rain. On the path, a fallen chaplet of kawakawa leaves lies.

Ahead, the mourners gather round the gateway to the graveyard. *Haere mai ki o tatou mate e.* They open up before my father, waving sprigs of greenery in their hands. The mourners glisten in the rain. Their hair is matted and they lift their faces to the darkening sky. *Haere mai, haere mai.* The women sway and keen a lament. They raise their arms toward my father.

So heavy he is; he is so heavy. And as I am carrying him, my feet slip. My grandfather gives me his strength. He steadies father for me. Then he comforts me. *You must make your father proud, mokopuna.* And one step further now, through the gateway into the graveyard.

Here, in this place, lie my whanau, my family dead. Here, among the flowering gorse they lie, beneath simple headstones.

And father comes to sleep with them. This is the afternoon of the third day.

Strange, the wind has ceased a moment. Strange, the clouds are still. Nothing moves in this world except the mourners following through the graveyard after father. *There is no sound. The tide ebbs silently away.* But a further step forward now. Past the headstones to the place where father will rest. Until I am standing with him at the newly dug ground.

The casket is laid upon the ground. *Death comes but I am not yet dead.* The mourners press close to it. To one side, Mum is standing with my brothers and sisters. My grandfather is with them too. He embraces her and then addresses the mourners. He is saying farewell for them. The mourners nod at his words. They brush at their tears. Once again they come forward, one by one, to bend and say haere ra to father. They kneel in the mud and whisper to him. And Auntie Ruihi kisses the polished wood. *I breathe, I live.*

Then my sisters come to farewell father. Ripeka the calm one, Mere the strong one, and Wiki the one whom father loved most. Finally, my mother bends to the casket. She caresses it softly. I join her. *Kua mate taku papa.* We link hands.

Uncle Pita motions me to help lower father into the ground. I take hold of the cord. It begins to rain again. Grandfather reads from the Bible, a hand raised in the air.

E pa, don't leave me...

Slowly, slowly the casket descends. Until the cord slackens.

The rain drives across the hill. The women clutch their scarves and the men bow their heads against the wind. So many are the mourning people who come to farewell father.

Petals fly loose from the flower wreaths. The leaves of the kawakawa chaplets swirl away in the wind. The black skirts of the women flap soundlessly in the storm. The mourners come forward to look upon father. Clay trickles upon the casket. *I bend toward him and my shadow falls across him.* My father's belongings, his clothes, suitcases of garments, cascade into the ground. So many photographs are thrown into the ground to crack and splinter across the casket. *E pa, farewell e pa.* One by one they fall.

And then the feather cloak falls, unfolding its glistening feathers to shimmer across father. *Your lips are cold, e pa.*

No sound, no sound. In the driving rain, I see my mother step forward. She bends to the earth and then she gathers some clay and casts it into the grave. The dirt rains upon him, upon the feather cloak.

And men begin to shovel earth over him.

Farewell, e pa...

Some of the women fling their kawakawa circlets to the ground. Auntie Ruihi struggles against the arms of Uncle Pita. My grandfather lifts his face to the bitter rain. Mere and Ripeka must hold Wiki back from the open ground. The dirt falls, *the rain falls.* The dirt falls, *the rain falls.*

I hold my mother tightly to me. She stretches forward for father.

And Earth reaches for Sky and Sky bends to Earth. One last fierce clasp in rain and wind and wind and rain. One last embrace of rage and fury and helpless grief. One last clinging of body to body, of Earth to Sky. One last meeting of lips to lips and tears to tears.

And then the slow drawing away, the slow tearing away, the slow wrenching away of Sky from Earth, of Earth from Sky, in the final, sorrowful separation...

Farewell, e pa. Haere ra, my father.

Whanau (Extract)

Rongo Mahana stops his car at a corner of the paddock. He gets out and takes some sacks out of the boot. For a moment, he looks over the paddock, the long rows of potatoes, a few of pumpkins and marrows, and the tall maize glistening yellow and green in the sun. A big paddock, stretching back to the road. One of four paddocks in the village which together form what is left of the Mahana land.

— Well, Rongo says to himself, may as well get started!

The Mahana land . . .

Until last year, the Mahana clan would get together at a family meeting, dub in some money and buy seed to plant in the family paddocks. Then they would fix a time for the planting, calculating it the old way by the shape of the moon and the position of the stars in the night sky. Once that was done, they would all come together at the planting.

It used to a good time. A family occasion. A gathering of the Mahana clan. Kids and all would come to follow the tractor and plant the seeds in the furrows. And although it was hard work it didn't seem to take long because everybody was too busy chucking off at each other to think of how hard the work was.

— Hey! Cover that plant properly with the dirt, ay!

— Worry about your own plant! And while you're at it, don't you know how to plant in the straight line?

— Who says I'm not planting straight! It's not me, it's the furrows that are crooked.

— Don't blame the furrows, ay! You must have had too much to drink last night!

— Me?

— Yes, you! And just look at the son of yours! Hey, Boy! You only have to dig a small hole for the plants. You think you're going to China?

— You watch your own son! He's not watering those plants at all!

— So? What with your boozing last night, you got enough water in *you* for all the plants!

And so it would continue all that day. The laughter and the light-hearted exchanges, and the constant bending into the planting. And at smoko times, the clan would all rest beneath a willow tree and eat some kai. Then back to the work again until night had fallen.

Sometimes, the planting would take a whole week, depending on how many paddocks the clan had decided would be planted with seed. One week among the very few weeks that all the Mahana families became one family. A happy week of shared muscle and sweat. Of laughter. Aroha. Until the planting was over.

243

Then would come the waiting time. The waiting for the maize and potatoes to grow. And each Mahana family would come out to the land to weed the growing plants and water them when it was their turn.

But once the crop was ready, the Mahana clan would come together again. They would gather at the harvest and there would be fulfilment of family reaping a shared labour.

This day, Rongo Mahana has come for this year's harvest. He has come with spade in hand to this paddock. He has come alone; he has come in sadness. There is no sense of fulfilment.

For last year, Rongo Mahana planted this one paddock by himself.

And this day, he has come alone to the harvest.

— Times are changing...

Rongo throws the sacks on the ground. He sits on one of them and unlaces his shoes. He puts his boots on. Then he stands with spade gripped in his hands and pushes it into the earth to uncover the potatoes clinging to the roots of an upturned plant. He bends and pulls at the potatoes, his fingers searching the soil for any others which have not been exposed by the cleaving spade. And he piles them in the furrow between this row and the next before thrusting the spade again beneath the next plant in the row. Spade turning earth, body bending and fingers scrabbling in the dirt. Spade cleaving earth, body attuning itself to the rhythm of the work. Plant after plant being upturned.

— Good spuds these...

Losing himself to the rhythm of the spade. Trying to forget the loneliness of the digging. Moving up the row leaving potatoes strewn in the furrow. His heart racing, the sweat beginning to bead his face. And an aching beginning in his bending body. Alone in the paddock. A solitary speck amid the expanse of furrows out into the earth. Alone. Alone under the hot sun.

And then the spade slips to cut into the roots of a plant and slide into the potatoes beneath. And with despair, Rongo grasps them and flings them at the sun. And the rhythm of this man to the land is destroyed...

A big clan, the Mahanas. Once they all lived here in the village. Seven brothers and three sisters. Rongo, the eldest. Growing up together, sharing life with one another. Marrying and bringing up families here. Until the land could not contain them all; until they began to leave the land. Of the ten families, only Pita and Miriama and Rawiri and his wife Teria, remain in the village. Rawiri and Teria and their seven children live in the old home, Mum and Dad's home. Rongo and the eldest sister have brought up their children in the nearby city. The rest of the clan are scattered throughout the country. A brother at Mataura in the South Island. Another brother in Hastings working the orchard during summer and odd-jobbing through winter. Two brothers and two sisters living in

Wellington, their children assembling engines or shifting endlessly from job to job. And another brother in the freezing works in Hamilton. Scattered. And the times of their gathering together as a clan are fewer now.

Times are tightening up. During the first years when the Mahana families had begun to leave the village, they would still come back when called for the planting, the harvesting, the family shearing. And when the village itself called them for the big huis or the tangi, they would return. That was when there were a lot of labouring jobs around, when you could tell the boss you were leaving and know that you'd be able to get another job easy when you returned.

But the gypsy life too, is diminishing. And it seems you need more money to live on these days. There is security in having and keeping one job, in having permanent employment. And living in the cities is nothing but an attractive trap. It binds you to itself with contracts: with high mortgages or steep rents, with hire purchase payments and threats of repossession. And it asks more of you: more of your money and more and more for things you did not really want. A Venus flytrap. And once you're caught, you can never escape. You must keep working and keep working to keep up the next payment. You can't afford to take a week or two off for something as ridiculous as the family planting.

Yes, ridiculous, that's what it is. And you say you want five days off to go to a *funeral?* Ridiculous! No, definitely not! No! You see our point, don't you? I mean the Company comes first, doesn't it? Heavens! What would happen if all you Maoris took off five days! The Company would be ruined, absolutely ruined. The quotas wouldn't be met, production would grind to a halt... And by *your* action, you would be putting *other* people out of work. The people who are waiting to assemble our product, the people who distribute it...It would be utter chaos. Can't you see that? No, definitely *no.* The Company cannot allow you five days off. If you persist in your intention, then we must terminate your services. And I'm afraid there would be little likelihood of your job being here for you when you returned. We have a long waiting list of applicants you know. I'm sorry, but that's the way it is. You Maoris will just have to learn to live with the times. You do understand our point of view don't you?

Yes, that's the way it is. So better to stay and not listen to the hearth calling you. Better to stay at the bench in the production line. Better to live with the times.

Rongo Mahana sighs. What's the use of feeling sad? What's the use of feeling angry? Can't do anything about it. Can't do anything at all. Things don't last forever...

The spade thrusts into the earth again.

And could you really put all the blame on the Pakeha life? Blame it for changing the Maori? That sister, that Ruihi, she'd promised to come out for the planting last year. And she broke her promise. Don't know why, don't know why.

On that first day of the planting last year, Rongo Mahana had waited alone in the paddock. He'd hoped that somehow, the others of the family would be able to come. Even though they'd told him they couldn't make it, he had still kept on hoping. The sun had sprung quickly in the sky. And he had felt his heart breaking. The time of the family planting was over but he had been too stubborn to realise it. He couldn't blame the others for moving from the village and destroying the rhythm of the land. He couldn't blame Rawiri and Teria for being in Hastings while he waited here alone, nor Pita and Miriama for being away shearing. He could only blame himself for waiting, for being so stubborn. For hoping.

And then he had not been able to wait longer. He had felt the earth crying out for seed. He had felt the yearning of the land for peace, for it had become accustomed to the rhythm of the yearly planting. And there had been a crying out of his blood too. The rhythm of the land and the rhythm of his blood had been one and the same. And he had begun the planting and both blood and land had gradually become calm. And he felt the strength of the land calling him. He had made a promise to himself and the land that day. That every year he would return to bring peace to the land and to himself.

A promise this, which Rongo Mahana remembers now, on this Sunday as he harvests alone. And when I am dead, what then? he asks himself. Who will come to bring peace to the land?

He laughs to himself and pats the earth affectionately.

— Don't you worry! he says. For Tama will come to you when I am gone...

Tama, the eldest son of Rongo. In Wellington now, confused between two worlds. But the pull of the land in his blood will be the stronger. And he will come back. He *will* return.

Rongo Mahana decides to have a little rest. He sits on the ground and looks back over what he's done. Not too bad for an old man. And the spuds are good this year. How many sacks should he fill today? Better dig up as much as he can today. Take some round to Rawiri and Teria. Maybe they'll be able to give a hand with the digging tomorrow. No, tomorrow's Monday and they're both working. Ah well, that Huia, that lazy wife, she can come out here tomorrow instead of sitting around the house.

— Well! Better start again! Rongo says to the land. Times may have changed, ay land! Me and you are getting old. But pae kare, we're not giving up yet, ay?

His laughter is a challenge ringing from his lips.

The House With Sugarbag Windows

Watene couldn't help it. He burst out laughing.

He'd been standing at the curved bay window watching with wine-warmed eyes as the rain lashed across Kelburn. All of a sudden he'd felt cold and the thought had come to him:

— Better close the sugarbags so the rain doesn't come in.

He'd reached up to grab the sugarbags and the heavy drapes had surprised him. Not like sugarbags at all, not rough nor having the earth smell of kumara and kamokamo. Then he had looked at his hands — one was holding the drapes and the other was grasping, of all things, a delicate-stemmed wine glass.

And he'd laughed. After all, it was so amusing to remember those sugarbag windows, especially after all these years. Amusing? Once upon a time he would have used the words funny or hardcase.

Bemused, Watene let go of the drapes. Even the words he used had changed. Just like the sugarbag windows.

He remembered where he was. At Alan and Janet's place — a party for a mutual friend, Colin, who was going to Washington on a diplomatic posting.

— That was some laugh. What's the joke?

Alan. Standing there beside him, crystal decanter in hand.

— Aah, Watene grinned. Just in time.

He held out his wine glass to be filled. Behind him he could hear the social chatter of other guests, muted to a tasteful murmur by the surrounding sound of quadraphonic Vivaldi. Circling through the strains of *L'Estro Armonico No 9*, the guests dipped and swayed and described elegant figures across the room as if engaged in some delicate courtly dance. Their conversation was illumined with grace — baroque music always seemed to have such effect, unlike loud rock mixed with beer which brought out the brash and blatant in people. Here the tone was as smooth and as rich as the red wine and as polite as the music. As ingratiating too, and so deeply satisfying to Watene's palate he could almost believe he'd been born like this, standing here with wine glass in hand amid these people in the house in Kelburn.

He lifted his glass in salute to Alan.

— And now? Alan asked. The joke?

— It was nothing, Watene answered. It wasn't important. Just something I remembered.

— About what? Alan persisted.

Watene shrugged his shoulders. He looked round the room — wood panelling, old colonial furniture, expensive paintings in ornate frames, roses in a crystal vase, Persian carpet, circular stairway, glittering chandelier, latticed windows — and fingered the drapes. His eyes began to twinkle again.

— Oh, he answered hesitantly, I was just standing here and all of a sudden I remembered the house I was born in. It's raining outside, you see, and I thought I'd better draw the sugarbags across the window and....

—Sugarbags?

— To stop the rain from coming in and....

Watene hesitated. He looked at Alan. Smiling. Amused.

— I knew you wouldn't understand, Watene said. It was nothing. Nothing important.

— Hmmmn, Alan answered. It was certainly important enough to take you away from the party. Aren't you enjoying yourself? You're not bored are you?

— Oh no, Watene said.

— Thank God for that, Alan smiled. Well don't stand here by yourself for too long. It doesn't do my image as a host any good.

Watene nodded. He saw some new arrivals at the door and indicated them to Alan.

— Must look after my image, Alan sighed. I'll come back to you later. All right? In the meantime, Watene, circulate. Meet my friends. You should find much in common with them.

Watene watched as Alan left him, moving towards the arrivals, dispensing wine and greetings on the way. He began to envy Alan his gift, for it was a gift to be able to divert people and make them feel at home. Alan made it seem so simple too, that was his great achievement, socialising with ease and assurance as if he was accustomed to it. But after all this was his home, these were his people, he had been born to this life and to this style and was secure here whereas Watene.... He turned to the window again. He sipped his wine thoughtfully and a gradual sense of satisfaction and pride began to well within him as he saw his reflection shimmering across the landscape. Kelburn on a wet winter afternoon. The epitome of colonial elegance set with grace and taste amid the green of native bush. Red brick and tile tilting with the waving fern. White plaster and wood panelling and windows paned with emeralds. Wide empty streets, concrete pathways and well-kept gardens. Select. Secure. Beautiful storeyed houses for upper-floor people. And here he was, for all the world to see, part of it.

With confidence he made to rejoin the party. He saw Colin waving to him across the room. He grinned back and took a step away from the window.

It happened again. The curtains. Sugarbags across the windows. Rain thrumming like heavy knuckles on the tin roof and splashing through the windows onto the dirt floor. Outside, within the rain-dark square of window, blurred by the rain, Mum and Dad hurrying home.

Startled, Watene looked round him. For a moment it seemed that he and the other guests were sipping wine and chatting in a large room lined with newspaper, treading expensive shoes across a dirt floor and exchanging greetings over a trestled table. A single oil lamp swayed from the exposed beams of the ceiling. Smoke billowed out of the open fire where huge black pots swung on wire hooks over burning wood. Apparently unaware of their surroundings, the guests gossiped on long benches or apple boxes and took cheese delicacies and olives from tin plates. The smoke did not seem to bother them as it curled with the wind through the room. The door was open and in the doorway, shaking the rain from themselves, were Mum and Dad, being ushered in by Alan.

— How are you, Watene?

Colin with his girlfriend, Francesca, clinging to him. The smoke cleared. The chandelier twinkled again. The scuff marks of the dirt floor resolved themselves into the curlicued patterns of the Persian carpet.

— Oh, hullo, Watene answered, distracted.

— We saw you coming over to us, Francesca said. But then you just stopped. So we decided to come to you.

She smiled but her eyes were sad at the prospect of Colin leaving her. The Vivaldi was not an accompaniment to joy but more like a pavane for steps measured with sorrow.

— I hope things go well for you, Watene said to Colin. How long will you be in Washington?

— Four years, Colin answered.

— A lifetime almost, Watene said. Things will have changed by the time you returned. We'll have changed. You'll have changed too.

Things will have changed. The echoes of the word sprang upon him. Although he continued to chat with Colin and Francesca, Watene began to feel those words resounding through his mind, nudging him persistently, plucking like pincers at his heart. Try as he might, he could not rid himself of them, shake them off, tell them begone. His body became a tuning fork softly humming and scattering the years with its vibrations.

As he stood there, wine glass in hand, listening to Colin, he began to remember his childhood and where it started. In that house. The one with the sugarbag windows.

That house. It stood in the middle of nowhere at the top of a dense-forested valley overlooking the river where his mother washed the clothes. He had been born there, during an early morning when the mist was steaming across the hills. In that solitary place, his eldest sister had delivered him. She'd been eleven at the time. Later, his father had buried the afterbirth in some secret place. Watene had been the fourth child and first son.

It was a small house. More like a tin shed. He had been a sickly child until his parents had taken him to see an old kuia well-known for her healing powers. In later years, Watene's mother had been reluctant to tell him about that visit except to say that the kuia had hooked her finger into Watene's mouth and pulled strings of hard phlegm from his tiny throat. Although he improved, his early years were filled with sickness. His mother had fed him by first chewing the food in her mouth and then pushing it with her tongue into his.

His first memory was of being carried down to the river on his mother's back and sitting and watching while she and his three sisters slapped clothes on the rocks and dipped them in the water. All the years they lived in that place of his birth he associated the river with the slap slap slap of clothes against stone and soap swirling in the currents. The family did not have a washing machine because they did not have electricity. Even if they did have electricity they would not have been able to afford a washing machine. Washing machines, like flush toilets, modern stoves, refrigerators, gas fires, electric lights and hot water cylinders belonged to the world beyond where the hills turned blue, where the occasionally-glimpsed DC3 pointed its droning flight as it descended from the drifting clouds.

Yet his father could joke at their poverty. When you're as far down as we are, he used to say, there's only one direction to go — up.

Up? Where was that? As a young boy, Watene had been mystified by his father's words. He and his sisters accepted the world as it was because it was the only world they knew. The concept of an up or down direction was puzzling; the world just *was*, the way they lived was, simply, the way they assumed things were supposed to be. After all, whenever they went into the village twelve miles away the people there lived exactly like themselves, didn't they? Yes, they did know of others who had more than they had — the local school teacher, the owner of the general store, the big farmers — but these weren't people. They were Pakehas and their world was so distant, so remote, that the children could never comprehend their way of living as being normal. What was normal was what the children saw: the way their relations and friends lived, in houses just like their own. And in that world there was no up or down, no basis for comparison with their own lives. Everything was the same.

It wasn't until some years later, when Watene had started school, that he'd discovered where up was, what poor meant and how his kind of people were regarded.

Until he was three, Watene had slept in a small wooden cot in his parents' room. There were two bedrooms in that tin house: his parents and he slept in one, his three sisters slept in bunks in the other. They slept on mattresses stuffed with horsehair and their blankets were grey army blankets made smooth and soft by incessant washing. Then his mother had given birth to another child, the second son, and Watene had begun sleeping with his eldest sister in her bunk.

The only other room had been their kitchen, dining room and sitting room all in one. One entire wall was their fireplace providing them with both a cooking place and source of warmth during the cold winter. Wire hooks were strung along an iron beam running the length of the wall, and from the hooks dangled the black cooking pots. The fire was kept going morning till night, the smoke billowing grey through the tin-sheeted chimney. The smoke-baked earth was the floor. A wooden table, two benches and makeshift apple-box chairs, a meat safe and a cabinet were the only furniture in the room. In an attempt to make the room look more colourful his mother had pasted newspaper and pictures from magazines on the other walls. And, with the help of his sisters, she had made her curtains from sugarbags.

From the exposed rafters hung the oil lamp and fading decorations of some long ago Christmas. Dark-framed photographs of his parents and the children were propped above the doorways. The prized possession, a whalebone mere, lay on the window-sill. Beside it was the family's one book, the Maori Bible.

The life of the family was centred on that room. In it, Watene had learnt to crawl and then to walk. He'd watched as his mother woke every morning with the sun to nurse the glowing embers of the fireplace into flame and prepare the morning kai. He'd sat in its doorway with his sisters who bathed him and then themselves with water from an outside tank. He'd played on the floor while his sisters dressed for school after having done the morning duties — the milking, feeding the fowls, and the dish-washing in a tin tub by the outside tank. He'd farewelled them as they walked the six miles to the bottom of the valley where they would wait for the bus into the village. Sometimes, if he'd found work, his father would accompany them. If so, then Watene would attend to his brother during the long hours while his mother swept the floor with manuka brush, bottled fruit, salted meat, baked bread from flour and water, and did all those daily tasks in calm acceptance of their need to be done. Then it was down to the river to wash the clothes or across the fence to till the gardens, baby slung on her back and Watene ambling after her, until the sun was half way in its downward flight. Back from the river or gardens she would hasten with her children to stoke the fire, prepare the night's food, feed the baby at her breast and await the return of the rest of her family.

251

This had been the normal routine of her days, patterned with sweat and the dull throb of fatigue. Yet she did not feel any fury or rage against the way she lived. Sweat, fatigue, pain and sometimes hunger were to be borne because they were part of the only life she knew.

But in that life there had been laughter too and joy in her family. During the long winter nights, by firelight and the lamp's glow, she and her family would sit round the table and play cards or knucklebones with smooth stones from the river or just talk while her girls ironed their clothes, her husband carved wood with a pocketknife and her two sons chased each other across the floor. She was content enough. Her family had been her life. Her family and working for them.

His father, Watene supposed, had been what would now be called a 'seasonal worker', a rather glossy term to describe someone who worked when there was work to be had and who eked out his existence by tilling the soil. (When Watene had needed to fill in forms seeking financial help to get him through high school and university he'd been so embarrassed about the question of his father's occupation that he'd written: 'farmer'.)

The family lived on tribal land, a small patch of thin soil which lay on the periphery of the expanse his people had once held in common. The rich and fertile lowland now belonged to the Pakeha.

Only remnants of the ancestral land, like pieces of a broken biscuit, remained to his father and others like him. On this land his father and mother raised the subsistence crops — the kumara, corn, kamokamo — which composed their staple diet. They supplemented these with puha, mushrooms, wild blackberries and cabbage tree leaf stalks picked during their ranging over the hills. During fruit season, the children and their mother would work in the local orchards and bring home boxes of peaches, pears and apricots to be bottled for eating during the following year.

The river supplied eels and the hills wild pig. His mother raised hens and his eldest sister — until Watene was old enough to take her place — milked two cows morning and night.

The earth was good to them and kind but even she could not sustain them through all her seasons. Winter, when earth grew old, was the leanest season of all, leaner still if Watene's father was too long without the paid work which would enable them to have mutton, sugar and other groceries most families took for granted. Then it was a matter of keeping warm, carrying on and waiting for the earth to grow young again.

But it was the way of things. The family lived in stoic acceptance, knowing that after winter summer always came. And with the summer would come work — shearing in a gang with others who, like themselves, had been waiting for the winds to warm.

In this manner they had lived. In that tin house on that piece of land in

252

the middle of nowhere. From that place and life ruled by the seasons, Watene had one day departed with his sisters and walked down the valley to catch the bus into the village to begin school For a while he had continued to accept life as his family lived it as the way life just was.

Then, when he was seven, Watene had brought home his school report. It had been a good report. He'd asked his mother to sign it for him. She told him he should wait until his father got home but Watene had not wanted to wait. He'd set his face with stubbornness and, angry, his mother had grabbed a pencil. Asking him where she should sign, she had stabbed an 'X' in the place. Then, although it was dark, she had gone out of the house towards the gardens to push at the earth under the thin moon.

With that single act, Watene had remembered his father's words. Yes, the only way for them was — up. He'd committed himself with anger to that climb. He'd fashioned for himself an image of the life he wanted. And he'd pursued it down that valley road leaving behind that house with the sugarbag windows.

Watene's fingers tightened on the wine glass.

And he'd finally caught up with the image and, although he did not like all about the person he'd become, he was at least true to the image.

He was back at the bay window again after having circulated among the people Alan had wanted him to meet and spoken to all those others with whom Alan averred he'd much in common. The hardcase thing about windows was that one could look out and fill the landscape with the figments of one's own imagination, colour it according to one's mood and animate it as one wished. *Hardcase?*

— I've been ordered to rescue you, a voice said beside him.

A reflection joined his in the window. A girl with small black eyes and magenta lips and the rain sweeping through her face. Pretty in the fashionable manner.

— From what? Watene asked.

The girl glanced at him, amused, and licked her wine glass with the tip of her tongue.

— Perhaps sugarbags? she said.

Watene's fingers tightened again. Alan must have mentioned it to her. No, Alan would never understand. Nor this girl.

She saw his discomfiture and smiled like a cat.

— Well you must admit it does sound rather curious, she continued. But then you're rather curious yourself. Alan has told me all about you. An honours degree and an important job in Treasury — I must say I am suitably impressed.

— I'm glad for you then, Watene answered somewhat puzzled at the cutting edge in the girl's voice.

— It's just that you're so unexpected, she said. But I imagine you come from a better background than most.

— I'm sorry to disappoint, Watene tried to laugh.

— Oh dear. You mean you *are* a poor Maori boy who's made good?

Her tone was mocking. Watene remembered an encounter he'd had in a hotel a few weeks before. A girl, just like this girl, had witheringly accused him of being a middle-class Maori. He'd asked himself: what was wrong with that? He wanted what he'd never had. He visualised it in terms of a two-storey red brick house, money in the bank and two cars in the garage. Nothing was going to stop him from getting it.

— Yes, he answered the girl. But don't let that stop you putting me down.

— I won't, the girl answered.

— But I must warn you, Watene continued, that I've met your curiosity and your kind before. Always wanting me to conform to your image of what a Maori is supposed to be. And when I don't conform then you look for convenient reasons, for surely there must be some explanation for my being such an — aberration?

The girl laughed. Her laughter was like an eel flicking its tail and eluding his grasp.

— Well it won't work, Watene said. Whether you like it or not I'm here to get exactly what you've always had, to compete with you at your own game.

— Oh dear, the girl said again. You sound just like one of us.

— I am, dear lady, Watene whispered as he kissed her lips. So there's no need for you to be curious about me, is there?

He made a low bow and walked away. He went to a table where a decanter of wine was sitting and poured wine into his glass. Then he stood there, listening to the hum around him.

— So you've met our Nicola, Alan grinned. Bitchy isn't she! Sometimes I wonder whether she is actually as naive as she appears to be.

— She just likes playing games, Watene answered. Why the hell did you tell her about the sugarbags?

— She was curious about you. It just slipped out. Look, what on earth is wrong with you today?

Watene shrugged his shoulders.

— I guess you could say that I've caught up with me, he answered.

— Oblique answers and nonsensical words, Alan sighed, are all it appears I'll be getting from you.

Other friends came to join them and talk. The Vivaldi was replaced by Mozart. Outside it began to get dark but inside the atmosphere remained gay under the glittering chandelier.

That house. His family had finally left it when Watene was nine years old. They had moved to a large coastal town where his father got a job on the wharf, loading and unloading cargo from ships that plied the coast. His sisters had married among their own kind while he, Watene, continued in his climb. His mother had died during his second year at university. The strange thing was that she'd always pined for that house in the valley and had always wanted to return.

But he could never return. In a way it would be like taking a step backward. And yet. . . .

Watene smiled ruefully. In some respects, the girl he'd met in the pub had been right. He was middle-class. But he wasn't going to be middle-class forever, no. For the time being, maybe, but he hadn't finished yet.

— Come and join us, Watene!

He heard Colin calling him to where he and Francesca were playing some silly game. He nodded.

But that house hadn't finished with him yet and as it continued to nudge his memory he felt a sudden flood of affection for it. For nine years it had kept him, nurtured him and looked after him. No matter how far he went he would never forget it because it had been at the beginning of his life.

Anyway, it seemed that it would never let him forget.

He grinned and looked towards the windows. Sugarbags fluttering in the wind. Smoke billowing through the room.

— Yes, he whispered. I need you to remind me and to make me remember who I am. And I will need you more as I keep on climbing. Never leave me.

He joined Colin and Francesca. The wine burst within him and lifted his spirits.

— You're back with us are you? Colin asked

— I suppose I am, he answered.

He lifted his wineglass in a secret toast and whispered the words to himself:

— To houses with sugarbag windows, he said.

WITI IHIMAERA (1944; Te Aitanga-a-Mahaki, Rongowhakaata, Ngati Porou, Whakatohea, Tuhoe, Ngati Kahungunu) was born and brought up in Gisborne. He began writing seriously in 1970 while at Victoria University. In 1972 he published *Pounamu, Pounamu* — the first collection of short stories by a Maori writer. A year later he released *Tangi*, the first novel to be published by a Maori writer. It won the James Wattie Book of the Year award in 1974. The novel had been completed while Witi was living in England. Also in 1974 he published his second novel, *Whanau*. In 1975 Witi was the Robert Burns Fellow at the University of Otago and published *Maori* (an historical essay) and wrote *The New Net Goes Fishing* (1977), a second collection of stories. It is the fourth book of a projected six-book series on Maori life and the first of the urban trilogy.

Witi is a past member of the Queen Elizabeth II Arts Council and in that capacity he established the Council for Maori and South Pacific Arts. At his instigation the Maori Affairs Awards for writers were established and he helped set up the Maori Artists' and Writers' Society in 1975. His work has been translated into German, Russian, French, Japanese and other languages and a number of his stories have been used on radio and on television. In 1973 Witi was invited to the Victorian Writers' Conference in Melbourne and the following year the SPACLALS Conference in Brisbane. He has read his work at the 1979 CACLALS Conference in Montreal and the 1980 Pacific Rim Conference on Children's Literature in Melbourne. His work can be found in *Contemporary Maori Writing* (1970), *Short Stories by New Zealanders* (1972), *Ten Modern New Zealand Story Writers* (1976), *New Zealand Short Stories* (1975), *My New Zealand Junior* (1974), *My New Zealand Senior* (1973), and *NZ Listener Short Stories* Vol. One (1977). His third novel is provisionally entitled *Maui/Mauri/Maori*.

Peter Croucher

The Good Old Days

we never worked
one full week in all that time.

but we drank — how we drank.
we drank on boats
and brawled with sailors,
drank in bars
and fooled with women,
drank in streets
and out-ran policemen,
seagulled and played poker
small-time bets with a wild joker.
dreamt in ships' holds
fished on wharf sides
wished for nothing
apart from good times.

needed nothing
for our living
except enough food to keep us standing.

and we did it — most of us.
we're still standing...a
little shaky of foot,
weary of heart,
but with our eye on the future
and our hand on the helm
prepared to meet the storm.

Work

captured
in the silent air
a seagull
stretches out above
the low tide high
up this river estuary

the black mudflats
unfold
down to the silver river
that finds its way
on weary feet down
to the foot of bracken covered hills that rise

and fall into the sea.

PETER CROUCHER (1952) was born in Masterton. Educated at Palmerston North Boys High School and Wellington Polytechnic he now lives in Carterton. He started writing in 1970.

Keri Hulme

E Nga Iwi O Ngai Tahu

Where are your bones?
    My bones lie in the sea

257

Where are your bones?
They lie in forgotten land
stolen ploughed and sealed

Where are your bones?
On south islands, sawed by discovering wind

Where are your bones?
Whisper
Moeraki, Purakanui, Arahura
Okarito, Murihiku, Rakiura...

Where are your bones?
Lying heavy on my heart

Where are your bones?
Dancing as songs and old words in my head
Deep in the timelessness of mind

Where are your bones?
Here in my gut
Strong in my legs walking
Knotting my fists, but

Where are your bones?
Aue! My bones are flour
ground to make an alien bread...

October

Moonbeshotten, the silver sheep
stare and stare and shiver,
and whitebait with moonlight eyes
are running up the river.

How can I share that moon with you?
It was still, warm, the stars far wicked points;
the houses dark, gutted of life;
the ghost hour when souls slip easily
from sleeping bodies;
and the moon brooding over the land.

Nightsounds steeped in moonshine,
sea-roar, tree-frog, morepork,
and the steady drop of water off the roof.

That night was the moon's creation
and I an intruder,
afraid to stay too long awake
in the solid shadow...

    And moonbeshotten silver sheep
    stare and stare and shiver,
    while the whitebait with moonlight eyes
    go running up the river.

First Sleep In Te Rangiita

Alone in a sea of breathing
with a hook dream
waiting in the dark.

The wind bangs the door like a stranger
and the rain clatters
clawfooted on the roof.

Aue! Moeraki, Okarito —
my sea-rock people
are miles fogged with distance
long silences away.

Whakatu

Eh man!
They like us on the chains
we do a good killing job
and we look so happy

    Hei tama tu tama
    tama go away

They like us in the factories
cleaning floors and shifting loads

    hei tama tu tama

they like us driving trucks and dozers
and working on the roads

    hei tama tu tama

Hey boy!
They like us in the pubs
we drink up large
and we look so happy

    Hei tama tu tama
    tama go away

E tama!
They like us
they like us
drinking & shouting & singing
when it's someone else's party
or swinging plastic pois
in a piupiu from Woolworths
and thumping hell outa an old guitar
Because we look so happy

    Hei tama tu tama
    tama go away
    Aue, tama go away.

Nga Kehua

I carry my ghosts on my shoulders
wet-eyed and tight with teeth
I am immune to cooked charms.

    Motoitoi, who joined with a sailor
    until her bruises broke her heart;
    Emma, who drew a plough

where a horse should be;
Tommy Rangikino shovelling coal
until the dust throttled him
with canker of the throat.

I carry my ghosts on my shoulders
though some have never been born:
did I have a silent cousin
Did I know tears?

> In grief, seaweed
> In grief, bleeding
> In grief, obsidian knives. . . .

> > Mary Matches, smiling over
> > her broken thighs.

I carry my ghosts on my shoulders,
O John my father why work
until your heart burst?

> The dead weight a lifetime,
> weigh nothing at all.

He Hōhā

> Bones tuned, the body sings—

See me,
I am wide with swimmer's muscle, and a bulk and luggage I carry curdled
        on hips;
I am as fat-rich as a titi-chick, ready for the far ocean flight.

See me,
I have skilled fingers with minimal scars, broad feet that caress beaches,
ears that catch the music of ghosts, eyes that see the landlight, a pristine
        womb
untouched except by years of bleeding, a tame unsteady heart.

See me,
I am a swamp, a boozy drain with stinking breath, a sour sweetened flesh;

261

I am riddled with kidneyrot, brainburn, torn gut, liverfat, scaled with
     wrinkles,
day by day I am leached, even between smiles, of that strange water,
     electricity.

See me,
I am my earth's child,

     and she, humming
     considers her cuts and scars, and debates our death.
     Mean the land's breast, hard her spine when turned against you;
     jade her heart.

Picture me a long way from here—
back bush, a rainbird calling,
the sea knocking shore.

It is cliché that once a month, the moon stalks through my body,
rendering me frail and still more susceptible to brain spin;
it is truth that cramp and clot and tender breast beset— but then
it is the tide of potency, another chance to walk through the crack between
     worlds.

What shall I do when I dry, when there is no more turning with the
     circling moon?
Ah suck tears from the wind, close the world's eye;
Papatuanuku still hums.

But picture me a long way from here.

Waves tuned, the mind-deep sings—

     She forgot self in the city, in the flats full of dust and spiderkibbled
          flies;
     she forgot the sweetness of silence in the rush and roar of metal
          nights;
     no song fitted her until she discovered her kin, all swimmers in the
          heavy air of sea;

     she had lost the supple molten words, the rolling thunder,
     the night hush of her mother's tongue;
     she had lost the way home, the bright road, the trodden beach, the
          mewling gulls,

the lean grey toe of land.
In the lottery of dreams, she gained prize of a nightmare, a singular
dark.

But picture her a long way from there,
growing quiet until she heard herself whispered by the sea on the
blackest night,
and echoed in the birds of morning.

Keening, crooning, the untuned spirit—
I am a map of Orion scattered in moles across this firmament of body;
I am the black hole, the den where katipo are busy spinning deadhavens,
and he won't go, the cuckoo child.
Jolted by the sudden thud and shatter, I have gone outside to find
the bird too ruffled, too quiet, the barred breast broken, an end of the far
travelling.

Tutara-kauika, you father of whales, you servant of Tangaroa,
your little rolling eye espies the far traveller — quick!
whistle to him, distract, send him back to the other island;
I don't mind ever-winter if summer's harbinger is so damaged,
damaging.

He turned full to face me, with a cry to come home —
do you know the language of silence, can you read eyes?

When I think of my other bones, I bleed inside,
and he won't go, the cuckoo-child.

It is not born; it is not live; it is not dead;
it haunts all my singing, lingers greyly, hates and hurts and hopes
impossible things.
And Papatuanuku is beginning her ngeri, her anger is growing,
thrumming in quakes and tsunami,

and he won't go, the cuckoo's child.

O, picture me a long way from here;
tune the bones, the body sings;
quiet the mind, the spirit hums,
and Papatuanuku trembles, sighs;
till then among the blood and dark
the shining cuckoo spreads his wings

and flies this hōhā , this buzz and fright,
this wave and sweat and flood,
this life.

The Kaumatua And The Broken Man

It is a long slow march, paced for a funeral, a march of death.

The kaumatua shuffles, bone-fingered hand grasping Joe's forearm. He moves blindly; his feet catch on sticks and stumble on stones. He mutters to himself continuously. He is failing horribly fast, the upright man of yesterday become this scarecrow of bones mere hours later.

> *I have seen dead people, but I have never seen someone die.*
> *What do you do? Hold their hand and let them get on with it?*
> *Pray? Tangi? Listen?*

The old man trips again, and nearly falls. Joe steadies him with his body.

'Corner. Left.' The words are forced out. Thick veins in the old man's forehead pulse alarmingly.

The beaten earth track forks. Joe helps him down the left-hand path. They come to rocks, worn and broken, but still towering above them. An ancient gorge where the river ran aeons ago, and carved this place for part of its bed. A silent place: ochre and slate-grey stones. No birds. No insects. The only plants are weeds, stringy and grey and subdued. The old man pulls on Joe's arm. He points with a trembling hand.

'Cave. In ground.' He tightens his lips and closes his eyes, concentrating. 'I don't. Want. To be put there. In the *town*...'

> *Burial cave...and his grandmother will lie up there.*
> *Somewhere. There's a rock like a saddle about fifty yards*
> *away, in a direct line with where he's pointing. I'll take a look*
> *later. Maybe.*

Joe shivers. 'E pou, don't worry. I won't put you there. You want to be buried in the town, I will take you there...but what marae? Who are your people?'

'No. People. They're dead. The town...'

'You want to go to the cemetery in the town?'

A whisper of sound, 'Ae.'

'So be it.'

The kaumatua edges forward again. 'Ki te tauranga atua...' he says softly. Under his breath, again and again, 'Tauranga atua, tauranga atua,' as though those words give strength and enable him to walk.

> *Tauranga...a resting place for canoes, an anchorage. For a*
> *god canoe, what anchorage?*

264

I remember a wet afternoon, when I was a child, and I read a magazine. It had the pictures and story of how they found an old canoe of the Egyptians. . . the sun ship of Cheops, that was it, a burial ship for a pharaoh to ride in. And I thought then — to think of it now! — how much more exciting it would be to find a ship of ours. . . not a dusty narrow craft in the desert sand, a river-craft if it sailed at all, but one of the far-travelled salt-sea ships, that knifed across great Kiwa centuries ago. . . guided by stars, powered by the winds, and the muscles of stronghearted women and men. . .

But Cheop's canoe travelled the way of the dead, and that's a journey and a half. . . coffined it was, confined between stone blocks.

Where will I find this ship? In stone? In water as he suggested?

Or only in the clouded remnants of an old man's mind?

The kaumatua's grasp on his arm tightens again. 'Here,' he says in a choked whisper, 'Here.'

The earth track goes on a way yet, turning a corner to head towards the sea. The sea is loud here, as though the diminishing rock walls by some freak of acoustics, channel in the sound. There doesn't appear to be anything different about this part of the gorge. Joe looks sadly round.

Mad and stricken after all. . .

'See. It?' The rasping urgency of the tired voice makes him stare at the bare surrounding rocks as hard as he can. Tears blur his vision.

I can't say even Yes for him. I can't tell him a lie.

The wind blows a little more strongly, and the white streamers of cloud shift away from the face of the sun.

Over by the cliff, something glints.

'Is it water?' asks Joe sharply.

The old man sags. 'Haere. . . .' Pushing himself away from Joe, 'Go, you go, I cannot go.'

As gently as possible, Joe helps him lie down at the side of the track. He takes off his parka and wraps it into a pad, a pillow for the kaumatua's head. The old man's eyes are closed.

'I'll come right back.'

Don't die yet, he thinks fiercely. He clambers over the rocks towards the glint, his heart pounding.

A weathered stratum of rock makes an overhang. It is almost a cave, but it hasn't a floor. A great natural well, like a sinkhole, a cenote, has been formed in the rock.

The water is pale green and milky, as though it contains lime dust in suspension. It is opaque at first glance. But in a very short time — trick of the light, or his eyes adjusting — he can see shadows in the pool. He can't tell how deep the water is, or how large the things that show as shadows are. They cover the bottom of the pool, with patches and gaps between them. Long angular shadows mainly, with two round ones at the far side.

> *It can't be one of the great ships...the pool's only, what? twenty feet in diameter...but there's something down there...rock debris? Old logs? Dunno... where does the water come from? Underground spring maybe...there doesn't seem to be any outflow or overflow...*

He puts his hand in the water cautiously, meaning to see whether the water is coloured or contains stoneflour, and snatches it out again before his fingers go in past the knuckles.

Jesus Holy! It's like ten thousand tiny bubbles bursting on his skin, a mild electric current, an aliveness. He notices that the water is not still at the far end of the pool. Fine tendrils, filaments of clearness, rise and meld with the pale green, like an ice-cube melting in whisky and spinning lucid threads into the surrounding colour. He edges back from the side of the pool. Peace, peace, I'm just looking...maybe I should introduce myself? Feeling foolish, squatting on his haunches by the overhang, he tells the water his name and his tribe, that Tiaka Mira has named him as his replacement.

> *Stupid fool, Ngakau...what do words mean to, whatever it is? If it's anything...*

He says 'E noho ra' before he goes, though.

The old man is sitting, back against a rock, when he returns.

'Not dead yet!' He calls cheerfully, triumphantly. 'I am staggering on the edge of corruption, but I'm not dead yet!'

Fresh strength has been infused into him, from the rest or by Joe finding what he was sent to find. His eyes are bright and see the present again, and he no longer mumbles unintelligibly to the ghosts that surround him.

He produces Kerewin's last cigar from the pocket of his greatcoat, and lights it, passing it then to Joe.

> *E hoa, if only you could see where your smokes went...where are you now? And the last time I shared a smoke, it was with Haimona... O boy, what are they doing to you? Though maybe you can't know...*

They smoke in silence, sharing the cigar puff and puff about.

'Pity we didn't bring the tea,' says the kaumatua suddenly. 'It's a good place for a picnic nei?'

Joe looks at him sideways. 'A bit too quiet for my liking.'

'O, it's not like this all the time...plenty of noise in a thunderstorm! It booms and echoes all up the gorge like giant men yelling...and when there's an earthquake! Ahh, I've been here when the earth was creaking and groaning as if she were giving birth...and sometimes, on long summer evenings when the flies are humming, sometimes,' the bantering note is gone, and his voice is low and dreamy, 'the old people come back. I've seen them standing round the mouth of that shelter up there, watching and talking softly. With their long oiled hair, and their fine strong bodies, and proud free-eyed faces...sometimes they talk, and sometimes they walk, filing away down a track that isn't there anymore, silent under the sun...maybe they don't come back, maybe I've gone into their time, because they've looked to where I sit and shaded their eyes, squinting, as though they could see something but not enough. And once, a woman threw a piece of cooked kumara at me and I ducked, and laughed...and once I looked at my dog, and he'd gone misty. Insubstantial, until I put my hand on him, and he whined and licked my hand, and when I looked back, the old ones had gone...mysteries, O Joseph. All the land is filled with mysteries, and this place fairly sings with them.'

'I don't think I'd like to meet any of the old folk.'

I don't think I could look them straight in the eye. I'd feel like a
thing of no account, less than a slave.

'You may, and you may not.'

The old man shrugs, and begins talking about other days and happenings, when he was younger and spent much of his time hunting pig and deer through the scrub.

'Fishing and hunting and looking after my garden,' he finishes, 'that's how my life has been spent. It has been a very easy life, I suppose. No wars or great doings. Just watching things grow, and catching things for food. No family worries after the old woman died. No money problems, always enough to eat, enough to smoke, a roof over my head. A man can find satisfaction with enough.'

'Yes,' says Joe. His thigh has started to ache after all the walking and scrambling over the rocks, and his arm is throbbing hard.

I'd like to stretch out in the sun and go to sleep while he talks,
but I can't do that.

He says with an effort, 'Your dogs, e pou? Where did you get them?'

'O, the old lady had a bitch, that somehow got herself in pup...a dog from a hunter's pack maybe? They bred among themselves, never too many, all good strong dogs, not a mean or bad cur among them. The last one, he died about two years ago, and I didn't have the heart to start again. Just as well, nei? It's not good for a dog to outlive his master...they were company as well as hunting companions. That last one, Tika he was called, must have been the only dog in the country who was brought up and lived

on fish, eh. I haven't hunted pig or deer for many years now, but I can still fish...oh, he used to get a bit of bird now and then, but mainly fish...'
He sits in the sun, his hands folded in his lap, remembering the dogs, retelling their exploits as they come into his mind.

It's maybe his last talk, Ngakau. Make it happy for him.

So he chuckles amiably at the funny stories, and clucks his tongue at the bad ones, and mourns with the old man over the deaths of long-dead dogs. The ache in his arm and leg grows, but he doesn't let it show on his face.

At last the kaumatua reaches out his hand to him. 'Help me up, O Joseph.'

When standing, he cries out in a loud voice, something that is gutteral and archaic and incomprehensible to Joe. The chant rings in the gorge, an echo dying seconds after the last word has been called out.

'A farewell,' says the old man, turning to him, answering his question before it is asked. 'I don't think the mauriora or the little god recognise we who watch over them as individuals. My grandmother through of us as an attendant stream of awareness, and said they knew when we left. Now, they'll know I'm leaving.'

Joe, rubbing his thigh awkwardly with his left hand says, 'I told them when I said hello. Sort of.'

'What did you see to say hello to?' asks the old man, grinning.

Joe flushes. 'What looked like long shadows in the water.' His words echoing the kaumatua's earlier words.

The old man says gently, 'It's all in pieces, you know...and not all of it is there. The old people managed to get the stern and the prows and a few of the hull sections to that safety...I know they used pieces of the hull to carry the little god and the mauri to the tarn.'

'They're the round shadows?'

He smiles with satisfaction. 'Ah, you're a discerning one after all...it took me days to see them properly. Yes, I think they may be unwrapped now, but when my grandmother brought them to the surface they were covered with the remains of cloaks. Red feather cloaks, too.'

'She swam in *that*?'

The old man smiles more widely still. 'You touched, eh? It's a surprise isn't it! No, she called them to the top, and the little god came with the mauri on his back, and they stayed there for minutes while she sang, and then sank back to safety. Believe it, or disbelieve it, that was how the matter was. I tried once, using the words she taught me, but the water started boiling, and that hadn't happened when she sang, so I was afraid and stopped. My grandmother was a very strong-minded woman, remember, and she had knowledge she maybe never should have had.'

Joe shivers, partly from the growing pain, partly from the magic. 'Where did she get hold of it?' he asks, not really wanting to know.

The old man waves a hand in the air. 'From her girlhood, she was curious about this place...her grandfather doted on her, and told her many things from the past. What he told her of the burial of this canoe, and what it contained, fascinated her mind. She sought out the people who had knowledge, and one way or another, obtained all she needed to know. She had the right to this piece of land, through her mother's sister, who never was married. She had to wait years until she got it though, and when she got it, she made sure, Pakeha fashion, that it would never pass out of her hands except to someone she was confident would look after what it bore. Me. Now you.' He looks up to the strange well in the gorge-side.

'Remember, it was a time of flux and chaos when she sought her knowledge. No one can be blamed for giving her information that she maybe should never have known. And she can be praised for having that staunch courage and intelligence to preserve something she believed, as I believe, to be of unusual value. Incalculable value. How do you weigh the value of this country's soul?'

Joe shakes his head. He doesn't want to think of what could be lying there in the cool green and stinging water. He does say, tentatively as they're walking slowly away, "If it is, the heart of Aotearoa...why isn't this whole place...flowering? Something as strong as that, would make the very stones flower, nei? And there is nothing at all...no birds...flies, you say, but...flies?'

The kaumatua waits until the halting sentences are finished.

'It despaired of us, remember. It is asleep...maybe its very sleep keeps the living things away, except for flies, who come to the sleeping and the dead alike. Aue! The one thing I regret about dying is that, secretly, in the marrow of my heart, I have always wanted to see what happens when it wakes up.' He sighs. 'Maybe we have gone too far down other paths for the old alliance to be reformed, and this will remain a land where the spirit has withdrawn. Where the spirit is still with the land, but no longer active. No longer loving the land.' He laughs harshly. 'I can't imagine it loving the mess the Pakeha have made, can you?'

Joe thought of the forests burned and cut down; the gouges and scars that dams and roadworks and development schemes had made; the peculiar barren paddocks where alien animals, one kind of crop, grazed imported grasses; the erosion, the over-fertilisation, the pollution...

'No, it wouldn't like this at all. We might have started some of the havoc, but we would never have carried it so far. I don't think.' He adds thoughtfully, after a pause of seconds, 'I can't see that,' nodding back towards the hidden well, 'ever waking now. The whole order of the world would have to change, all of humanity, and I can't see that happening, e pou, not ever.'

'Eternity is a long time,' says the kaumatua comfortably. 'Everything changes, even that which supposes itself to be unalterable. All we can do is look after the precious matters which are our heritage, and wait, and hope.' The lively glint is back in his eyes. 'Well, at least *you* can do that...this one is going to take things easy from now on!' He rubs his belly. 'Though I might wait long enough for tea, Joseph. Yes, I think I'll take you through my garden, and we'll gather food for tea. We'll eat a last good meal together, and you can tell me all about your dead family that was, and your live one which you have lost, and I'll be as polite as you were while I was boring you with tales of my dogs, hei?'

Joe grins shamefacedly.

'I wasn't that bored...I hope it's not our last meal. Maybe you won't be called away so fast now they,' gesturing with his hand to the pale shining sky, 'know how inept and unlearned I am.'

'Ah, you'll do, you'll do,' says the old man cryptically, and they walk on, limp on, in silence.

In the garden, under that bright sky, the kaumatua clutches at his chest, and falls heavily to the ground. 'Ahh,' he gasps, trying to regain his breath, but with each exhalation there is less left. His body jerks spasmodically. Then slowly, he curls up, withering round his anguish like a burning leaf.

Joe starts to run towards the whare, turns and comes back. No phone no nothing no doctor what good would a doctor be? He kneels by the man.

His face is suffused and his eyes are screwed tightly shut. One hand scrabbles on the ground. It is a deliberate motion, Joe realises after a moment. Writing...aie, the will...

'Where is it? The will you want? Where?' he asks urgently, bending over and loosing his voice like an arrow into the old man's ear.

Somehow the thin shaking limbs are drawn together, driven by an inordinate effort of will. He is nearly to his knees.

Joe unstraps his right hand from his belt, and clenching his teeth against the tearing ache, picks him up, cradles him, arm beneath back, head lolling, arm under the long legs.

For the strength in my shoulders, praise, going one half step after the other, for the strength in my shoulders, praise, arm feeling like it is breaking anew; for the strength in my shoulders, praise, a slow torturous ripping apart of bone and muscle fibre; for the strength in my shoulders, praise, staggering, skinning round the doorframe, grating against it, using it as a prop to hold himself up a little longer.

He stumbles across the room and lays the old man on his bed. The sweat rolls into his eyes, stinging them blind.

A whistling croaking voice, pausing after each word, an inhuman voice, says, 'In. The Bible. Pen. On clock.'

He wheels round and lurches over, fingers fumbling, words ticking like an inexorable clock, 'Bible pen bible pen bible pen.' He shakes the bible and a piece of folded typescript falls out, snatches the pen off the clock knocking over a key a candle butt, and races back to the bed. 'Ahh!' he calls wildly, 'somethingtowriteon!' He picks up the fallen bible and brings it back. He is dizzy and sick, both with his own pain and the knowledge that the old man, however strenuous and gallant his effort, is too nearly dead to succeed in writing his name, drawing his secret design.

Like a puppet lifted by its strings, the old man rises up. His hand outstretched, he receives the pen. His eyes stare fixedly ahead, looking at the end of his bed.

'Where?' Pen poised.

Joe stares at him, cold with horror. For it is as though the old man has already vacated his body and he — or something else — is directing it from the outside.

'Here,' he whispers, through numb lips. Blinking against the tears and sweat of pain, he guides the stiff hand. 'My name,' he whispers, 'here.'

In beautiful copperplate, the letters form: mechanically, each letter separate then joined by an eerily serene curve: Joseph Kakaukawa Gillayley, Kati Kahukunu...

'It is done. Where?'

The voice is not the kaumatua's, the eyes still stare blankly ahead.

'Here.' He is shaking and trembling, his voice chilled to an almost noiseless whimper, fear growing in him like crystals of ice.

The signature flows swiftly, appearing on the paper as if tipped from a strange container. T. M. Mira, a flourish, two dots. The pen falls.

As though someone struck him, the old man winces and jerks. For a second he is present again. Joe seizes the pen and returns it to the cold grasp, ice deep in his heart now as he touches the fingers to close them round the barrel. Seeming to have eyes, the fingers take the pen back to Joe's name, and quickly draw a complicated maze of spirals and spreading lines. Too quickly. No calligraphist could have drawn the moko so perfectly in the short time the fingers execute it. With the same horrid fluidity, a second pattern is drawn over the kaumatua's signature.

'Yours...Joseph. My. Blessing.'

Joe eases the paper away, avoiding another touch of the living dead hand. The pen falls. As though a string has been cut, the thin body flops bonelessly on the bed, the eyes closing.

'Aue,' Joe says softly, 'it is ended. It is done.'

But the old body convulses once, twice, and the bowel contents spurt out. The stench of excrement is overpowering. The old man moans, his fingers twitching helplessly by his sides.

271

'Not like this,' a husky thread of protest, 'not like this...aue...aue, the shame, the shame...'

Joe takes hold of the hands, enfolding them. He says, weeping, 'E pou, tipuna, we all die like this, do not worry, I will be a son to you, be content to let a son perform this office for you, there is no shame, no shame.'

His words strangle in his sobbing.

'Aue, te whakama,' says the kaumatua wearily.

'No shame, no shame,' but he is talking to empty ears.

> Today I shall cry, 'Kia koe, Rehua! Rehua, kia koe! Aue, te whakama...'

He washes the body. He clothes it in a pair of his jeans and his shirt. The jeans are short, and the thin ankles stick out ridiculously. The shirt could be wrapped round the body twice. There are no shoes he can put on the body's feet, no shoes anywhere in the whare.

He walks out and waits by the side of the road. A passing motorist stops, and when she hears someone has died, she is shocked and sympathetic. She takes him right to the police station in Durville. Joe doesn't speak. He feels as hollow and dry as a cicada husk.

He watches as they casually pick up the brittle old body and tuck it up on the stretcher, blanket across the face.

> The roots of the tree
> snake down the cliff.
> There is nothing beyond them
> but the endless sea.

Hooks And Feelers

On the morning before it happened, her fingers were covered with grey, soft clay.

'Charleston,' she says. 'It comes from Charleston. It's really a modeller's clay, but it'll make nice cups. I envisage,' gesturing in the air, 'tall fluted goblets. I'll glaze them sea blue and we'll drink wine together, all of us.'

I went out to the shed and knocked on the door. There's no word of welcome, but the kerosene lamp is burning brightly, so I push on in.

She's pumping the treadle potter's wheel with a terrible urgency, but she's not making pots. Just tall, wavery cones. I don't know what they are. I've never seen her make them before. The floor, the shelves, the bench —

the place is spikey with them.

'They've rung,' I say.

She doesn't look up.

'They said he'll be home tomorrow.'

The wheel slowed, stopped.

She looked at her clay-covered hands.

'So?'

'Well, will you get him?'

'No.'

The wheel starts purring. Another cone begins to grow under her fingers.

'What are you making those for?'

She still won't look at me.

'You go,' she says, and the wheel begins to hum.

Well, you can't win.

I go and get him and come home, chattering brightly all way.

He is silent.

I carry him inside, pointing out that I've repainted everywhere, that we've got a new stove and did you like your present? And he ignores it all.

But he says, very quietly, to his ma, 'Hello.' Very cool.

She looks at him, over him, round him, eyes going up and down but always avoiding the one place where she should be looking. She says, 'Hello,' back.

'Put me down please,' he says to me then.

No 'Thanks for getting me'. Not a word of appreciation for the new clothes. Just that polite, expressionless, 'Put me down please'.

Not another word.

He went into his bedroom and shut the door.

'Well, it's just the shock of being back home, eh?'

I look at her, and she looks at me. I go across and slide my hands round her shoulders, draw her close to me, nuzzle her ear, and for a moment it's peace.

Then she draws away.

'Make a coffee,' she says brusquely, 'I'm tired.'

I don't take offence. After grinding the beans, I ask, 'What are you making the cones for?'

She shrugs.

'It's just an idea.'

The smell from the crushed coffee-beans is rich and heavy, almost sickening.

273

His door opens.

He has his doll in his hand. Or rather, parts of his doll. He's torn the head off, the arms and legs apart.

'I don't want this anymore,' he says into the silence.

He goes to the fire, and flings the parts in. And then he reaches in among the burning coals and plucks out the head, which is melted and smoking. He says, 'On second thoughts, I'll keep this.'

The smoke curls round the steel and lingers, acridly.

Soon after, she went back to the shed.

I went down to the pub.

'Hey!' yells Mata, 'c'mon over here!'

'Look at that,' he says, grinning hugely, waving a crumpled bit of paper. It's a Golden Kiwi ticket. 'Bugger's won me four hundred dollars.' He sways. 'Whatta yer drinking?'

I never have won anything. I reach across, grab his hand, shake it. It's warm and calloused, hard and real.

'Bloody oath, Mat, what good luck!'

He smiles more widely still, his eyes crinkling almost shut. 'Shout you eh?'

'Too right you can. Double whisky.'

And I get that from him and a jug and another couple of doubles and another jug. I am warm and happy until someone turns the radio up.

'Hands across the water hands across the sea . . .' the voices thunder and beat by my ears, and pianos and violins wail and wind round the words.

The shed's in darkness.

I push the door open, gingerly.

'Are you there?'

I hear her move.

'Yes.'

'How about a little light on the subject?' I'm trying to sound happily drunk, but the words have a nasty callous ring to them.

'The lamp is on the bench beside you.'

I reach for it and encounter a soft, still wet, cone of clay. I snatch my fingers away hurriedly.

'Are you revealing to the world what the cones are for yet?'

I've found the lamp, fumble for my matches. My fingers are clumsy, but at last the wick catches a light, glows and grows.

She sniffs.

'Give me the matches please.'

I throw the box across and she snatches them from the air.

She touches a match to a cigarette, the match shows blue and then flares bright, steady, gold. The cigarette pulses redly. The lamp isn't trimmed very well.

She sighs and the smoke flows thickly out of her mouth and nose.

'I put nearly all of them back in the stodge-box today.'

What? Oh yes, the cones. The stodge-box is her special term for the pile of clay that gets reworked.

'Oh,' I add after a moment, apologetically, 'I sort of squashed one reaching for the lamp.'

'It doesn't matter,' she says, blowing out another stream of smoke.

'I was going to kill that one too.'

I take my battered, old, guitar and begin to play. I play badly. I've never learned to play properly.

He says, out of the dark, 'Why are you sad?'

'What makes you think I am?'

'Because you're playing without the lights on.'

I sigh. 'A man can play in the dark if he wants.'

'Besides I heard you crying.'

My dear cool son.

'...so I cry sometimes...'

'Why are you sad?' he asks again.

Everlasting questions ever since he began to talk.

'Shut up.'

'Because of me?' he persists. He pauses, long enough to check whether I'm going to move.

'Or because of her?'

'Because of me, now get out of here,' I answer roughly, and bang the guitar down. It groans. The strings shiver.

He doesn't move.

'You've been to the pub?'

I prop the guitar against the wall and get up.

'You've been to the pub,' he states, and drifts back into his room.

My mother came to visit next day, all agog to see the wreckage. She has a nice instinct for disasters. She used to be a strong little woman but she's run to frailty and brittle bones now. Alas; all small and powdery, with a thick line down over her face that manages, somehow, to protrude through her makeup. It'd look so much better if she didn't pile powder and stuff on, but I can't imagine her face without pink gunk clogging the pores. That much has never changed.

She brought a bag of blackballs for him. When he accepts them, reluctantly, she coos and pats him and strokes his hair. He has always hated that.

'Oh dear,' she says, 'your poor careless mother,' and 'You poor little man' and (aside to me) 'It's just as well you didn't have a daughter, it'd be so much worse for a girl.' (He heard that, and smiled blandly.)

She asks him, 'However are you going to manage now? Your guitar and football and all? Hmmm?'

He says, steadily, 'It's very awkward to wipe my arse now. That's all.'

For a moment I like him very much.

My mother flutters and tchs, 'Oh, goodness me, dear, you mustn't say . . .'

He's already turned away.

As soon as my mother left, I went out to the shed.

'You could have come in and said hello,' I say reproachfully.

'It would have only led to a fight.' She has no doubt about that. She sits hunched up on the floor. Her face is in shadow.

I look round. The shed's been tidied up. All the stray bits and pieces are hidden away. There's an innovation, however, an ominous one. The crucifix she keeps on the wall opposite her wheel has been covered with black cloth. The only part that shows is a hand, nailed to the wooden cross.

'Is that a reminder for penitence? Or are you mourning?'

She doesn't reply.

Early in the morning, while it's still quite dark, I awake to hear him sobbing. I lift the bedclothes gently — she didn't stir, drowned in sleep, her black hair wreathed about her body like seaweed — and creep away to his room.

The sobbing is part stifled, a rhythmic choking and gasping, rough with misery.

'Hello?'

'E pa . . .' he turns over and round from his pillow and reaches out his arms. He doesn't do that. He hasn't done that since he was a baby.

I pick him up, cradling him, cuddling him.

'I can feel it still pa. I can feel it still.' He is desperate in his insistence and wild with crying. But he is also coldly angry at himself.

'I know it's not there any more,' he struck himself a blow, 'but I can *feel* it still . . .'

I kiss and soothe and bring a tranquilliser that the people at the hospital gave me. He sobs himself back to sleep, leaning, in the end, away from me. And I go back to bed.

Her ocean, her ocean, te moananui a Kiwa, drowns me. Far away on the beach I can hear him calling, but I must keep on going down into the greeny deeps, down to where her face is, to where the soft anemone tentacles of her fingers beckon and sway and sweep me onward to the weeping heart of the world.

He stays home from school for another week. It's probably just as well, for once, the first time he ventured outside the house, the next door neighbour's kids shouted crudities at him.

I watched him walk over to them, talk, and gesture, the hook flashing bravely in the sun. The next door neighbour's kids fell silent, drew together in a scared huddled group.

'What did you do to stop that?' I ask, after he has stalked proudly back inside.

He shook his head.

'Tell me.'

'I didn't have to do anything.' He smiles.

'Oh?'

'I don't imagine,' he says it so coolly, 'that anyone wants this in their eyes.'

The hair on the back of my neck bristles with shock.

'Don't you dare threaten anybody like that! No matter what they say!' I shout at him in rage, in horror. 'I'll beat you silly if you do that again.'

He shrugs. 'Okay, if you say so pa.'

(Imagine that cruel, steel curve reaching for your eyes. That pincer of unfeeling metal gouging in.) The steel hook glints as he moves away.

How can he be my son and have so little of me in him? Oh, he has my colouring, fair hair and steelgrey eyes, just as he has her colour and bone structure; a brown thickset chunk of a boy.

But his strange cold nature comes from neither of us. Well, it certainly doesn't come from me.

Later on that day — we are reading in front of the fire — a coal falls out. He reaches for it.

'Careful, it's hot,' I warn.

'I don't care how hot it is,' he says, grinning.

The two steel fingers pick up the piece of coal and slowly crush the fire out of it.

It hasn't taken long for him to get very deft with those pincers. He can pick up minute things, like pins, or the smallest of buttons. I suspect he practises doing so, in the secrecy of his bedroom. He can handle almost anything as skilfully as he could before.

At night, after he's had a shower, I ask, 'Let me look?'

277

'No.'

'Ahh, come on.'

He holds it out, silently.

All his wrist bones are gone. There remains a scarred purplish area with two smooth, rounded knubs on either side. In the centre is a small socket. The hook, which is mounted on a kind of swivel, slots into there. I don't understand how it works, but it looks like a nice practical piece of machinery.

He is looking away.

'You don't like it?'

'It's all right...will you string my guitar backwards? I tried, and I can't do it.'

'Of course.'

I fetch his guitar and begin immediately.

'There is something quite new we can do, you know.' The specialist draws a deep breath of smoke and doesn't exhale any of it.

The smell of antiseptic is making me feel sick. This room is painted a dull grey. There are flyspots on the light. I bring my eyes down to him and smile, rigidly.

'Ahh, yes.'

'Immediately after amputation, we can attach an undamaged portion of sinew and nerve to this nyloprene socket.'

He holds out a gadget, spins it round between his lean fingers, and snatches it away again, out of sight.

'It is a permanent implant, with a special prosthesis that fits into it. The wrist tissues will grow round it, but the child will retain a good deal of control over his, umm, hand movements.'

He sucks in more smoke and eyes me beadily, eagerly. Then he suddenly lets the whole, stale lungful go, right in my face.

'So you agree to that then?'

'Ahh, yes.'

Later, at night, she says 'Are you still awake too?'

'Yes.'

'What are you thinking of?'

'Nothing really. I was just listening to you breathe.'

Her hand creeps to my side, feeling along until it finds a warm handful.

'I am thinking of the door,' she says thoughtfully.

You know the way a car door crunches shut, with a sort of definite, echoing thunk?

Well, there was that. Her hurried footsteps. A split second of complete silence. And then the screaming started, piercing, agonised, desperate. We spun round. He was nailed, piniomed against the side of the car by his trapped hand.

She stood, going, 'O my god! O my god!' and biting down on her hand. She didn't make another move, frozen where she stood, getting whiter and whiter and whiter.

I had to open the door.

'I know it's silly,' she continues, still holding me warmly, 'but if we hadn't bought that packet of peanuts, he wouldn't have spilled them. I wouldn't have got angry. I wouldn't have stormed out of the car. I wouldn't have slammed the door without looking. Without looking.'

'You bought the nuts, remember?' she adds irrelevantly.

I don't answer.

There are other things in her ocean now. Massive, black shadows that loom up near me without revealing what they are. Something glints. The shadows waver and retreat.

They stuck a needle attached to a clear, plastic tube into his arm. The tube filled with blood. Then, the blood cleared away and the dope ran into his vein. His eyelids dragged down. He slept, unwillingly, the tears of horror and anguish still wet on his face.

The ruined hand lay on a white, shiny bench, already apart from him. It was like a lump of raw, swollen meat with small, shattered, bluish bones through it.

'We'll have to amputate that, I'm afraid. It's absolutely unsalvageable.'

'Okay,' I say. 'Whatever you think best.'

They say that hearing is the last of the senses to die, when you are unconscious.

They are wrong, at least for me. Images, or what is worse, not-quite images, flare and burst and fade before I sink into the dreamless sea of sleep.

I went out to the shed.

'Tea is nearly ready,' I call through the open door.

'Good,' she replies. 'Come in and look.'

She has made a hundred, more than a hundred, large, shallow wine cups. 'Kraters,' she says, smiling to me briefly.

I grin back, delighted.

'Well, they should sell well.'

She bends her head, scraping at a patch of dried clay on the bench.

'What were the cones?'

She looks up at me, the smile gone entirely.

'Nothing important,' she says. 'Nothing important.'

When she's washing the dishes, however, the magic happens again. For the first time since the door slammed shut, I look at her, and she looks willingly back and her eyes become deep and endless dark waters, beckoning to my soul. Drown in me...find yourself. I reach out flailing, groping for her hard, real body. Ahh, my hands encounter tense muscles, fasten on to them. I stroke and knead, rousing the long-dormant woman in her. Feel in the taut, secret places, rub the tender, moist groove, caress her all over with sweet, probing fingers.

'Bait,' says a cold, sneering voice.

She gasps and goes rigid again.

'Get away to bed with you,' she says without turning round.

'I'm going to watch.'

An overwhelming anger floods through me I whip around and my erstwhile gentle hands harden and clench.

'I'll..."

'No,' she says, 'no,' touching me, warning me.

She goes across and kneels before him.

(I see he's trembling.)

She kisses his face.

She kisses his hand.

She kisses his hook.

'Now go to bed e tama.'

He stands, undecided, swaying in the doorway.

Then, too quickly for it to be stopped, he lashes out with the hook. It strikes her on her left breast.

I storm forward, full of rage, and reach for him.

'No,' she says again, kneeling there, motionless. 'No,' yet again.

'Go to bed, tama,' she says to him.

Her voice is warm and friendly. Her face is serene.

He turns obediently, and walks away into the dark.

At the weekend, I suggested we go for a picnic.

'Another one?' she asks, her black eyebrows raised.

'Well, we could gather pauas, maybe some cress, have a meal on the beach. It'd be good to get out of the house for a while. This hasn't been too good a week for me, you know.'

They both shrugged.

'Okay,' he says.

'I will get the paua," she says, and begins stripping off her jeans. 'You get the cress,' she says to him.

'I'll go with you and help,' I add.

He just looks at me. Those steely eyes in that brown face. Then he pouted, picked up the kete, and headed for the stream.

He selects a stalk and pinches it suddenly. The plant tissue thins to nothing. It's like he's executing the cress. He adds it to the pile in the kete. He doesn't look at me, or talk. He is absorbed in killing cress.

There's not much I can do.

So I put on my mask and flippers and wade into the water, slide down under the sea. I spend a long peaceful time there, detaching whelks and watching them wobble down to the bottom. I cruise along the undersea rock shelf, plucking bits of weed, and letting them drift away. Eventually, I reach the end of the reef, and I can hear the boom and mutter of the real ocean. It's getting too close; I surface.

One hundred yards away, fighting a current that is moving him remorselessly out, is my son.

When I gained the beach, I was exhausted.

I stand, panting, him in my arms.

His face is grey and waxy and the water runs off us both, dripping constantly on the sand.

'You were too far out. . . '

He cries.

'Where is she?'

Where is she? Gathering paua somewhere. . . but suddenly I don't know if that is so. I put my mask back on, leave him on the beach, and dive back under the waves, looking.

When I find her, as I find her, she is floating on her back amidst bullkelp. The brown weed curves sinuously over her body, like dark limp hands.

I splash and slobber over, sobbing to her, 'God, your son nearly died trying to find you. Why didn't you tell us?'

She opens her brown eyes lazily.

No, not lazily: with defeat, with weariness.

'What on earth gave you the idea I was going to drown?' She rubs the towel roughly over her skin.

I say, haltingly, 'Uh well, he was sure that. . . '

(He is curled up near the fire I've lit, peacefully asleep.)

'Sure of what?'

'I don't know. He went looking for you, got scared. We couldn't see you anywhere.'

A sort of shudder, a ripple, runs through her.

'The idea was right,' she says, very quietly. She lets the towel fall. She cups her hand under her left breast and points.

'Feel there.'

There is a hard, oval, clump amidst the soft tissue.

'God, did he do...'

'No. It's been growing there for the past month. Probably for longer than that, but I have only felt it recently.' She rubs her armpit, thoughtfully. 'It's there too and under here,' gesturing to her jaw. "It'll have to come out.' I can't stop it. I groan.

Do you understand that if I hadn't been there, both of them would have drowned?

There was one last thing.

We were all together in the living room.

I am in the lefthand chair, she is opposite me.

He is crooning to himself, sprawled in front of the fire.

'Loo-lie, loo-lay, loo-lie, loo-lay, the falcon hath borne my make away,' he sings. He pronounces it, 'the fawcon have borne my make away.'

'What is that?' I ask.

'A song.'

He looks across to his ma and they smile, slyly, at one another, smiles like invisible hands reaching out, caressing secretly, weaving and touching.

I washed my hands.

I wept.

I went out to the shed and banged the door finally shut.

I wept a little while longer.

And then, because there was nothing else to do, I went down to the pub.

I had been drinking double whiskies for more than an hour when Mata came across and laid his arm over my shoulder.

He is shaking.

'E man, don't drink by yourself. That's no good eh?' His arm presses down. 'Come across to us?'

The hubbub of voices hushes.

I snivel.

'Mat, when I first knew, her fingers were covered in clay, soft grey clay. And she smiled and said it's Charleston, we'll call him Charleston. It's too soft really, but I'll make a nice cup from it. Cups. Tall fluted goblets she said.'

His hand pats my shoulder with commiseration, with solicitude.

His eyes are dark with horror.

'I'll glaze them sea blue and we'll drink red wine together, all three of us.'

We never did.

KERI HULME (1947; Kati Tahu: hapu Ngaterangiamoa, Ngaiteruahikihiki) was born in Christchurch and grew up there and at Moeraki. She has been a fish and chips cook, TV director (for Television One), law student, tobacco picker and woollen-mill worker and is now a whitebaiter and writer at Okarito on the West Coast.

In 1973 she won the Te Awamutu Short Story Award and in 1975 a Katherine Mansfield BNZ Short Story Award. She held a mini-Burns Fellowship at the University of Otago in 1977 and received a Maori Trust Fund Award for writing in English in 1978 and Literary Fund grants in 1973, 1977 and 1979. In 1979 she was invited to the East West Centre in Hawaii.

Her work has appeared in *The NZ Listener, NZ Listener Short Stories Two, Islands, Te Kara, Broadsheet, Hawaii Review* and in *Coast Voices* as well as on Radio New Zealand and Television One.

'The Kaumatua and the Broken Man' is an excerpt from her unpublished novel *The Bone People*; she is currently at work on two other novels. A collection of short stories is in preparation as well as *The Silences Between (Moeraki Conversations)* which is a collection of poetry and prose.

Along with eight other contemporary Maori writers her work is soon to appear in a Swedish anthology of modern Maori stories, translated by Bengt Dagrin.

Teremoana Pehimana

Untitled
(parts of this sequence are dedicated to the memory of my kui Roka Pehimana and to Joyce Hall of Weipa)

I

4 white people
    grey hair
        dark glasses
drive up Capitol Hill
    to look at the view. . .
ignoring the humble tents
    and broken burnt bedsteads

of a dispossessed people.
Yes, they drive past in their Volvo
  a painting class
Of Volvo men and women
  elegantly clad
    bohemianesque even
casually trying to find
    an Australian image
ignoring also
    the people
      who have been
        pushed aside
      trodden over
  killed off
wiped out in the wake
    of prosperity
        mining companies
        and progress

Yes, i watch
    them
    walk
    awkwardly
    full bellies
    heads without lice
    bellies full of food
    and not full blown
    by
    flies
    and
    malnutrition
they walk
    over
to
the
fireplace
hearth
stand
awkwardly
arms
akimbo
whilst
their

obese
wives
stare
in puzzlement
at bedsteads
  stacked
protectively
over
an aboriginal
hearth. . .

they look up
at the sky
    glasses gleaming
read the noticebox
then walk
    off
heavily
    grossly
to their
white Volvo car
satisfied?
puzzled?
bemused?

they don't have to worry
the future is theirs. . .
below
me
the ants
(yes
i
walk
over
life
too
and in my human bigness
kill
tiny
creatures
with
weight

and
aggression)
(i'm
dreading
returning
to
Aotearoa...
fat's
  in
  the
  fire
  now
and
  i
lack
heart
and
courage).

Tourists
come
and
go
row upon row
well clad
well shod
well spectacled
MANACLED
with
cameras
and
equipment...
  they even drive
right up
now
in huge
gasguzzling
limousines
and
retreat
  leaving me
  wondering how

        much
changed
    their
    souls
are
    by
the paradox
presented
to them
here
in
wealthy
Canberra...

II

this morning
i wake
as usual
    early.

Can't get over the thing
        of being alone,
Tane (5) and me in this land
        when i come
from
such family people
        across the sea:
            the sadness of life
haunts me.
        Last night Joyce Hall
of Weipa crying for her
                lost people
        lost lands
            lost kangaroo
lost birds
lost plants
lost waters
lost life

287

      gone taken destroyed
            forever
by C.R.A.
      CONZINC RIOTINTO
      COMALCO...

      bulldozers/machinery/mines
haunted my dreams
      her sad face
            imprinted itself on
my soul and i think of my
      class of black children
            last year
on a NORTH QUEENSLAND
      RESERVE
and just cry at their plight

      how can people destroy
            this race?
it's heartbreaking...

how can we all help
      we who're so comfortable
            in CANBERRA
            by comparison?

can't sleep peacefully
      knowing those little
            children suffer
            those adults have little
to live for
their   past ⎫
      present ⎬ all haunt me
      future ⎭

            such destruction on
            such a scale...

will people never learn
      Joyce's wisdom?

Her sad face

            haunts me
                  her tears pierce
                  my psyche
how dare people here
     become so incensed
       about conditions
            in countries
       other than the lucky one
when the lucky one
       does this
       to its own?

me, i think western
       so-called civilisation
has had its day
            doesn't question the power
       it possesses now
to destroy. . .

its faith seems to lie
       in logic
       reason
       science
       technology
       + things money can buy

Oh Joyce may your
       face/sanity
be shown
       to the world
and shame us all into
       ACTION
       not words
       not promises
       not treaties
       not intentions
       not laws
JUST SILENT ACTION
       For the damage done
can never be repaired
            the innocent world
has been destroyed utterly

                    gaping void
            in the soul
                of the destroyers
can never be filled...
            unless we band together
        the writing is on the wall
                clearly, finally,
                    FRAMLINGHAM CASTLE, SUFFOLK
its photograph falls to the floor
                symbolic
                    of peoples' rise and fall

we lie, we cheat, we destroy
            we hate, we undo
our creations
            we need to take stock
                    right now
of our actions
            i don't think destruction
of people is ever justified...

Pakehas tell me violence is necessary
                quote Marx to me
                quote other thinkers to me
me, i want only to follow the wisdom
                of my forebears
and of TE WHITI, TOHU, KUI ROKA who
            taught peace, not war
and for this i feel so out of kilter
            at odds with society
        in general in
Aotearoa or Australia.

Yes, this morning i wake as usual
                early
        just can't get over the thing
            of being alone,
of the sadness of life
        of sufferings of Joyce
of Joyce's wisdom
            AROHA
and beautiful simplicity

tears streaming down her face and mine
and weep, weep without ceasing, at thoughts of
        WEIPA
and cry for my lost children of Hopevale,
North Queensland.

III

    this morning
rising early to watch
        sunrise over Mt Majura
i think of how much
        (paradoxically in view of
                previous poem)
Australia
        has given me
and how much i like this
place and its people
of all origins...

    i'm so ambivalent:
a typical gemini
        8 days before
my birthday
        fearful of being alone
        of passing years
        of precious time wasted
        of loves lost
        loves' labours lost...
but Teremoana now
(i say to myself severely)
LET'S BE POSITIVE!

i love Sunday mornings
        early
sunrise coming soon
        lacebark leaves yellow
                in frost
Mrs Webbie's oak tree opposite
        coppery/magnificent
Mrs Webbie peppery

with life
86 years old
now raising her
great grandson
one year old next Friday...

how i love this city
in autumn
this house/refuge
has become my
home away from home
hate
it at times i do
love it often
unexpectedly
and surprise myself

love the landscape/birdscape/
treescape
creativity of it all
hope my sisters and brother
can see it too
now that my aging parents
pass their years
in contemplation
philosophic realists
both of them

they visited me twice
in my first year
i was so sad when they left
so new as a mother
so ignorant of my role
so fearful
so alone
the new land felt vast and
uncaring
i, like so many others
was lost in a wilderness
of my own suffering
unable to cope
breaking down
shrinks had kept me

         on lithium
carbonate
         4 years long
what a diagnosis
         manic depression
             Katherine Mansfield
             Virginia Woolf
             Kui Roka Pehimana
         you kept me going
as did my parents
    a poor husband
         unable to cope
             wrung his hands
wept with despair;
             me, i sank into depression
a well of blackness...
Black holes? Wot are they
         astrophysics holds
             those answers
i know only many black holes
    in people's lives
and watch with anger
         how people in power
         care so little

now Ainslie Mountain
    (must learn its true name)
         turns purple
             over Mrs Webbie's house
and Milia, my Croatian
         neighbour's spotless
             place
looks friendly across the
             road...
i look out at the new
         cumquat
cosy, i hope in its
    black
    plastic
    hood
surrounded
    by
    clods of soft earth...

this morning
  rising early
    i watch RA
rise over
  Mt Majura.

IV

 here i am
      back home
      blubbering
with grief
  an unknown letter
triggers off
    memories
of my nephew; and of
suffering
often borne stoically
by my family.

i feel weighed down by
the pain of life;
time passes so swiftly and cuts so
cleanly
so swiftly; it, like death is so
final
there is no arguing with time
no bargaining with it
heed its warnings we must, for
it will not pass this way again.

i look out at the sky this cool summer's evening
it's such a soft blue,
teal or aqua, i don't
recall the hue
and watch the soft green lacebark
leaves awash with evening-sun gold
and think of you my friend always so
far away
and think of Lorca's words

Cordoba, Cordoba, far away and alone

Cordoba, Cordoba, I shall never reach
Cordoba.

one son,
and a broken marriage are some
of what i have to show
of life's path
my mother tells me
that my life's passing
is what hurts her...
my sentiments exactly.

and so now the
firm resolve
and, at times a
brave front

to start life anew, ah, yes
that's what must be done. But how
to do it?
    It's simple really,
back in the land of one's birth
at least one doesn't have to look for roots
or family, or friends,
but but the hard reality
lies
across the Tasman...

TEREMOANA PEHIMANA (1942: Te Atiawa) was born at Te Puke. Educated
at Tokomaru Bay and Te Teko Maori schools she trained as a teacher in
Wellington. With her son she has been working on an Aboriginal Reserve in North
Queensland but currently lives in Canberra. Teremoana has read her poetry at the
Women's Art Registry (Canberra) and at the opening of the Women's Gallery
(Wellington).

Rawiri Paratene

Mary's Dream (Extract)

Mary is alone

The men will come
and replace the hills with nothing
Their equipment
like giant insects intent on destruction
will move the hills to oblivion
Their hoppers and caterpillars
and centipedes and yellow praying mantis
will eat the hills
and the hills will bleed . . .
like crisp apples.

Last night I dreamed I walked in the hills
alone and softly
I made no noise
as I trod on the remains
of the trees and birds and life that was
I looked up at the life that is
and in my dream the bush was calm.
It was just as in my painting —
blobs of colour and sound and smell,
thick blobs I could stroke with my fingers
and tongue
And I was happy
Happier than I had ever been

Then, in my dream
I closed my eyes, my redundant eyes
and I saw
what I thought at first was an opossum,
scampering down a tree
When it reached the ground it stopped
and looked at me
I could see it was a stoat
It was sweating and panting
and in its mouth were three white feathers

There beside the stoat
lying on that blanket of decay
was a tui
It was dead
Its throat was ripped

The stoat looked at the bird
then at me,
Then scampered up the next tree
Down fell another bird
a thrush this time
Soon the trees were full of stoats
ripping the birds apart
There was crying and screaming and panic

A fantail went mad
and flew round and round my head,
until I opened my eyes
and saw a carpet of freshly killed birds.

I was running
and could feel the dead birds between my toes
When I woke I was crying out
'Leave them! Leave them!'
and I was here
looking at the hills.

enter David

The sun was rising...
but it didn't fool me.

The Proper Channels (Extract)

NEWSREADER: ...Mr Hone Te Rangi Porter, Spokesman for the newly
formed Maori Liberation Front, said in Wellington today,
that the organisation was primarily concerned with the
'blatant denial of Human Rights by the present legal
system.' Mr Porter said that too many young Maori
people were going through the Courts unrepresented and
being convicted without what he considers a 'fair trial'

Mr Porter said 'it should be against the law for a person to stand in the dock and enter a plea without any legal advice.' The M.L.F has with the assistance of the Wellington Law Society, set up a legal aid service to assist the Maori Welfare Officers on duty in the Courts. That concludes the local news, here's the latest weather.

T.V. is switched off.

PETER: You're on the news more than Muldoon now.

HONE: The huas missed out half of what I said.

PETER: Everyone back home would've seen that. You're a big star up there.

HONE: Yeah?

PETER: Yeah. Mum'll be saying, 'Good on you Hone, ka pai. Kia kaha e tama.'

HONE: Bloody old battle axe. What's your old man think?

PETER: He reckons you're a communist. When you were on that Brian Edwards show about Maoris he said, 'Here comes Mao tse Porter again.'

HONE: (*laughing*) Mao tse Porter eh? I like that. Hey, you should come along to some of our meetings.

PETER: Me?

HONE: Be good for your journalist course.

PETER: I'm not into politics.

HONE: We need some Maori journalists.

PETER: But I don't want to be a political reporter. I want to be a sports writer. I've got no time for politics. Half the time I don't understand it.

HONE: Ignorance is no excuse.

PETER: But I'm more interested in tennis and athletics and rugby.

HONE: That's pretty political.

PETER: (*trapped*) I mean reporting on how the play went. League, squash, racing — any sport. Even cricket. I know about sports. Politics, it's like...well...it might as well be a play by Shakespeare. I just don't understand it.

HONE: Proper Uncle Tama, just like your old man.

PETER: Eh?

HONE: Why don't you just come and have a listen. There's a meeting tomorrow night.

PETER: Nah. I wouldn't be any use. Anyway I've got classes most nights.

HONE: Fair enough, I'm not gunna twist your arm...you want a kai?

PETER: What's the time?

HONE: Just gone seven.

PETER: I better get back. I'm a family man don't forget.

HONE: Your missus a coastie?

PETER: Yep. One of the Baileys.

HONE: Oh yeah, Hohepa Bailey's crowd.

PETER: Yeah.

HONE: What's her name?

PETER: Hine.

HONE: Good looking?

PETER: Course.

HONE: Bring her and the kids around. Weekends are the best. My cook works nights during the week.

PETER: Who looks after the kids when you've got meetings?

HONE: We have the meetings here most of the time.

PETER: Where are the kids?

HONE: Oh they're all flako. I get them in bed by six. You haven't met Joan eh?

PETER: Who?

HONE: My cook.

PETER: No. Where's she from?

HONE: Johnsonville. She's a pakeha.

PETER: I know. Should hear what Dad says about that.

HONE: I bet.

PETER: How come anyway? How come you're always going on about pakehas, and yet you're married to one?

HONE: I'm not anti-pakeha. I'm pro-Maori.

PETER: (*laughs*) Well I better get crackin'.

HONE: Righto Peter. Thanks for calling in.

PETER: It's all right, by the way, Mum sent her love.

HONE: You make sure and send mine back.

PETER: I'll do that.

Door opens.

PETER: (*fading*) See ya Hone.

HONE: Yeah. Good luck with your course.

           Panel fade out.

SCENE 2 (*The* TETTIRA'S *flat*)

Fade up a radio.

HINE: Are you going to that meeting?

PETER: Yeah.

HINE: Have you joined up now?

PETER: No, I just go along to listen.

HINE: What happens?

PETER: Talking mainly. They're organising some sort of cam-
           paign. Handing out leaflets in shopping centres, that sort
           of thing.

HINE: It says in the paper they're communists.

PETER: Nah, most of 'em wouldn't know what that meant.

           Fade to a meeting.

HONE: We *are* talking about a class struggle. It's quite clear that
           the moneyed class (a minority) is privileged and the
           workers (a majority) are oppressed.

           Fade back. Radio in background.

PETER: They talk about people's rights, y'know?

HINE: What rights?

PETER: Legal rights. They've done this pamphlet called 'What to
           do when approached by the Police.'

301

HINE: What for?

PETER: To hand out.

Fade to meeting.

HONE: It must be remembered that workers have *no* rights. There
          are no laws to guarantee you any rights. However, the law
          gives the police wide powers.

Fade back as before.

HINE: Who's all in it?

PETER: All sorts. Students, truckies, there's even a lawyer.

HINE: All Maoris?

PETER: Yeah...oh there's a couple of Islanders too. Quite a few
          have been beaten up by the police.

HINE: Really?

PETER: So they say.

SCENE 2A (*A Meeting*)

Fade to meeting.

HONE: Understanding the powers given to the police can help
          resist harassment. The police, however, daily overstep
          these powers. The system allows them to do so in order to
          maintain consistent class and racist oppression. Our
          pamphlet isn't designed to give the impression that justice
          can be achieved under this system. It is simply designed to
          help our brothers and sisters, to defend themselves against
          police harassment. Particularly our younger brothers and
          sisters. In order to change the system, which after all is
          our ultimate aim, we must first educate those who suffer
          under it. Hence, our pamphlet which we will hand out
          tomorrow night. No reira, ka mutu taku korero. Kia kaha,
          kia maia, kia manawanui. Kia ora koutou katoa.

Saturday Morning (Extract)

(Scene X: a city prison holding area.)

BILL: They got me for vandalism...

You see I got home very late and very pissed. I went to go inside but the front door was locked. Banged on the door a coupla times but, no answer. Went round the back door and bugger me days if that wasn't locked too. Banged away at that one for a while, louder this time, still no answer. By now I was getting a bit hot under the collar. See it was cold and I had no shirt. Puked all over it in the pub toilets earlier on. Went back to the front door.

There I was banging on the bugger getting hotter and hotter. Well a man'd feel a right prick wouldn't he? Neighbours' lights were starting to go on one by one just like that bit at the end of the Flintstones.

Anyway, I went right round the house trying all the windows but they were locked too. So I went to the bedroom window and started yelling out to the missus. I knew she was in too. She never goes out, she's a bit of an invalid you see.

Anyhow, I went around to the shed. Thought about shacking down there but changed my mind. Why the hell should I? My house too. So instead I took a beer crate around to the bedroom window, climbed up and looked in. Sure enough, there she was pretending to be asleep. I knew she couldn't really be asleep 'cos of all the noise I made. So I went around the backyard, found a brick, went back to the bedroom and threw it at the window.

Of course the bloody thing missed which made me even hotter so I picked it up again, took careful aim, and this time I hit the bullseye.

CRRASHH! Smashed to smithereens.

I climbed up onto the crate, reached through, opened the window and climbed in. As soon as I got inside the missus gets up, takes half the blankets and goes into the sitting room. Which suited me down to a tee 'cos I was in no state for shacking up on the settee. So I took my clothes off and hit the sack.

Just as I was dozing off the missus comes back in, turns on the light, which played bloody havoc on the old eyes, and then she starts tidying up the broken glass. Then she

303

goes out again. Left the bloody light on, too, so I had to get up and switch the bugger off. Then I musta flaked.

Next thing I know this young cop with a mo was standing next to the bed prodding me with his truncheon saying, 'Oi, wake up old fella, you're under arrest.'

Well, I didn't know what to do. Thought I was dreaming, but he was real all right. Well, I got outa bed. I was just in me jockeys so the young cop threw me some strides, gave me time to sorta hitchem up, shoved the handcuffs on and we were off like a shot. Not even time to put some shoes or a shirt on.

On the way in I was trying to remember what the hell I'd done all night. Nothing came to mind but I guessed it must have been pretty bad.

Well anyway, to cut a long story short, when we got in here I found out that the missus had charged me with bloody vandalism.

(*Pause*)

JACK: Oh, have you finished?

BILL: Yep.

JACK: Boy, if that was my missus I'd've bloody vandalised her face for her.

BILL: Oh no. Never hit the missus. She's too good to me.

RAWIRI PARATENE (1954; Te Rarawa te iwi, Whirinaki, Hikatu te hapu, Motukaraka, Ngai Tupoto te hapu) was born at Motukaraka and grew up in Otara. After Hillary College he went to the New Zealand Drama School in Wellington in 1972. While he was the Wellington chairman of Nga Tamatoa he was the national co-ordinator for the first Maori Language Day (1972). In 1973 he joined the Mercury Theatre Company as an apprentice actor and became involved in over 30 productions during the next three and a half years. In 1976 he appeared in Television One's series *Joe and Koro*. Since 1977 he has been a freelance actor working mainly for live theatre.

Rawiri is also well-known as a radio actor. He was company writer for 'Stagestruck' in 1978 and spent six months workshopping his play *Directions* at Downstage in 1979. He directed his first radio play, *The Proper Channels*, in 1980. In 1976 his first play for theatre, *Saturday Morning*, won a Maori Writers' Award;

it was performed at the Newtown Community Theatre in 1980, whence it transferred to Downstage. Currently he is working on a new play, *Kingi Ria*. He lives in Lower Hutt.

Michael Stevens

Kapiti

Between the road and the windlashed sea near Paekakariki squats a low stone wall constructed to confine the battles between land and ocean to a shellthin stretch of rocky coast. At intervals the monotony of stone upon stone beside stone eases where the wall and road separate. Here the traveller may stop, and, rain and cloud permitting, gaze awhile across the waves to Kapiti. In one of these places between the road and the weathered sea wall, my father would stop our car, and surrounded by the sea's crash and its particular smell, with the salt taste wet on our lips, we would crablike scramble over slick black rocks that burst the salt waves to gullhigh spray, and we would crouch to seek and find the secret treasures of the restless waves: the sea-eggs and -snails and, if in luck, a halfsack of fat, black paua, each the size of my father's outspread hand.

Now days are spent with pool cues and jugs of beer, and friends far from Kapiti. The wall no doubt survives, and the rocks and waves continue their eternal battle, but I do not think the food remains. No more the eager scrambles over the wetback rocks; no more the seagifts melting in the mouth. Only sea and rocks persist, and Kapiti riding the waves as always, beyond the low stone wall, below the high gulls.

On Your Dying

Not rains falling, nor thunder,
nor unnatural darkness
announced your passing, for you,
after all, were just a man.
But the tears shed and the
darkness of mourning pervading
this land are evidence that

the reverberations of
your days will continue
so long as great and peaceful
men are remembered by we
to whom your life was given
and those who are yet to come.

Prayer

Let feathered psalms
soar skyward:
may no dark clouds
impede their paths
nor black smoke nor choking dust
coat their bright singings.

Tangiwai

There are some people born
with greenstone eyes: I name you Tangiwai
knowing the allusion is lost,
would call you Kahurangi, instead
call you friend; wear my illusion like greenstone
warm against my chest, smile
my fractured smile, and
rub the sandstone beneath my lids.

*Sister, he said, take this
and grind until the rough is smooth.
He did not know it was himself he gave
until they moved together.*

I am washed away
in your serpentine stream. The sand
washes in and out of my eyes.
I call you friend, have named you Tangiwai
knowing I am lost.

Koru

of rain and sunrise let us sing,
of fire and whale (inscrutable),
feather, tree and fern.

           silence
yet the ears ring/air's ring (?)
and wind move leaf wave feather
fireflame leaf

           unfurl
and let us sing of these and every song:
our singing carves our names
across their names

embracing the earth.

we, cruciform, an ocean
carved by song

           unfurl
and each small death proceeds.

the wind, the planting moon,
an ocean, the whale's spume.

from the east come singing
from the east with red feathers
from the east singing with a whale's tooth
like a river singing (rain in mountains)

           wake!
the night has rained mushrooms
white as whalebone, and curled fern.

and so we carve our song
        we carve our name
on treed hills, under leaf of fern,
flaxblade also, and the fire's blaze,
bright feathers, and the whale's spout

embracing the earth.

Let The Moon And The Sea...

Let the moon and the still
sea conspire and rising
reclaim these shores from the
impotence of sun and men.

is this the turning

This fish has not moved through the
sea's pull, nor yet the moon's suck
wave-flooded her belly: men,
not water, brought her drowning.

is this the turning is this

Like the sea your people covered our
land: you were as *nga tai a Kupe*
and we were not prepared. We have
become like the seagulls upon the rocks.

the turning is this

So let the moon-gathered waters
begin their rising: the tides of
sea and men change always. Let it
be known: the time for turning is come.

ko tenei te whatinga o te mata o te tai

MICHAEL STEVENS (1954; Ngati Raukawa) was born in Stratford and grew up in Taupo. He was educated at the University of Otago. A former teacher at Darwin Community College he is now lecturing in social anthropology and history at the National College of Choueifat in Abu Dhabi. His poems have appeared in *Critic, Koru, Otago University Review* and *Pacific Quarterly Moana*.

Maarire Goodall

Waiata Aroha

Ka tonga te kiri
  i te anu matao,
Ka pakia te tamaroto
  ki te haukoeoeo.

Inake te ngakaukore.

Te hau-kaika
  i whakaarohatia mai
E toku kanohi tonga;
  E matawaia.

Moea iho nei e au
  ko te hokiwai
  rere po.

MAARIRE GOODALL (Kati Mamoe, Kati Tahu, Takatapora) composer of the waiata aroha, was born in western Southland and grew up in Fiordland. Educated at Otago Boys' High School and the University of Otago, he has taught at the Institute for Medical Research of the Chicago Medical School. A past president of the NZ Society of Oncology, member of the WHO Expert Panel on Cancer, and chairman of the Cancer Research Trust, he is at present Director of Cancer Research at the University of Otago. Goodall belongs to Otakou Marae and is a trustee of the multi-tribal Araiteuru Marae in Dunedin. As well as his publications of scientific papers and waiata he recently released, with George Griffith, *Maori Dunedin* (Otago Heritage Press) for the opening of Araiteuru Marae.

Acknowledgements

The editors would like to thank the publishers of the following books and periodicals in which the works listed first appeared.

ARAPETA AWATERE: 'Kepa Anaha Ehau', *The New Quarterly Cave.*

HERETAUNGA PANANEHU PAT BAKER: 'A Prophecy Fulfilled', *Behind the Tattooed Face* (Picton, Cape Catley Ltd, 1975).

KINGI M. IHAKA: 'Poi' and 'Haka Taparahi' were performed by the Auckland Anglican Maori Club at the Third New Zealand Polynesian Festival at Whangarei in 1975.

HARRY DANSEY: *Te Raukura — The Feathers of the Albatross* (Auckland, Longman Paul Ltd, 1974). Dansey's English translation of 'Poi Raukura' first appeared in *Marae.*

HONE TUWHARE: 'Reign Rain', 'Ron Mason', 'Child Coming Home in the Rain from the Store', 'Heemi', 'Old Comrade', 'Taniwha', *The NZ Listener.* 'Drunk', 'Haiku', *Come Rain Hail* (Dunedin, The Bibliography Room, University of Otago Library, 1970). 'Ron Mason' and 'Heemi' were reprinted in *Something Nothing* (Dunedin, Caveman Press, 1974) and 'Reign Rain' and 'Taniwha' in *Making a Fist of It* (Dunedin, Jackstraw Press, 1978).

TE AOMUHURANGI-TEMAMAAKA: 'Te Hunga Kua Riro Ki Te Po', *Koru*; 'E Tō E Te Rā I Waho O Mōtu', *Te Kaea.*

ALISTAIR TE ARIKI CAMPBELL: 'Walk the Black Path', 'Grandfather Bosini', *The NZ Listener*; first collected in *Kapiti* (Christchurch, The Pegasus Press, 1972). 'Waiting for the Pakeha', 'Flowering Apple', *The NZ Listener*; first collected in *Drèams, Yellow Lions* (Martinborough, Alister Taylor, 1975). 'The Manner is to be Deplored', 'Friend' (earlier called 'Epitaph'), *Landfall*; collected in *Dreams, Yellow Lions.* 'Burning Rubbish', 'To My Grandson Maireriki Aged One Day', *The NZ Listener*; 'A Woman in Love', *Eve*; both collected in *Collected Poems* (Martinborough, Alister Taylor, 1981).

MERIMERI PENFOLD: 'Marituu', *Koru.*

SAANA MURRAY: 'My Decree', *Te Karanga a Te Kotuku* (Wellington, The Maori Organisation of Human Rights, 1975).

PATRICIA BELL: 'Kuia', *Landfall*.

KATERINA TE HEI KOKO MATAIRA: *Te Ātea* (Wellington, School Publications Branch, Department of Education, 1975).

ROWLEY HABIB: NGA PITIROIRANGI: 'Moment of Truth', Radio New Zealand. 'Orakau', *The NZ Listener*. 'Ancestor', *Landfall*; reprinted in *Poet International*. 'Jacko', *Landfall*. 'A Coloured Man Addresses a White Protester Against Apartheid', *The NZ Listener*; reprinted in *Poet International*. 'Go Home Maori', *Rongo*; reprinted in *The Week*. 'Another Kind of Wilderness — Mount Eden: Summit and Prison', *The Week*. 'Memorial Day', *Sunday Times*; reprinted in *Koru*, and on Radio New Zealand and Television One. 'Dole Day', *Landfall*; reprinted in *Ten Modern New Zealand Writers* (Auckland, Longman Paul Ltd, 1976). 'Strife in the Family', *Te Maori*; and on Radio New Zealand. 'Motu', *Short Stories by New Zealanders* (Auckland, Longman Paul Ltd, 1972). 'A Young Man Feeling His Oats', *Te Maori*. 'The Gathering', Channel Two (Television New Zealand).

HAARE WILLIAMS: 'Go East Of Your Mountain', 'Koru', *Koru*.

BRUCE STEWART: 'Boy', *Alumni*; reprinted in an altered form in *Shirley Temple is a Wife and Mother — 34 Stories by 22 New Zealanders* (Whatamongo Bay, Cape Catley Ltd, 1977); broadcast by Radio New Zealand. 'Papa', *Te Kaea*; recorded for Radio New Zealand.

VERNICE WINEERA PERE: 'Bitter-Sweet', 'At Porirua', 'The Boy Named Pita', 'Songs from Kapiti', *Mahanga: Pacific Poems* (La'ie, The Institute for Polynesian Studies, 1978).

BUB BRIDGER: 'The Stallion', *The NZ Listener*; reprinted in *Shirley Temple is a Wife and Mother* (Whatamongo Bay, Cape Catley Ltd, 1977) with 'Girl in the River'.

HENARE DEWES: 'Tihei Mauriora!', 'Whakarongo', *Rongo*.

PATRICIA GRACE: 'A Way of Talking', *Landfall*; collected (with 'Parade') in *Waiariki* (Auckland, Longman Paul Ltd, 1975). *Mutuwhenua* (Auckland, Longman Paul Ltd, 1978).

HIRINI MELBOURNE: 'He Whakaaro Huri Roto', *Rongo* (in an earlier form).

ATIHANA MOANA JOHNS: 'He Pakete Kanara', *Short Stories by New Zealanders One* (Auckland, Longman Paul Ltd, 1972).

RANGI FAITH: 'Corrosion of Values', *Pacific Quarterly Moana.*

WITI IHIMAERA: 'The Child', *Pounamu, Pounamu* (Auckland, William Heinemann Ltd, 1972). *Tangi* (Auckland, William Heinemann Ltd, 1973). *Whanau* (Auckland, William Heinemann Ltd, 1974). 'The House with Sugarbag Windows', *The New Net Goes Fishing* (Auckland, William Heinemann Ltd, 1977).

KERI HULME: 'E Nga Iwi O Ngai Tahu', *Te Kaea.* 'Hooks and Feelers', *The NZ Listener*; reprinted *The NZ Listener Short Stories Two* (Wellington, Methuen, 1978). 'October', 'Nga Kehua', *Coast Voices* (Greymouth, Walden Books, 1979). 'The Kaumatua and the Broken Man' is from the unpublished novel *The Bone People.*

RAWIRI PARATENE: 'Saturday Morning' was first performed at the Newtown Community Theatre. 'The Proper Channels' was first broadcast by Radio New Zealand. 'Mary's Song' is from the play *Directions*, first workshopped by the Youth Theatre Workshop at Downstage in 1979.

MICHAEL STEVENS: 'Kapiti', 'Let the Moon and Sea', *Critic*; reprinted in *Koru*. 'Prayer', *Critic*. 'Tangiwai', *Otago University Review*; *Pacific Quarterly Moana.*